P9-AOM-571

Brenner, Marie.

Intimate distance

DATE DUE

Intimate
Distance

Books by Marie Brenner

Tell Me Everything

Going Hollywood

Intimate Distance

Marie Brenner

William Morrow and Company, Inc.
New York   1983

Library of Congress Catalog Card Number: 83–61856

ISBN: 0–688–02137–9

Printed in the United States of America

First Edition

1 2 3 4 5 6 7 8 9 10

BOOK DESIGN BY ANN GOLD

For Jonathan

Contents

Introduction

The vacation was to have been short, two weeks in London in June of 1977 for the Queen's Jubilee. I had no intention of working, which is to say "reporting" on the events, interviewing the participants, filling notebooks. None of that for me this time, just a pure holiday all alone. But something happened: I stayed two years. After the first few months, I began to think of myself as a semipermanent exile, affecting the customs of the culture, pleased to be able to write out drafts for sterling from my branch of Lloyds. I started placing dates on these pale pink checks as if I was to Hempstead born: 23 October 1977.

My activities became pan-European as well. The time I once spent pursuing a New York free-lance writer's life I now spent filling journals with the minutiae of the alien—jottings of style and detail taken in at hot meals and on country weekends, baroque descriptions of dramatic moments between people who were strangers to me but not to one another. Writing it down was the only way I could begin to understand what was going on. I thought the information in the journals would help me. If I had been looking to reinvent myself, I was wasting time. I had been a journalist in one culture and I remained a journalist in another. In London I hadn't yet realized that a state of semipermanent exile was a condition of the métier.

9

An entry from my journal of the time:

15 July. I think I am going to survive here in the following manner. Think of everything as material and don't take anything personally. Today I went to lunch at Mrs. D's, a famous hostess and aging American expatriate—she's one of the last holdouts of Chester Square. Mrs. D. even looked like a relic, thin and haunted, wafting through her drawing room, offering her guests peach juice and champagne with a Mississippi voice. Her large house was filled with period furniture. In the library, one of the guests, a Mr. P., an English art dealer, stopped before a Louis XV chair covered in shocking pink peau de soie. "It's a contrived color accent, isn't it, E. dear?" And then he asked the hostess, "E., have you seen the new Fragonard?" Right before lunch Tennessee Williams arrived. He was passing through London on his way to Australia. In these rooms, everyone always seems to be on his way somewhere and has just seen Manoli, George, or Swifty in Paris, Rio, or at the Carlyle. Mrs. D.'s guests had travel advice for Tennessee Williams. In Sydney, he was to meet Lady Fairfax and to avoid Lady Docker. Williams acted dazed or drunk and wobbled badly as he went in for lunch. Mrs. D. is "known for her cook," according to one of the guests, and the cook didn't fail. He laid on a spinach soufflé, grilled sea bass, and baby everything—snow peas, cress, and chèvre. Everybody made a big fuss about how young the goat cheese was. But Mrs. D. wasn't having a good time. She was furious that one of her guests hadn't shown up and kept carping about it. "Why didn't he ring?" "What could have happened to him, Tennessee?" Just before the raspberries, Williams took her arm. "My poor dear, you're so desperate. You really are." Everyone got very quiet. Williams kept his grip on E.'s arm. "This is your whole life, isn't it? These entertainments . . . seeing people." "That's not true," Mrs. D. said. "I told you just the other night there were two parties I absolutely refused to go to." "Yes, that was very good of you, dear," Williams said. The art dealer interrupted. "Tom," he said, "I don't think E. is nearly so desperate any more. E. does wonderful things for people. She always finds people that are needy and organizes their lives." Mrs. D. turned on Williams. "I'm not like you, Tennessee. I don't have anything to do. I don't have any work." Dessert resumed. In the drawing room over coffee, someone said that E. had just returned from Zurich where she'd had her face done. "She told her doctor that when she was young she used to be taken for Susan Hayward," the guest said.

The lunch itself was insignificant; I doubt that Tennessee Williams or any of the others would have remembered it. But it exists in my notebooks as a piece of sub-rosa journalism for one reason only: I wrote it down. It is not anything more important than an entry put there to mark, perhaps, an encounter with the weary and the jaded. I was at Mrs. D's strictly on a tourist visa—a friend brought me. The occasion wasn't unusual. In London, among a certain world, weekends that are not spent in the country are spent going to lunch.

In this alien setting, my defense mechanism went into high gear. As the fur flew, I can remember getting very quiet at the table and focusing on the cheese. I couldn't wait to get home. But when I got back to my flat and wrote up what had happened, I didn't write about that. None of my responses were recorded. Where was I in that scene? I was clearly at the table, but there is no "I" in the entry. Was I impressed to be in the same room with Tennessee Williams? You won't find that here. Was I dazzled by a look in at a rarefied existence? No trace of that. Did I feel sorry for the hostess? If so, I didn't find that worth mentioning.

I was there alright, but distanced. The inadvertent, but perfect journalistic stance. The record of the event makes its own comment, of course. As the outsider, my feelings were not the issue. I knew a good scene when I saw one and just wanted to get it down. *For the record.* The "I" was latent, beside the point. There was no need to insert myself into the drama, no need to scrape the inside of the coconut. Overt judgment—these people are vile—would have meant I couldn't have gone back to Chester Square, wouldn't have wanted to or felt comfortable there.

I retreated into the clouds of the third person, obliterating my presence and in my own diary became a journalist. In that way, I was safe. My distance meant I could return. My distance was terrific self-protection. Protection is needed by tourists, and journalists always travel tourist class. My status as a visitor made my place at the table in Belgravia—at any table, for that matter—suspect. Like every other reporter, often I'm not paying attention or even listening, but that doesn't matter. We are always considered aliens, even when the off-duty sign is on.

Another entry, almost four years later. By this time I'd gone back to putting dates in the right place.

January 26, 1980. Johannesburg. At dinner we were entertained by a handsome couple in an enormous house. The husband owns a diamond mine. All conversations among rich people sound the same here. They all torment themselves, or so they say, with the endless debate about staying on. They use expressions like "moral choices." But they all stay. The T.'s' house was way out of the city, surrounded by woods, their own waterfall, nature preserve, the works. During dinner it began to rain, a gentle summer shower. Suddenly, howling alarms sounded all over the grounds. Mr. T. got up from the table. "Don't worry. Just the rain. It trips the alarms." This could have happened anywhere—in fact, it happens all the time in New York—but the fact that we were in an 18K enclave of South Africa changed the mood at the table. The talk became very dark. Then Mrs. T. attempted to lighten things up. "Several weeks ago I was at a conference here and a real Afrikaner came up to me—the kind of fellow from the Orange Free State who wears yellow socks with a comb stuck in them—and I don't know why I did it, but I chose to tell him the name of another American journalist who had come to dinner. The Afrikaner flirted with me and I must say I was flattered, although I didn't tell my husband. Well, a few weeks later he actually called me and invited me to lunch, and I got so excited I went into Sandton and bought a new dress and did my hair. Do you know that at lunch he told me he was a member of BOSS, our secret police?" Mrs. T. laughed and passed the lamb. "He asked me if I would tell him when any other American reporters came to call. . . . What upset me was not that he was a member of BOSS, but that I thought he was interested in me as a pretty woman when it was merely my connections he was after."

I was in South Africa traveling with family—the dinner was a social call. Back at the hotel, I thought about the evening, how despicable South Africa was. Imagine living in this police state! Imagine an agent from BOSS wanting a private citizen to play spy. While that was true, so was something else. I had missed Mrs. T.'s entire point. The intimacy of the surroundings fooled me. Mrs. T. had threatened me. In case I missed it, she had been saying, "You might be here as an intimate, but as a journalist you are a danger, an unpredictable element that might threaten our way of life. We don't acknowledge your off-duty sign."

No choice was offered. The profession made me the outsider, but being the outsider (by disposition) gave me the profession, made me understand the tacit rules, like: There are no secrets. Everything starts from there. This is not to say there aren't temporary bonds of trust, but the bonds are fragile. As long as someone is getting it down, what is said today can be recycled, camouflaged, turned into material for tomorrow. Another rule: Anyone who tells an outsider anything has his reasons, often mysterious at the time. Sometimes it's vanity. More often, the secrets are spilled because the teller needs someone to bear witness, and who better than an outsider, a stranger, the exile who by trade knows how to ask questions? The act of telling can become an act of self-perpetuation. The secrets are out, but so are the facts of existence.

July 15, 1978. Munich. A local editor introduced me to a reporter named Ron H., whom he called "the David Halberstam of Germany." The German Halberstam was blond, Aryan, nervous, thin. I wondered about his English name. He talked mostly about his hangover. "I've been up since six talking to every doctor in Munich about my pancreas." Like everybody I've met, he spoke exquisite English, right down to the American syntax, as if he wanted to buff out his German cultural ties. That's common too. At lunch, I asked if he would go with me out to Dachau. "Why go there?" Ron asked. "Have you ever been to Sing Sing?" Ron offered to drive me back to the hotel. In the car I asked him how he learned to speak such perfect English, and instead of answering me he pulled the car off to the side of the road. I thought I had said something wrong. He asked me if I was familiar with the Stockbridge School in Massachusetts. I said I was. "It's very progressive, isn't it?" "Yes," he said. "It's where all the Jewish intellectuals send their children." Then, "That's where I went." Before I could react, a long explanation: "Can I trust you not to discuss this with anyone in Germany? My name is really Z. and my grandfather owned the largest publishing house in Berlin; he published Hitler before the war. Like a lot of families, mine thought they would be safe, but they wound up in Auschwitz. Never mind. They survived. I was born right after. Today, I'm a Catholic. It still isn't safe to be a Jew here. Certainly, as Z. I could never work in Germany as a reporter. So, I lead a double life. You could only get away with that here. That's how disparate a country we are. Half of the week I'm in the south, in Munich and Bavaria, working as the reporter, Ron H. The other half I'm in Berlin and Frankfurt where I'm known as Z. By my proper name."

I am still not sure why Ron H. told me this or even if the story is true. I do know that if he was making it up to provide me with a good dose of local texture, he was playing career roulette. How could he know I wouldn't have talked about this all over Munich? What would have been the purpose of such a game? A visiting American reporter, who happened to be Jewish, was hardly the person to hear a confession. I was in Germany working, not searching for my identity or looking to be a priest. Ron H., who made his living asking questions, remaining "neutral," distanced, felt the need to spill. He didn't want anything out of it. After he dropped me at the hotel, I never saw him or heard from him again. I've often thought of our talk in that car. Was Ron H. telling me these things because I was on my way to Dachau and he was consumed with guilt? Was it because I was safe, an American, no more threatening than if he had sat next to me on a plane? I don't know what his reasons were, but I suspect they had something to do with the fact that he was a reporter too, a member of the club. He could feel safe because I was just passing through his fiefdom, using the club facilities for the day. And something else: However melodramatic Ron's confession was, the parallel was irresistible. The intimate hidden self and the distant other, the camouflage that is *de trop* for an exile, imperative for the refugee. A necessary reporter's tool. We call this neutrality, and pride ourselves on transcending the base emotions of the subjective—although still getting the point across. The self is effaced as well. "She's a real pro," they say about the journalist who can get the copy in while undergoing a nervous breakdown, a divorce, a life-threatening disease.

The club is intimate, the membership select. In this fraternity, psychological distance is more than a norm, it is an ideal state. It took me a long time to begin to understand this and to learn that distance is not in all cases a condition to be corrected; that it has its time and place.

November 17, 1978. Paris. Lunch today with S. who was in a festive mood, off for Iran tomorrow to report on the revolution and the bloodshed, the demise of the shah. To celebrate, he ordered the "special number-ten belons. These are the last oysters I'll see

for a while." Typical S. behavior. So full of his own drama. His
bloviations foamed over the glass and hit the table. But he was
elated to be going to Tehran just in time to see its fall. "Aren't
you scared?" I asked him. "It's going to be a blast!" he said. "Everyone is going to be there. R. is coming in from London, T.
from Rome, W. will be showing up from Washington to cover it
for the *Post.* It's going to be incredible. Just like being in Vietnam
again."

I knew this was absurd—distance to the *n*th degree—but
somehow, away from home, I almost found the notion of the
traveling fraternity seductive. I was beginning to flounder in
Europe, unsure of my next move, not at all certain that I
wouldn't be happy existing amid the bomb blasts, surrounded
by my intimates from the club. I was reading a lot of Martha
Gellhorn and listening to the boys griping about how "shallow" the papers had become in New York, how "Nobody
cared about news anymore," how they had to fight for space
and usually lost out to features on pâté. A press strike was im-
minent. Each time I'd call my editor, he would say, "Nobody
cares about what's happening in Europe. That's over. The
news is here. Come home."

Then a letter arrived from a friend, Ward Just, who had
once been a foreign correspondent of the *Washington Post.* He
had given it up, saying he was "too old to be running around
anymore"; he'd gone home and turned his attention to writing
novels. I had written him for advice.

Back came this reply:

When I was twenty-eight I was in London, my career crumbling
around me, my marriage going to pieces. I was rescued by the
war in Cyprus. I'd finally found something I could do better than
anybody else. I was an OK political writer, a pretty good feature
writer, but war was really my profession and I think Cyprus saved
me from the ax, at for Christ's sake, *Newsweek.* Went there

twice, then took a six-month leave at the end of 1964 to go to Spain to write short stories. However, a familiar bearded figure was hovering over my shoulder, so I spent most of my time going to bullfights and drinking wine and thinking soulful thoughts. Silly as hell. Came back to Washington, had a detached retina repaired, left *Newsweek,* joined the *Washington Post*—still burning to write fiction, but broke now—until one afternoon I read about Vietnam and proposed to Benjamin Bradlee that I go there. 1965 at the *Post* had not been a conspicuous success either, and so I was saved a second time by gunfire, but that was an extreme. The same may not be true for you.

It wasn't. Ward's letter pointed up the obvious: There was nothing inherently attractive about the need to go to Southeast Asia to find a war; you had better understand your motives. Romantic notions were not enough. I had had my Spain period, only it had gone on for two years and sent me enough places to come back to the place I knew best: New York. I lightened up and I learned that I didn't have to be an expatriate to be an exile; there were plenty of foreign spheres close to home.

So I stopped keeping journals unless I was paid for it. Larger ambiguities gave way to smaller ones. I was back in New York working under the pressure of a weekly deadline in a period of such social and political retrenchment that often it seemed the same cast that used to lunch in Belgravia wondering about the new Fragonard were now running the country. People talked about "style" a lot. The jargon was everywhere: "Just like the Eisenhower years" or "Turning the clock back." Manners were important. I could have imagined I was in the precious and decadent atmosphere of SW 1, except I wasn't. Putting a gloss on any change and shining it up to a trend was as American as hula hoops. That made life easier. However retro life seemed, it would be temporary. Besides, I was happy: Rich people make good copy. The shift in the country meant there

would be loads of good material—exiles and immigrants, ty-
coons anointed to papacies, the newly powerful and famous,
the social arbiter, climber, and refugee. My nicely honed technique of journalistic distance could get a strong workout.
Where once I looked for meaning, now I found it without effort, and with a notebook for protection, I could dip in and out
of this world at will.

All of these pieces were written during 1980–83 for *New
York* magazine and its editor, Ed Kosner. There was no grand
design to the subjects—just anything or anyone Ed and I felt
was interesting or making news at the time. Luckily, we share
certain attractions: titans, the flamboyant, snake-oil salesmen,
the social, the insecure. This group makes good copy too.
Like pilgrims on the via Dolorosa, they flock to the city, eager
to pay homage to the kindred gods—power and career.

Kosner had been the editor in chief of *Newsweek* before he
took over *New York*. The phlegmatic rhythm I was used to in
magazine journalism no longer applied. No more lolling
around hoping to pick up pearls. You had to be ready to take
off on a dime and get your five thousand words ready for a
Wednesday close. When it came time to go back to London
to cover the royal wedding—five days to report and file—I
told myself that my long period of exile meant I could at least
read the London street guide, A–Z. I knew about all the essential nonessentials: what the General Trading Company
was, the proper attire for the queen's garden party (hats and
gloves), who to bribe at *The Times* with what brand of Scotch
to get to the telex, and that Patrick Litchfield was a cousin of
the queen's. I knew what is requisite for any reporter—how to
get in.

All that note taking in the journals, later redacted for *New
York* magazine, had taught me the importance of getting
close, the better to be there when "the moment" comes. The
moment is what every journalist lives for, when the subject
breaks down, reveals himself, drops his guard, unbends. Social

events are wonderful for observing these moments—that's where the spontaneity is. The spontaneity is never in a prearranged, set-up interview. That's where you get the party line. In an office, a man has his trappings. All the props are there. John Y. Brown, governor of Kentucky, looked impressive behind his large desk, flanked by pictures of John F. Kennedy and the Kentucky flag. It was only when he got to Appalachia and an uncontrollable environment that the cracks appeared. The same with Henry Kissinger. Talking stiffly in a suite at the Ritz-Carlton in Boston, he was very much a statesman, aware of notebooks and tape recorder. Outside in Boston Common, and among his friends, he dropped his guard. The luxury of working for a magazine is that you are allowed to hang around.

The luxury of a collection of pieces is that you are finally allowed the last word over your editors. So I have reinstated lines, words, and phrases that were cut for space. I have deleted expressions that certain gremlins who reside at magazines can insert in copy after pages have gone to type. ("We've changed the word 'distinction' to 'claim to fame',", one of these gremlins inevitably will announce as the presses roll.) Where this was particularly galling, I've gone back to my own words. These are just minor bits of polish, nothing which changes meaning or the substance of remarks. And wherever it was possible, I've added afterwords and updates because once in a while, as with Henry Kissinger and John Y. Brown, another bit of illumination can come with the subject's response.

But the ultimate luxury of a second life for what was meant to be magazine journalism is the ability to thank special colleagues, friends, and family. I am immensely grateful to the following: Ann Arensberg, Julie Baumgold, Sarah Lewis, Jesse Kornbluth and my parents, Milton and Thelma Brenner. A special thanks to Edward Kosner, a fine editor, who is always generous with his time and advice. Rhoda Koenig performs valiantly at *New York* under deadline pressure. And most especially my love and gratitude for the person who deserves it more than any other: my husband, Jonathan Schwartz. He is always there as reader, benevolent guide, cheerleader, and dearest friend.

To each reporter, her own Geiger counter, her own bag of tricks. Mine are simple. I prepare a few questions that I rarely ask. I know everything I can possibly know in advance. I listen. I pretend I'm in a social situation: "Let's have tea." I mind my manners. "What a beautiful house. What a lovely chair." No attacking, no journalism as assassination, no name-calling, no "How did the ax come to be held in your hand?" I compliment and, in the face of outrage, feign indifference, poker-faced, properly distant in my response.

This is precarious methodology, but for me, anyway, it works. It is precarious because a subject can be deluded and later, feel tricked. A smile can hide an icy edge. Eventually you get inured to the follow-up belligerent phone calls, the nasty letters, the remarks—they're just hazards of the trade. You get unflappable, more or less, because your concern is for the material, not to make a set of friends. Besides, you're too busy searching for the *next* moment, which means putting yourself in intimate settings, then waiting, before you are allowed to step all the way back. All you have to do is be there. The moment always comes. The trick is getting in.

Eventually, Henry Kissinger will talk about his analyst. Prince Charles will mock one of his subjects. Phyllis George Brown will show up in a see-through blouse at a courthouse in rural Kentucky. The rector of St. Bartholomew's, embroiled in an explosive real-estate controversy, will attack Brooke Astor and Mrs. Onassis. President Reagan's son, Ron, will blurt out, "I'm not going to shake hands with Jimmy Carter at the inauguration. . . . He has the morals of a snake." These incidents are mere incidents, nothing more. Like journal entries, they are *never* the whole story or even the partial story, but they are the moment when your heart beats faster, when you know you're close to striking gold.

There is no duplicity. My intention is always clear. It is my job to get the story. Facts and fairness. The line between the social and the professional can get blurred by the subject, but should never by the reporter. We are there to work. Anything else is their problem.

—M.B
January 1983, New York

Exiles and Immigrants

Henry Kissinger

Henry Kissinger had problems in the spring of 1982. *Years of Upheaval,* the second volume of his memoirs, was set to be published in May. In March, news of another book circulated: Seymour Hersh, the former *New York Times* reporter and Pulitzer prize winner, was coming out with his own work—an exposé of Kissinger's White House years. The Hersh book was not to be published any time soon, but an excerpt of it would appear in *The Atlantic* at just about the time *Years of Upheaval* hit the bookstores.

Kissinger had not granted any magazine reporter a lengthy interview since Oriana Fallaci visited him in 1972, but he was in a bind. He told friends that he was worried about the Hersh piece, and for good reason—a bombshell could have badly damaged *Years of Upheaval.* Kissinger had other troubles as well. He was recovering from open-heart surgery, and his father had recently died. His relationship with the current secretary of state, Alexander Haig, was complex. Kissinger had enjoyed inordinate personal prestige since his days in Washington, but now his former assistant was in charge. There was some talk that Haig might try to shut Kissinger out. With all this at work, it took some weeks to get Henry Kissinger to see me—and I think he finally agreed because he was feeling so vulnerable—but agree he did.

Just before we began, Kissinger surprised me. We were already seated in the living room of his suite at the Ritz-Carlton in Boston, the tape recorder was running, my questions prepared, when the following exchange took place:

HK:—Can we agree on some ground rules? That if you quote me, you will check the quotes with me?

MB:—We can do that.

HK:—I don't want to get into the position where Kosner [Edward Kosner, editor of *New York*] decides if I can change a quote or modify it or alter it. I mean, if I want to change something, it is my decision, not Kosner's decision. Or I'm going to be very careful. That's how I do it with the *Washington Post* and *The New York Times*. If I want to change the answer . . .

MB:—If you want to modify it slightly . . .

HK:—*No!* In *The New York Times* and the *Washington Post,* they let me rewrite the whole answer. I'm serious.

MB:—Dr. Kissinger, you must be the only person in history who has this agreement.

HK:—Why not? It should be the purpose of an interview that I say what I want to say.

MG:—Well, if *The New York Times* and the *Washington Post* allow you to do this. . . . If they do it, we'll do it.

HK:—I just want to make sure that we don't get into a situation. . . . And you cannot edit the answer without clearing it with me.

I knew I had protected myself with the sentence, "If they do it, we'll do it," and I was fairly sure that the papers had no such policy. If they did, that would be news in itself. As soon as I got back to New York from Boston, I called Arthur Gelb, the executive editor of the *Times,* and Ben Bradlee, the editor of the *Post.* I repeated to each of them what Kissinger had said—that their papers gave him the right to change his quotes. The editors were both emphatic. Arthur Gelb said, "Outrageous! There is absolutely no such agreement." Ben Bradlee said, "Total bullshit! You didn't fall for that one, did you?"

I wrote the piece, and before it was published, a *New York* researcher dutifully called Kissinger to read him his quotes. This is a courtesy the magazine extends to certain subjects, if the writer agrees. Kissinger was one of those subjects where quote review was a necessity. He wouldn't have allowed an interview unless his remarks were read back to him. But that's just about where the courtesy ends; we will correct grammatical bloopers, but we won't change nuance. When Kissinger heard his quotes, he was furious. He never denied he had said anything—after all, I had him on tape—but he demanded changes and deletions, tinkerings and shadings, on just about everything. His performance was astonishing and his requests out of the question.

*   *   *

*T*he habits of the diplomat die hard, so they were just a shade late. They said that Billy Graham had stopped in to visit on his way to the Soviet Union, and that had thrown off the schedule. As they walked briskly through the lobby of the Ritz-Carlton, heads turned, and the sprinkle of Bostonians began to react: "It's Kissinger, the Kissingers . . . *There goes Henry Kissinger*"—the aura still glowing after years out of power. The bodyguard followed at a discreet distance. As the Kissingers moved toward the waiting limousine on Newbury Street, they passed the hotel newsstand, and, of course, there it was—the dread *Atlantic,* with his face on the cover as the illustrator had imagined it, bloated and evil, shadowy, filled with wiretaps, Ellsberg treason, and secret weakness, staring out like some kind of memento mori. Chipping away at everything he had contributed to the world, after he had survived so much: Cambodia and Morton Halperin, the congressional committees and the shah. It was all back again to give succor to his enemies, pause to his friends. Yet another assault just after he had come through the triple-by-pass heart surgery and another tragedy, probably the worst blow, the death of the father he revered.

It was the operation that had brought Kissinger to Boston for a checkup and to Locke-Ober this night to honor his surgeons from Massachusetts General Hospital. He had dieted off twenty-seven pounds since the operation in February, and he was planning to go a little crazy, chucking the poached sole for the evening, feeding his heart doctors on steak and béarnaise. Upstairs waited a long table and eleven specialists with their wives; later would come, for the host, *Wiener schnitzel à la Holstein,* and his mood, despite *The Atlantic,* was soaring, his spirit, like his body, almost light.

Kissinger understood very well that he was not welcome in some Boston circles, but this group was not one of them. Far from it: These men had had the most intimate relationship with him. He had given himself over to them with great success. He could relax. Kissinger knew nobody at Locke-Ober was going to demand whether he had, in fact, put the taps on his friend Marvin Kalb. He could kid his doctors about "taping me in intensive care" and "leaving the tubes in to control me." He could be the Kissinger who charmed Chou and Sadat and Jill St. John, who regaled tables at Chequers and the Elysée with the self-deprecating wit, a survival technique he had used for years, deflecting all potential adversaries, even when there was no adversary to deflect.

And so Kissinger laughed loudest of all as he told a story about his father and how he had dealt with the metacelebrity his son had become. Thirty-two scrapbooks Louis Kissinger had filled with articles detailing his son's activities. His method was precise. "When a writer wrote three critical things about me," Kissinger said, "then my father would retroactively cut out all the rest of the writer's stories, so that through all the books there were gaping holes. The fault in my father's system was that he was very literal and guileless. So if a writer would describe me as 'Henry Kissinger, the brilliant states- man, the architect of foreign policy, responsible for the mass murders of Cambodia,' my father would leave *that* article in. At least they had called me 'brilliant.' He never understood what the real meaning was."

Louis Kissinger had survived ninety-five years not under- standing real meanings; his son had his own methods. No matter that all the scurrilous tales about his early years with Richard Nixon—and some new ones—were being told again. That night, Kissinger seemed beyond it; there was no tension around him, no shifty eyes. He was transcending, as he would phrase it, the latest barrage in his own way, talking Falkland Islands strategy and Sadat, reliving his operation with his doc- tors even though he had no tolerance, he said, for the sight or memory of blood.

That Kissinger would survive as a strong figure out of office was never in question—his mind was too subtle, his in- telligence too developed, his defense mechanisms too sophisti- cated for him to be anything less. The surprise is how much prestige he commands, how sought-after he is. Not for Henry Kissinger the oblivion of other ex-secretaries of state, clois- tered in a law firm, locked away in an investment-banking house. He has kept his influence over foreign affairs by his constant lecturing, at fifteen thousand dollars an appearance; his consulting work; and the publication of two exhausting volumes of memoirs. Lest we forget, here is Chile, Moscow, San Clemente, Le Duc Tho, China, Israel, Brezhnev, and Mao, Super-K hurtling from crisis to crisis, shuttle to shuttle, detailed in three pages for every day in office. If there is little perspective in any of it, there is the image of how smart and how powerful he really was, all of it confirming what he told me recently. "I had to act for a time as a substitute Presi- dent."

As Washington flounders, Kissinger's reputation ascends,

his management of foreign affairs, however controversial, inspiring a nostalgia for him in many circles. If he were renamed secretary of state tomorrow, the stock market would probably shoot up a dozen points. This, despite all the criticism, despite Cambodia, Iran, the wiretaps, the fawning over Nixon, the war-criminal talk. Yet, Kissinger seems to levitate above everything, and there are many reasons for this: his brilliance, his personality, the charm he can exude.

Kissinger's survival tactics have been masterly. His best defense has been no offense: He rarely answers a charge, issues a denial, or lets a mea culpa slip out. What he does is quite clever: He questions the motive of the accuser, usually with a wry smile. Kissinger has alienated both the far right and the far left, a perverse accomplishment few others could have managed. Perhaps each side cancels the other out. While no one has been paying much attention, the revisionism of the times has revised Kissinger too, enabling him to move beyond his critics and endure not as a pariah—far from it—but as a figure of eminence, a one-man A list.

His escape to New York may have saved him. Here the lone cowboy can protect himself from the political cross fire, the who's-up-who's-down, as he puts it, of Washington life. Here he can be shielded from Harvard and its moral pieties; anyway, Cambridge didn't welcome him back. That kind of intellectual rigidity has never found favor on the New York dinner-party circuit. It's a rare Manhattan guest who might be discomfited watching the butcher of Cambodia across the table spooning up his sorbet. Accomplishment, brains, and power banish moral ambiguities in Manhattan drawing rooms. And so, at fifty-eight, Henry Alfred Kissinger is surrounded with friends from every world—Brinkleys and Buckleys, Ribicoffs and Rohatyns, Arthur Schlesinger, Lane Kirkland, Mollie Parnis, Isaac Stern, Zubin Mehta, Simcha Dinitz, Barbara Walters, even the De la Rentas. He is a refugee no longer in exile, cosseted by his wife, Nancy; a blond Labrador named Tyler; bodyguards; a Georgetown house; a staff in Washington; a River House duplex in New York (with, it is said, bulletproof windows); and an income of more than five hundred thousand dollars a year.

Only rarely now do the accusations of the past come back to haunt him, as they have in the *Atlantic* piece, by Seymour Hersh, all of it gruesome and assiduously detailed. There is the word of Roger Morris and Morton Halperin, from Kissinger's staff. Kissinger is portrayed as devious, double-dealing, out to sabotage his subordinates to stay in good with his boss. Leakers were to be destroyed. Kissinger, Hersh says, ordered almost every wiretap. It's all there: Richard Nixon's drinking, Daniel Ellsberg's sex life, the duplicity of small men struggling to win vicious power games.

The irony was that Kissinger would wind up in Boston just after the hometown magazine hit the stands, the perfect setting to observe the Kissinger defense strategy in action. When he was quizzed, his behavior was paradigmatic. He was sitting in a wing chair at the Ritz-Carlton on a beautiful spring morning, trying to describe his foibles, how, he said, "I have never been able to gauge my enemies." It seemed the moment to bring up *The Atlantic*.

"Have you read the piece?"

"I have. I don't want to comment on it."

"But being characterized as so evil, that must upset you."

A pause. "But in this case, if you read the statements of the author, which he made when he started this article, and what he said to people—this is the view with which he began."

"Do you mean that you feel Hersh was out to get you?"

"That is what he has said. I don't know him. Did it upset me? Yes. But I don't want to get into a debate with him."

"Is this like a final chapter of Watergate for you?"

"I don't think this is a final chapter of Watergate. It doesn't bring back the experience, because it has no relation to reality, not the reality I know."

So, by saying nothing, he had said something, put the screws into Hersh without a real accusation, yet tried to rise above the substance of the text. All the same, Kissinger was in a very good mood. He had strolled on the Boston Common, down Boylston Street, and he had been recognized several times. As he walked, he chatted about Nixon, saying he had yet to hear from him, although he thought he had treated the ex-President very kindly in his book.

"So, what *was* the story with Nixon's drinking?" I asked, and for Kissinger no simple answer would do. Clearly, he felt the need to defend. "You know," he said, "these assistants of mine like Roger Morris, who Seymour Hersh quoted in *The Atlantic,* only worked directly for me for six months in 1969. How can they remember what went on thirteen years ago? How can they remember one incident when I might have said something about Nixon having had too much to drink? At any rate, it isn't true."

Fairly cool, but not for long. The next day at the River House, in New York, there was the magazine, opened, right by Kissinger's unmade bed. He must have been rereading the article and worrying what to do. And so he rescheduled an appearance on the Phil Donahue show he had canceled some weeks before, even though he had been told by friends, "Henry, you're too big for daytime TV." Kissinger wanted to talk about his book; Donahue wanted to talk about Hersh. So his performance was out of pattern: Boxed into a bad situation, he gave a brief answer, calling the Hersh piece "gossip and innuendo." That was about it. Even that little was uncharacteristic; Kissinger is usually very measured in his responses. But he may be less so since his father's death. He is suffering terribly, his friends say, and might be reexamining his modus operandi, wanting to indulge in self-justification, wondering if he could have been a better son.

That he would be so disquieted shows how much he has changed from the Other Kissinger, the corseted "secret swinger" who issued White House edicts. That Kissinger's style, with its undertones of Metternich, he capsuled elegantly in *Years of Upheaval:* "There are many occasions in diplomacy when dedication is measured by the ability to pretend indifference when every fiber strains for getting to the point."

Pretending indifference is useful for Kissinger now only in rare situations. He no longer needs to strain at much of anything. Or so he says; "My life in New York is very relaxed. New York is so different from Washington. In Washington, you are always onstage, you always have to consider that what you say at dinner will become part of the political landscape. Here, people do not go to dinner in order to measure their virility or to take your temperature—at least not the ones I go to."

And he goes out a lot, "five nights a week," he says, always within a circle of friends, favoring certain hostesses: Mollie Parnis, Brooke Astor, Francoise de la Renta, and Happy Rockefeller, who recently invited three hundred people to her Fifth Avenue apartment to celebrate Kissinger's new book and to nibble pretzels and finger sandwiches on the requisite white bread. His hostesses are aware of his "paradoxical vulnerability," as one called it, and they protect him, surrounding him with other potentates, most of whom are already his friends. "In all the years I've known him," Mollie Parnis says, "I have never once heard anyone attack him at table. Once, when Henry wasn't there, one of my guests said, 'I never want to meet Henry Kissinger,' and later I said to that man, 'By saying that, I can assure you that you never will.' " The hostesses' reward is the revelation of Kissinger's *haimish* side. "Sometimes he is so open at dinner," Shirley Clurman, wife of public-policy advisor Richard Clurman, says, "I will be just staggered. I will say, 'Henry, if someone heard you say this, you would be in terrible trouble.' "

For Kissinger, the process is, as he says, "very ecumenical. There is always a collection of noncompeting people in their fields. To go to a small dinner for Alec Guinness—that's fun. I don't have to talk about foreign policy if I don't want to. Conversely, when I do talk about foreign policy, it is with someone who is interested, who really isn't part of the power process. My friends don't want anything from me, and I don't want anything from them."

Except, often, just a good time. As with a lot of self-made refugees, there is a side to Henry Kissinger that is terribly innocent, still back in the old country. At times, the innocence is almost childlike, as if the boy who was deprived of a real childhood by persecution might still be in there, struggling to get out. At Locke-Ober, the doctors surprised Kissinger with a belly dancer, who gyrated for him and wrapped him in veils. Kissinger loved every moment—he was neither cynical nor fretful, even when the dance went on a bit long. Robert Evans, the producer, another Kissinger friend, tells the story about being in Washington for a state dinner the night John Ehrlichman resigned. "Henry and I sneaked away from the dinner and crept into the Oval Office," Evans says. "He wanted to show it to me, and so we tiptoed around and wound up in Nixon's john. There by the toilet was the phone list. Everybody had been scratched off. Henry was laughing. He said, 'Look, Bobby, I'm the only one left.' "

In New York, all facets of his personality can be indulged. He can be ponderous or innocent, grotesque or merely brilliant. In New York, he can have dinner with Danny Kaye, or he can be the statesman emeritus. On a recent Saturday night at the River House, the Kissingers' table was set for dinner. Three close friends were expected: Simcha Dinitz, the former Israeli ambassador, Bette Bao Lord, the writer, and his agent, Marvin Josephson. A nothing-special evening, Saturday night at home. In the Kissingers' navy-lacquer dining room, not a picture warms the veneer, only recess-lighted shelves of Chinese *objets*. Silver service plates rested on lace settings, along with a pair of crystal candelabra, matching floral arrangements, and, for accent, a cluster of Chinese figurines. A formal setting for an informal evening, a reflection of the Kissingers' private tastes, a modified state dinner no matter whom they entertain.

The private statesman style extends through the rest of the Kissinger apartment, a large, elegant duplex with swags of silky maroon curtains, matching sofas, a Siqueiros over the fireplace, an eighteenth-century Chinese screen. It's a kind of standard-issue royal residence—the ultimate in assimilation— surprisingly without photographs or family keepsakes. Until you get upstairs to Kissinger's study. The small room is stacked high with professional papers, government documents, memos, and dropoffs—Billy Graham's speech on nuclear weapons rested on a table, waiting to be read. On one wall is a large TV screen for Kissinger's beloved Yankee games. In this room are a few talismans: the tiny pillow needlepointed POWER IS THE ULTIMATE APHRODISIAC; photographs of his children, David and Elizabeth; and a carton of *White House Years* shoved almost out of sight.

It is in this room, with its sloppy comforts, that Kissinger conducts most of the business of his day. "Early mornings from seven-forty to eleven I set aside for meeting people, the consulting I do." Heads of large corporations seek him out, wanting his advice on international affairs. Half call him cold: "Dr. Kissinger, please." On a typical day, he works on his memoirs, writing in longhand on legal pads, from eleven to five. Soon he will start volume three—his Washington staff will pull almost every document detailing the invasion of Cyprus, the fall of Vietnam, the Ford years. Every report, diary, memo, and phone log will be piled up in the study at the River House, ready for Kissinger and his legal pads. In the late afternoon, he must rest. Since his bypass operation, he also must walk four miles a day.

The Kissinger phone continues to ring. "I've shut it off," Kissinger says. "It rings too often. I have my security people get it. I try to get all the calls routed through Washington. There are fifty or so calls a day. There is always a residual list." A lot of the calls are the skim-off off fame—a radio station in Oakland wanting his opinion on the Falkland Islands dispute, a gold trader wondering if there will be a war in Angola, that kind of thing. There are other calls: Yamani and Mubarak and every other world leader frequently check in. "I am on the tour for visiting Israelis," Kissinger says. "Shimon Peres calls me occasionally, but he doesn't ask, 'What should I do about Begin?' He might say, 'What should I do?' about a particular problem. Not only Peres but also Abba Eban. Mr. Begin always knows where I stand, if he cares."

For all of this, there is a strict etiquette. "In the first two years that Henry was out of office, if, say, Sadat would arrive, he might call Henry first to discuss a matter of diplomacy," says Bob Evans. "Henry would say—and I know, because I've been in the room—'I would like to take your call, but it is not protocol. Please call the State Department first.' "

In the small room upstairs at the River House, there is perspective. Here he tries to think like his models, David Bruce and John McCloy, "without malice and with compassion," about those who wield power. "In a funny way," he says, "I understand the thing I did in Washington better now that I am out of government. Some of the things that seem world-shaking to you when you are in government—somebody leaking something, for example, doing something that at that moment you find almost unendurable—I can smile at now." Here there is distance and no treachery. "One of the aspects of leadership is that you are often, as in a nightmare, on a railway track with a train heading toward you, and the question is, can you get off the track before the train hits you? You know very well the train is coming and you will die. I must have had those dreams then. Now I don't dream."

In the past, he says, there was no relaxation—he couldn't even read. "I was an illiterate. All I could read were psycho-

logical thrillers, like Le Carré." Now he can spend some days
reading history and biographies—he even finds time to indulge himself in a bit of trash. "I tried to read Judith Krantz,"
he says, "but I found it too boring. I didn't find it very sexy.
To simply say 'They went to bed' is not sexy. And I read
Ninja. I suppose that was trash, but it was more like a thriller.
To be sexy, for me, there must be an element of mystery."

Still, with all the new calm, the illusion of power is somehow preserved. It is almost as if Kissinger is trying to function
as a shadow secretary of state. His Washington staff describes
his "scheduling problems"—he must wedge visitors in at
twenty-minute intervals, not give them a second more. It
seems a bit purposeful, almost calculated. Certainly, the approach to selling his memoirs was a ploy. "When Henry was
going to start writing his books," Bob Evans remembers, "I
said, 'You simply cannot be represented by an agent. That is a
terrible comedown.' To have been represented by a lawyer
would have been wrong too. So I called Marvin Josephson." It
was Josephson, the head of a conglomerate, who negotiated
the million-dollar-plus advance.

There is a compulsiveness to all the activity and the travel,
but sometimes, in his desire to remain in the public eye, Kissinger can slip and behave like any other celebrity. At the moment, a lot of his domestic travel has to do with giving
speeches and sitting on boards. He is on an advisory board of
the Chase Manhattan Bank, where his duties include analyzing loans for foreign countries; it meets twice a year. He sits
on the board of Twentieth Century-Fox, but "That's just for
fun, because Jerry Ford asked me to." And he's on the board
of the Trust Company of the West, a position that led to a recent embarrassment. Kissinger was in Los Angeles for a
meeting and was asked to give a speech. It turned out to be for
an opening of a savings-and-loan branch. Kissinger was made
to look foolish by the publicity, and he was furious. "The
problem was, because of my operation, nobody checked out

the nature of the event," he says. "This kind of thing will never happen again."

Indeed, the illusion of power is too important. The bodyguard is omnipresent, and there is all the talk of logistics, where the car will be, where the guards will be, details that say nothing really has changed. And something else: As long as the image is retained, soon, he too might be.

Nancy at home: The towering nurturer is barefoot in a cotton caftan, pleased to have a few days "to clean out the closets," since Henry has gone to the Coast. She is curled up on the couch, smoking incessantly, eating smoked salmon and cream cheese. All of it leaves an impression: Nancy Maginnes Kissinger seems coltish, confessional, a girl's girl and a scholar, an ideal roommate to find sharing your suite at Mt. Holyoke. Sometimes in New York one hears cavils. Nancy, people will say, is obsessed with clothes. Or; if Nancy is so smart, why doesn't she work? In fact, she would, she says, if only the right person would ask. "It's very hard to find a job when you're a Kissinger," she says. "And I am an awful putterer. I'm both phlegmatic and nervous. I've been offered things, but I don't want to work seven days a week."

Perhaps by the time she turned forty-two and decided finally to marry, Nancy Maginnes was ready to retire, no longer eager to draft Rockefeller position papers or ruminate over the influence of the Tang dynasty. She was ready to hit the racks at Adolfo, ready for the nice rich-lady touches, like being able to wander into Mollie Parnis's showroom to buy Henry's assistants gifts of Ultrasuede suits. Kissinger courted her for six years—"He knew right away he wanted to marry me," Nancy says—but she held out, phlegmatic again. She might have been waiting for the proper credentials. It's one thing when you grow up in White Plains across the road from Punch Sulzberger to marry a refugee professor, however brilliant; it's quite another to become Mrs. Secretary of State.

Besides, life with Henry is hardly without incident. Her performance at Newark Airport, defending Henry against an offensive demonstrator, has made her a heroine. Soon she will have her day in court. Nancy has an explanation. The few days before weren't idyllic, she says. Her husband had come home from Boston with a handful of nitrogylcerin pills having been told there was something "seriously wrong." His doctors said, "Don't let him move a block." It was Nancy's responsibility to see that his blood pressure did not go up one point. "The whole weekend before we left for Boston so Henry could get his angiogram I kept thinking I wasn't really nervous. I was in an altered state. Then, when we got to the airport, Henry couldn't carry anything, and he had to walk a long way. Then this boy came up and said, 'Can I ask you two questions?' and I said no, and Henry waved him away. I was loaded down with books, his edits for the *Time* excerpts. It was typical Henry—a two-day trip and he packs like it's two weeks. So when the woman came up and said, 'Do you sleep with young boys at the Carlyle?' I just snapped. I pinched her neck. I only had two fingers free. I said, 'Get out of my way.' " She sighs. "It was about the way two eight-year-olds behave."

For Nancy Kissinger, a departure. She has her own wife-of-Kissinger strategies. She avoids all confrontations, all complaining, doesn't even hound her husband about losing weight. She is used to his domestic frailties, such as losing his glasses at least once a day. She doesn't get upset when she walks into the kitchen and sees the nocturnal tableau: Henry and Tyler staring into the icebox, analyzing the remains.

"Sometimes when I see Henry slathering five pounds of butter and strawberry jam on his English muffins every morning, as he used to do, I might say, 'Henry, can't we do without the butter and jam?' But that's about as far as I go." Instead, she worries, smokes, contracts ulcers—the stress caused her to lose half her stomach in her second year as the wife of the sec-

retary of state. And she wears braces to correct an overbite—
the result of too much teeth grinding.

Nancy is, she says, inured to Henry's critics by now. That,
too, requires strategy. A while ago she ran into Mort Zucker-
man, the new owner of *The Atlantic.* The Hersh issue had yet
to come out. "What are you going to say about Henry?"
Nancy demanded. Has she finally read it? "Only the first few
paragraphs. I'm a total coward. I figure, why get upset? If Abe
Ribicoff attacked Henry, that I would take seriously because
he is a man of integrity we respect." The friends protect her
too. "Most of my friends think, 'Why upset Nancy?' or they
will call up and say, 'Don't let this upset you.' "

The technique seems to be working. All looks fairly serene
at the River House, but there are indignities suffered, insults
for the man who opened China, slights that can't be rational-
ized away. Like the one from Harvard. Kissinger says he was
invited back, "but in such a way I would be guaranteed to refuse." Sometime after he left the government, a letter from
Cambridge arrived. "The letter was from a department chairman. He offered me a teaching post with a full course load, no
clerical help, and no assistant. Then he said in this letter that if
I was interested *I* should contact the dean. Neither the president of Harvard nor the dean invited me. It was an absolute
insult." ˙

That situation he couldn't control, and it was, he says, quite
painful, especially since Harvard had rebuffed him years before, in his first try for tenure. In those days, the early 1950's,
Kissinger had made up his mind to follow the advice of his
mentor, Fritz Kraemer. Tenacity is everything, Kraemer said.
So despite the early rejection and an offer from the University
of Chicago, Kissinger remained at Harvard. After Kissinger
became a consultant to the Council on Foreign Relations and
published the acclaimed *Nuclear Weapons and Foreign Policy,*
tenure came. Surprisingly, he showed no signs of resentment.

"Henry has the remarkable ability to not become bitter about any slight he has suffered in life," Nancy says. She is convinced that this is an inherited trait. "Henry's father never allowed the bitterness of the past to seep into the present," she explains.

For the Kissingers, father and son, this was a crucial strategy for overcoming their worst injury, their persecution in Germany and their subsequent flight. Louis Kissinger had been a *Gymnasium* teacher in a small town in Bavaria, a respected man of high position who could afford full-time servants. By 1933 he had lost his job. His son "Heinz" was beaten up. Louis Kissinger's three sisters were to die in concentration camps. The Kissingers' ordeal was fairly typical, but they got out of Germany, although late, just before Kristallnacht, in 1938. Henry Kissinger was fifteen, his brother Walter fourteen, and it is for this reason—linguists say a year can make the difference—Kissinger says, that he still has an accent and Walter does not. (Walter has his own explanation. "Henry never listens to anybody.")

For Kissinger, to survive this past was not to dwell upon it. Kissinger rarely discusses those years in Bavaria, even with good friend Henry Grunwald, now editor in chief of Time, Inc., whose background, although Austrian, was very much the same. "What is there to discuss?" Kissinger says. "Certainly, it was something that was an important experience in my life, but not one that we discussed frequently. It didn't need to be discussed," he says. This is more than tactical diplomacy: How could Kissinger be an internationalist if his heart harbored hate? (Recently, his Little, Brown editor, Genevieve Young, had an idea: Why not a memoir of childhood, a portrait of the statesman as a young man? She mentioned it casually to Peter Rodman, Kissinger's assistant. "He couldn't do that," Rodman said. "There is no research in the area.")

"My childhood is probably the reason I feel more deeply about America than some homegrown intellectuals who focus on its failings," Kissinger says. "I am very conscious of what hope America gave me when I was a boy in Germany." By concentrating on the people who had helped them in their hometown, Kissinger was able to go back to Bavaria with his parents some years ago. Ironically, it was Nancy, of all the Kissingers, who was nervous about the visit. Her husband said, "If all the rest of the Kissingers can go back, so can you."

Only rarely does melancholia creep in. During one of Nixon's last nights in the White House, Kissinger watched him standing at the window staring out at the Rose Garden. Kissinger writes, "I knew the feeling from the time when as a boy I had left the places where I had been brought up to emigrate to a foreign land: attempting to say good-bye to something familiar and beloved, to absorb it, so to speak, so that one can never be separated from it. In the process, sadly, one loses it imperceptibly because the self-consciousness of the effort destroys what can only be possessed spontaneously."

Forward motion also destroys any inclination to look back, as does desire for complete domination. Kissinger tells a story about several sessions he once had with an analyst. "When my first wife and I divorced, part of the agreement was that I would see a psychiatrist for four sessions, and I agreed. In our first session, I told the doctor, 'I am not the kind of man who can free associate or look within myself. But I have a proposition: We will meet four times. Each time we will discuss a different topic. We will alternate between the choice of topics. You can pick two, and I will pick two. Then, at the end of these four sessions, you will know as much about me as if I had free associated.' To his credit, the doctor agreed. He was a very intelligent man. One of the subjects he chose for me to analyze was a poem by Yeats. We never did talk about my dreams."

The master negotiator is also a master manipulator, pressing for advantage, often at times when there is no need. His doctors were not allowed to touch him until he knew every step of the surgical procedure, every risk, every graph. "He could almost have done the operation," Dr. Austen says. His interviewers are told that, if he should desire it, he will have complete control over his quotations. "That is the arrangement I have with both the *Washington Post* and *The New York Times*," he says. (As it happens, this is not true.) Even his mother was told on the night before he was sworn in as secretary of state, "Whatever happens tomorrow, no matter what, you are not to cry." And so, according to Bette Bao Lord, as Kissinger became the first refugee to be in the Cabinet, Paula Kissinger had the only dry eyes in the room.

Kissinger's control is most evident when he is asked, as he is frequently, for his opinion on foreign affairs. Here is where the Other Kissinger emerges. His voice becomes flat, didactic, without nuance or vocal gestures. The diplomatic *we* takes over. He still refers to Alexander Haig as "my former deputy," as when he says, "Haig was my deputy, and one can never be sure how one's deputy will perform." He monitors his former deputy's performance from afar, but he does notice the obvious, like the number of *I*'s used in any Haig statement. And he is careful not to criticize and to say the appropriate thing, such as, "Every secretary of state has his own style." Although Kissinger's policy is "not to initiate calls to senior officials," as Haig was leaving on his own shuttle during the Falkland Islands dispute, Kissinger phoned him. "I really called just to wish him good luck. In this case, knowing the feelings of uncertainty, I thought I should wish him luck. In that context, he gave me a rough idea of where he thought things stood. He quite literally didn't know what he would find."

Kissinger is cautious, rarely criticizing his former deputy or the deputy's boss, careful not to comment on Jeane Kirkpatrick's dining with the Argentineans the night of the Falkland invasion. Only once has he spoken out, during the crackdown in Poland. "When an issue becomes overwhelming and things seem to be going off the rails, then one has an obligation to say something," Kissinger says. His discretion is purposeful; he knows speaking out is no way to get back in. "This country is very wasteful about the people it has with experience," he says. "Every four to eight years there is almost a total change, so that people who are out of office are almost never seriously consulted or used."

This has to rankle the private statesman, whose foreign-policy quarterbacking is now limited to spheres of living-room influence and occasional calls. "Henry still worries intensely about the state of the world, just as he did when he was secretary of state," Nancy says. He has even revised some of his more recalcitrant opinions. On nuclear weapons, for example. "For a time, I thought that perhaps one could have limited nuclear warfare instead of mass extermination. This may still be theoretically possible, but nobody has ever come up with a proposal of how it would work. . . . Most of the new anti-nuclear people will not face the fact that the ideological and political conflicts of the period contribute to the nuclear tensions, that they also have to be addressed."

That is Kissinger in rare revisionism; his mechanism allows for little ambivalence. What's more, he genuinely believes that as secretary of state he made few mistakes. "Fundamentally, I tried to think through problems as carefully as I could at the time. . . . Some of these decisions were very difficult. It would be ridiculous to say now, five years after, ten years after the event, I was wrong. I was wrong on some tactical things, like the anti-war movement." The "tactics" of Iran? "The mistake we made in Iran was to not look at the political evolution more carefully. I remember in 1976, which was my last official trip to Iran, I told the newsmen on my plane, 'A country going through this rapid industrialization would normally have a revolution, but I see no sign of it.' That statement shows I just didn't understand it."

"I think the dominant failing of most people in the government is confusion, not evil," Kissinger says. "The man who said, for example, there was a light at the end of the tunnel in Vietnam wasn't lying, he was wrong. Most of the time you face, especially in a crisis, a lot of conflicting information. On top of that conflicting information are the conflicting pressures of the bureaucracy, of the various bureaucratic elements which have often not been made explicit, which are often not even explicitly understood."

That, in essence, was Kissinger's problem: the difficulty of controlling the bureaucracy, the petty malice, the leakers, other governments, dictators, left-wing journalists, domestic revolutions. Kissinger left the Ford administration exhausted, he says. And two hundred thousand dollars in debt. "He had no money when he was in Washington," Bob Evans says. "I used to tell him, 'Henry, your tux is terrible. That tie is horrible.' He would say, 'I know, but I don't have enough money to buy a new tuxedo.' " (He was able, though, to buy his apartment in River House—a bit rundown then, but expensively remodeled since—at a bargain price: a little over a hundred thousand dollars.) Perhaps this is one reason he maintains he really doesn't want to go back. Both Kissingers say this is no ploy. "There was so much responsibility all the time, there was real worry rather than joy. Power does not guarantee you a lot of fun," Nancy Kissinger says. "After the first six months on that level of the government, you feel so grim, so weighed down with responsibility, that it overcomes any feelings of grandiosity that you might have. But if the President called and said, 'The country needs you'—well, that nobody could turn down," she said.

As he pads through the River House in his Wallabees and shetland sweater, there seems to be very little that haunts Henry Kissinger in, as he calls it, "this new phase of life." Only one thing disturbs him—the death of his father. The closeness of family had been instrumental in Kissinger's ascent, as had Louis Kissinger's approval and pride in his son's life. It was unmitigated and undemanding: As successful as both sons became—Walter is a rich Long Island businessman—Paula and Louis Kissinger were secure enough to remain in Washington Heights. "However old you are, you are never ready for it when your father dies," Kissinger says. "My father was a complete innocent, unlike his son. He had no conception of evil. My father was not ready to die. He was totally alert at age ninety-five. He wasn't philosophical about it. I used to think when I saw people in their fifties when I was a young man that they were a different species. No one is ever prepared. I had called my father the night before he died to tell him to watch me on TV the next day. And then he was gone, just like that. His lungs filled, and he went very suddenly without suffering."

It is a few moments before Kissinger is due at Massachusetts General. He is stopped by a traffic light. The third man of the day approaches him. For a moment, Henry Kissinger looks scared. As with every encounter, it could go either way. The bodyguard tenses. "Henry," the man says, "Henry, we miss you. Go back to Washington." Kissinger smiles broadly and shakes his admirer's hand. The light changes, and he moves toward the hospital in front of a line of cars. "Maybe people are nostalgic for me," he says. "But it's like the nostalgia in the Seymour Hersh piece. They have nostalgia so they can finish me off."

May 1982

*   *   *

"The Importance of Being Henry" was published on a Monday in early May and by eleven that morning Kissinger had called my home looking for me. That's usually a bad sign; no one ever calls a journalist to say thank-you. Indeed, Kissinger was furious. When we finally spoke late that afternoon, he started the conversation off by yelling, *"I am outraged!* We had an agreement and you violated it."

Of course I knew he would be plenty irritated about his quotes, but I was irritated too: Kissinger had tried to pull a fast one. I told him about my conversation with Gelb and Bradlee. "They're lying," Kissinger said. "Bradlee has his reasons. But that's a whole other story."

"Our agreement was that if *The New York Times* and the *Washington Post* allowed you to change your quotes, then *New York* would allow you to change them too," I said. "Who was I to check with if not the editors of the papers?"

"I didn't think you were going to pull a legalistic trick on me," Kissinger screamed. "Anyway, maybe Bradlee and Gelb don't know the arrangements I made. I have these arrangements with Scottie Reston and Meg Greenfield. You could have called them and asked them."

Since this was the first mention of Reston and Greenfield, Kissinger's logic escaped me. "Well, Dr. Kissinger, you told me it was the policy of the newspapers. You never mentioned Meg Greenfield [editor of the op-ed page of the *Washington Post*] or James Reston. If you had told me that your deal was with them, I would have called them," I said. "Both Scottie Reston and Meg Greenfield let me edit my quotes," Kissinger repeated. "Why would I lie about such a thing?"

Kissinger was dogged. An hour later, he was still arguing with me. He never denied he had said what I printed, but what bothered him, as he kept saying, was that "someone might misinterpret my remarks. How is the board of Twentieth Century-Fox going to feel when they read that I have joined them just for fun?" he said. "No one will understand that I was joking when I said that the nostalgia people have for me as secretary of state is the same kind of nostalgia Seymour Hersh has—that they can finish me off." And, "I will not be called the 'butcher of Cambodia.' " "I will not be called a liar

in print." But Kissinger's main theme was our refusal to allow
him total control over his quotes. Finally, he said, "Look, we
could argue all day. You're going to have to realize something. You will never see me again."

Obviously I would never see him again. I was around
Henry Kissinger to do a story, the story was finished, what
more was there to say? Kissinger's tone—"You *vill* never see
me again"—was ominous. It was as if a form of social banish-
ment was his trump card, when nothing social had ever gone
on between us. Kissinger is surrounded by close friends who
are in journalism—Marvin and Bernard Kalb of CBS, David
Brinkley, Henry Grunwald—but these mandarins have been
his friends for decades, since he was the genius professor
working in the basement of the Nixon White House as national security adviser. Our conversation ended when Kissinger hung up on me.

But that wasn't the end of it. Later that day, Meg Greenfield called Ed Kosner at *New York,* and she was in a state.
Greenfield was in London and, that afternoon, Kissinger had
tracked her down. "I just want to reconfirm that I have this
arrangement with you," Kissinger told Greenfield. "I've told
New York that as a matter of policy you allow me to change
my quotes for the *Washington Post.*"

It was after midnight in London by the time Meg Greenfield got Ed Kosner on the phone. She was extremely upset
that Kissinger had involved her in his machinations. "Ed, I
must explain to you what this is about," she said. "Several
years ago when Rhodesia became Zimbabwe, I asked Kissinger to write a column for the op-ed page about what effect
the change would have on American foreign policy. Kissinger
said he didn't have time, he was leaving for Europe, so I offered to send over an editorial writer who could take down
what he had to say and then we could write it up with his by-
line. Kissinger thought that was a good idea except that he insisted on being able to change whatever he wanted in the piece

before we published it. Of course we agreed—what writers can't change their own copy? And that was our only agreement. The *Washington Post* does not allow anybody to change quotes."

A few days later, Kissinger phoned me again, this time to apologize for screaming. "I just get sick and tired of being called a manipulator," Henry Kissinger said.

Kentucky's First Couple: John Y. Brown and Phyllis George Brown

*T*hey had come to the tiny courthouse to ask their governor a lot of questions, extremely serious questions about their Medicare and why it had been cut in half, and about their Blue Cross and why it had doubled, and about the governor's wife, Phyllis George Brown. They wanted to know if she really spent twenty thousand dollars on state troopers each and every time she went up to New York City for her CBS football show. Maybe a hundred people filled that courtroom in Richmond, Kentucky, the women encased in sad, poverty fat, the men looking bewildered. As the governor spoke, a noisy farmer wandered in with a carton of eggs jammed into the pocket of his dusty jacket and sagged down near three black women, each wearing a startling combination of prints and plaids, proud as mynas.

The governor of Kentucky, John Y. Brown, kept looking toward the door, as if he were waiting for something to happen. He sat on a table in front of his constituents, twitchy, stroking his foulard tie with hands as graceful as a cardsharp's, dangling his legs as he would on the terrace of his estate at Cave Hill. He was trying to be soothing, like warm treacle on a cold day, but the jiggling tassels on his loafers betrayed him.

He seemed very bored. Awkward, even. Certainly out of place. He wasn't really answering anybody's questions, didn't seem to understand that what they were talking about was not being able to feed their families. He was just using the occasion of this rural drop-in—what he calls "government to the people"—to deliver his set piece about cutting waste, running the state like a business: Kentucky & Co.

But everyone had heard it already: how he had made all the millions in fast food—Kentucky Fried Chicken, to be exact—and how the money had qualified him to own basketball teams and run for office and deal with serious questions with a lot of ambitious-millionaire's twaddle about what he had said to Ed Meese the last time he was up in Washington. Everybody knew he had Washington on his mind. They also knew that Brown was in Richmond that day to push his succession amendment, selling it hard, as he sells everything hard—this notion that a Kentucky governor should be allowed to serve more than one four-year term. It escaped nobody's notice that should his amendment pass, the first Kentucky governor to be allowed a second term would be John Y. Brown.

The twitching accelerated as he went on to "little ole business" and how "if you put a tax on it, it's gonna move right out of the state," when suddenly attention seemed to shift. The trio of black women and the farmer began to look over the governor's shoulder, and a cloud of musk wafted through the court just as Phyllis George Brown entered, none too quietly. She was wearing about three-thousand dollars' worth of supple burgundy leather, as if Fendi had dressed her, and the pear-shaped diamond the size of a coal lump—all very ex-Miss America glamorous—but her forehead was deeply lined, as if the strain of trying to stay a beauty queen at thirty-two was beginning to tell.

And then the governor turned his head, the picture of spontaneity, and said, "Honey, what are you doin' here?" and Phyllis rushed to hug him, and everyone stared, which was the intention, because John Y. Brown knows that, next to Colonel Sanders, Phyllis George is his best asset. Her eyes sparkled, a lot of hi-y'all's and how-is-everybody's came out, and then she slipped out of her jacket to reveal a white blouse and bra so gauzy that from the back of the room it was possible to get a good look at the First Lady's nipples, pointing straight toward the portraits of Kit Carson and Daniel Boone. If her outfit wasn't appropriate, it did get everyone's attention.

"Phyllis, honey, why don't you take over for a while?" the governor said. "Oh, Johnny, I couldn't," she said. "Come *own,* honey, sure you could—they'd rather listen to you anyway." "Well, all right." She reached firmly for the microphone. "I'd love to tell you what I've been doin'. . . ." There was a buzz from the side of the court, where the governor was whispering with his aide. "Johnny, will you *hesh* your mouth so I can talk?" He did. Then Phyllis talked. "Johnny and I are complete partners in everything. A lot of people may not understand that, but we are equals in the marriage, and that is the way it is." That means they run the state together too. Phyllis had a lot of projects to talk about that day: bringing Hollywood people to Kentucky to make movies, selling the quilts and ceramics of the mountains to Neiman-Marcus in Beverly Hills. It was probably the first time in the history of the state that the phrase "Neiman-Marcus in Beverly Hills" had ever been heard in a small-town court.

Then she announced she was "going to play Phil Donahue." She roved the aisles with her mike, jamming it at all the constituents to get them to speed it up. She would tell her husband, "Answer the question, Governor," when he would wander off on some dumb tangent about his father, the way politicians tend to do. The "complete partners" worked the room, Phyllis's hand waving in the air,' the gauzy blouse, the diamonds, all of it bringing a curious kind of paralysis to the audience so that before long the questions were less about people's problems and more about how the governor liked his job. At the end, a few people asked for her autograph. Phyllis filled an entire page with her message: "Smile! Phyllis George Brown."

All of this would be fine if it were just regional theater. But John Young Brown has gotten awfully good at saying, "I'm not sure I want to run for President." He's being mentioned more and more these days as an attractive Democratic candidate. His uncertainty seems very studied, like a buildup, a soft sell. John Y. Brown is very good at selling. He went from selling encyclopedias to selling fried-chicken franchises. He made a lot of money—about thirty-five million dollars—when Kentucky Fried Chicken was sold. For a while he rewarded himself by buying a large share of the Boston Celtics. He wasn't so good at running that, but he did get to meet of lot of celebrities. Then he married Phyllis and decided to run for governor. He won with the help of a million dollars' worth of TV ads and his very energetic bride. Now he is back to selling again—Kentucky and himself. John Y.'s portrait has been seen in ads in the financial papers with the slogan KENTUCKY & CO.: THE STATE THAT'S RUN LIKE A BUSINESS. Phyllis George Brown is a pretty good saleswoman too. She's known from her appearance on CBS's top-rated football show, the *NFL Today*. Phyllis got herself out of Denton, Texas, by becoming Miss America. She's never looked back.

Phyllis and the governor are very happy. They have shared values. He fell in love with her when he saw her on TV. They started campaigning while they were still on their honeymoon. Now they crisscross the country like Kennedys. Their sirens wail through quiet Appalachia. Kentucky quilts hang in Bloomingdale's. Sometimes it's hard to tell exactly what their message is, but this is one of the rare times that any Kentucky politician since Lincoln has gotten national attention. The Browns don't shrink from the comparison. They named their baby son Lincoln. Brown brags that he wrote his platform on "the back of an envelope" on his return from his honeymoon (though he was not on a train, but on a plane from La Samanna, the grand Caribbean retreat). Cut waste, get rid of corruption, bring in economic development. No texture or nuance. A millionaire's simple answer for tough times. It could have come straight out of *Being There.*

The governor and his wife even talk about themselves in the language of self-help, as if their very style were emblematic of America in the eighties. "You know, the fashion in America used to be bitter and cynical," Phyllis says, "but now it's about being busy, getting high on other people the way John and I are. Now it is in to be the way John and I are. We've never been ones to go with the tide. There's a good quote for you: 'John and Phyllis have never been ones to go with the tide.' "

Brown's opponents thought he would make a fool of himself. He hasn't. John Y. Brown has in fact cut waste and has brought more money into the state in nine months than his predecessors had in nine years. He got rid of the old patronage system—Kentucky's infamous "personal-service contracts"—and has balanced the budget in the face of a huge revenue cut. Phyllis has just finished decorating their estate in red, white, and blue. They say those are their favorite hues.

A little perspective is useful. Officials of the last two state administrations are being investigated by grand juries. The state has traditionally been near the bottom in everything: education, per capita income, industrial development. Kentucky is a unique arena for an ambitious couple. The legislature meets but once every two years and for only sixty days. The big city isn't trusted: A candidate from Louisville hasn't been elected in forty years.

John Y. Brown, Jr., comes from Lexington, horse country, where his father was a one-term congressman, a failed politician, a New Deal supporter not accepted by Bluegrass society, a union lawyer, and a notorious poker player, but still very much a part of his small town. Kin is important in Kentucky. So is being part of the community. From the time John Y. was ten he campaigned for his father. Everybody in the state knew who he was. However much a self-promoter he grew up to be, he had a reputation for being honest. He was able to slide through a full slate of Democratic candidates because in bad economic times, with every state budget wobbling, a man with shiny new millions and a former Miss America for a wife seemed to have the key to the Robert Ringer dream. Theodore Roosevelt used to say that American voters lacked thoroughness. Brown, with no political savvy or experience, saying he detested the whole political process, swept his state in 1980 on an ooh-and-aah vote. A mandate. He ran, he says, because he didn't want to "carry Phyllis's bags." As unfocused as the governor's ambitions seem to be, his wife's are not. During the campaign, says Brown, it was "Phyllis who was good with crowds. I withdrew. I didn't like them much."

Brown knows to defer to her ambitions. He knows he wouldn't have swept anything or anybody without the indefatigable Phyllis George. She knows that too. They pose together for their official portrait. When you think about it, a former-Miss America-turned-sports interviewer and a fried-chicken millionaire aren't so different from an ex-movie star and a former actress. That couple started in a governor's mansion too.

Learning to be first lady: Phyllis made a lot of mistakes at first. Some of them were reported—her comment that there "wasn't much difference between politics and show business." All of Phyllis's gaffes have to do with her not understanding her audience, being in over her head. There was a testimonial dinner given in Louisville around the time that Brown was elected for Edward Prichard. "Prich," as he is known down there, is a famous Kentucky intellectual, lawyer, orator, Har-

vard grad—behind-the-scenes influential. A friend of Arthur
Schlesinger, Jr.,'s, John Kenneth Galbraith's, and Katharine
Graham's. Those three were at the dinner, as were about five
hundred others, a lot of whom got up to make speeches ex-
tolling Prich. Phyllis got up too. "I just want to share with
y'all that I'm pregnant," she said. "I just thought you all
would like to know."

There are a lot of stories like that. Once, in a boardroom of
Louisville leaders, Phyllis was going on about bringing "famous people" into Kentucky when one of the society matrons
turned in her seat and said, "Can't somebody shut her up?"
What's interesting about this is that the same woman is now
one of Phyllis's fans. Along with many other people in Kentucky, she sees that, despite the diamonds and the naive vul-
garity, Phyllis is doing a lot of good. Her crafts project is
encouraging the local workers. Her visits to child-abuse and
rape centers make the papers. Her energy has managed to
raise one million dollars so far to restore the dilapidated governor's mansion in Frankfort. She may not restore it to Petit
Trianon glory, but at least she'll get rid of the filthy carpets
and chartreuse bamboo wallpaper.

The jet-helicopter blades whirl, the grass shimmies, the
motors drone, the first lady is all over the place. There is a lot
of new-millionaire conspicuous consumption. Phyllis whizzes
through small towns, filling the helicopter with goods. She
says she gets all her clothes in New York, combs the antique
districts, spends. But she does more than that. Her house is
flooded with NFL handouts. She bones up before flying to
New York each Saturday for the weekend show. "Let's get
into that!" is what she says about every project; her staff is
working on a dozen things at once. She is probably the first
governor's wife to have her own office, much less a staff.

In that office are framed photographs of Andy Williams
and, in a place of honor, a letter from Ed McMahon. And a
Miss Piggy card: I DON'T EXPECT STAR TREATMENT, I DE-

MAND IT. Tuesday is the first lady's day to spend privately with her son. Phyllis is one of those women who believes in "quality time." She and Lincoln are often in the helicopter together.

The day of the visit to Richmond, the helicopter has brought her to Louisville, where she is to meet thirty women— vice-presidents, foundation people, community leaders, daughters of newspaper and distillery owners, the *crème*. Phyllis is nervous and her Denton, Texas, is showing: She explains that she's wearing all the leather and the tight, tight skirt because she "has to look good." By the time she arrives, the reception is already in progress—a serious meeting in a setting of Persian carpets and grand pianos, a view of the Ohio River, a scene of graceful Louisville life.

But before Phyllis addresses herself to the meeting's purpose, she tells the women she wants to explain a little about herself. She stands, twirls, stomps her feet. "I want y'all to see that I'm thin. Everybody writes that I'm fat—well, I'm not." She tells them that she feels like she's at a sorority rush. Perhaps out of nerves, she launches into her twenty-minute set piece, the fifth time she's presented it in two days: "You know a lot of people have a preconceived idea of me because I'm a former Miss America, former Miss Texas beauty queen. They all think I'm not going to be real. Well, I'm human too. Or they know about me from TV, where they see me as the most successful female sportscaster in America. You know, it was real controversial when I went to CBS. The men didn't want me there. I sure proved myself, though, and now our ratings are up something like forty percent over NBC. . . . I grew up in Denton, Texas. My parents are just plain people. Bob and Louise George. I was a cheerleader in high school, but also a leader, a good student. . . ." Phyllis then listed her high-school honorary societies and her sorority. She may be the only thirty-two-year-old who still uses Zeta as a credential.

Ten minutes after describing her days at Zeta House, she is

ready for Miss America. "My daddy told me, 'Phyllis, honey, put your knockers out when you go down the runway. That's what the judges want to see.'. . . I had been a prodigy on the piano but I had to give it up because I couldn't be both a cheerleader and a pianist, but when it came time for the Miss America Pageant I knew I had to really go for it, so I did a special arrangement of 'Raindrops Keep Fallin' on My Head' in six different musical styles, and I swear, y'all, I had no idea that Hal David, who wrote the lyrics, was going to be the judge."

The women drinking white wine were astonished, amused, in an odd way both repelled and charmed. The well-bred Kentuckians weren't sure how to react to her monologue. It was like a scene from *The Beverly Hillbillies.*

The set piece wound up with the inevitable, the story of how she dropped the crown on the runway when she was crowned Miss America. In front of all those millions and Bert Parks, and then she cried all night until her mother told her, "Phyllis, people will have to just accept you for what you are." She had a moral for the women in Louisville: "Look at my life. It shows if you get out there and take risks, it can happen. If it hadn't been for Miss America, I still would be back in Denton."

When she was going to school in Texas, she was already known, the way Farrah Fawcett was. She says, "I don't want to be stereotyped," but she has been since she was at North Texas State. Phyllis could have been an inspiration for *Vanities:* a Texas cheerleader with an upturned face, bound and determined to get out of her state, a small-town Methodist who inhaled her values by reading magazines at the Rexall. She finally got all the goods they had taught her to covet: beauty-contest prizes, a rich, malleable husband, some celebrity, a swimming pool, dinners at "21," access to Howard Cosell, Albert Capraro—he designed her fox-hemmed wedding gown.

It takes a real toughness to get out of Denton that way, an ability to lay saccharine over steel. Also, Phyllis is still young. When she was crowned Miss America she didn't know, she said, what a "feminist" was, but now she doesn't simp adoringly at her husband the way Nancy Reagan does, nor does she play aren't-I-lucky like Rosalynn Carter. She still has the need to keep up the beauty-queen coyness. It seems like such a pointless defense: Phyllis is genuinely good as a TV interviewer, she gets a lot done in Kentucky, and, as Edward Prichard says, "probably has good intentions and a good heart."

She and Bob Evans were a mismatch. He also liked what he saw on TV, pursued her, married her. But Evans is complicated, work-obsessed, moody. When a picture flopped, he would shut himself in his house in Beverly Hills, taking Nembutals and staring at old pictures of his former wife, Ali MacGraw. It's hard to imagine Flypaper Phyllis, as she was nicknamed in the campaign, being able to transcend that.

When Evans's film *Black Sunday* failed, Evans, says Phyllis, went into a funk. About the same time, she was given the anchor of the *People* magazine TV show. The show flopped, and her marriage fell apart after only eleven months, but, typically, Phyllis used the moment to talk to a women's magazine for an interview headlined "Making the Best of Sudden Failure . . . Meet Phyllis George, She's Looking for a Job."

She found one because she knew a lot about football, and there were other things she was looking for—"to be married and have a child." Her prince was fifteen years older, had a soft, callow face, an undisciplined body, and styled hair, but he was very rich, eager to spend, interested in sports, and, like her, had created his own myth. They married on St. Patrick's Day with nothing spared: Norman Vincent Peale, Studio 54, bagpipes at Tavern on the Green, Arnold Schwarzenegger, Bert Parks, Milton Berle, Eunice Shriver, Phyllis's low-cut, front-slit wedding dress, and, in case anybody missed the point, press releases and "photo opportunities."

"Most of John's celebrity came when he married me," Phyllis says. "All of this is new to him. I have to help him, teach him how to deal with it." As Phyllis was explaining this, we were approaching Cave Hill in the helicopter. The fog was coming in and Kentucky was spread before us like one of her quilts. Down in the garden of the mansion the pool gleamed, and you could just make out the Union Jack made out of tulips. Phyllis pointed out where they were going to put in the lake. She is a woman with every detail organized: the repairs of her bugle-beaded gowns, the pastrami she's having sent in from the Carnegie Deli for a "Save the Mansion" fund raiser, the airbrushed Rita Hayworth-like stills of herself she's ordered. She also thinks she knows her husband's flaws. "John," she says, "is both smart and too sensitive. A lot of times he doesn't understand certain things. He'd like it if I would go with him all the time, but I can't, you know. I have my own things."

Their helicopter is controversial—it is criticized in Kentucky as being a waste of money. That doesn't stop the governor. The helicopter drones for him too. He doesn't spend a lot of time in his office, preferring to bless expansions at steel plants, announce new bridges, and show up at small-town TV stations to give interviews. As he whirls through the state, folders and briefing papers surround him, but, unlike Phyllis, he hardly gives them a glance. The governor looks perpetually tired, complains of insomnia and of spending dawns reading "financial papers and government reports." It would be interesting to know what is in those reports, because during the campaign some fairly substantial issues got by him—once he drew a blank about the meaning of "affirmative action."

The gaps showed up again when he got to Huntington, West Virginia, recently. He was there to give a TV interview to push his succession drive—Huntington is on the Kentucky border. The interviewer was bright and she had something on her mind: formaldehyde. She said the formaldehyde in home insulation was ruining a lot of miners' lungs. The governor hadn't heard of this, although the issue had been widely reported. The interviewer pressed him on it, politely. The governor steered her toward succession, then on to Phyllis and her selling of Kentucky crafts. For a man whose father had been a New Deal populist and whose own election victory had come partially from the support of the United Mine Workers, his lack of interest was astonishing. Getting back into the helicopter, he said, "Can you believe that little girl? She must have taken up ten minutes of my time with that formaldehyde business."

Brown does understand a balance sheet. He's cut the state's budget by sixteen percent. He's gotten rid of the boondoggles, such as the road crew that used to go and see if the Kentucky highways were still there or the ninety-nine people who once sent out press releases on the governor's activities. He's cut education, cut services, cleaned up some shady state banking practices. He is apolitical—most of the businessmen in his Cabinet didn't even back him for office. That doesn't bother him. He refers to himself as "the front man, the chairman of the board," and he has infuriated many Kentucky Democrats because he won't even bother to shake hands with them at meetings. "I hate all that bullshit," he says. "The chicken fries, the fish fries, the backslapping. I won't be a part of it." Although the governor makes Democratic-party-reflex remarks about "needin' to help people," nobody much believes him. He has a large portrait of John F. Kennedy in his office, but his outlook is closer to Ronald Reagan's. "Reagan is the first President we've had who is secure," he says. "I'm secure too. People respond to that."

He is a go-go governor in a go-slow part of the country. He does not pause to reflect. He worships success, expansion, and the institutions that create them. He sees no flaws in the American system, little gray. The system enabled him to sell his way to millions, gave him the cockiness of speedy wealth. Brown is a man whose gods lunch at "21." His sudden money seems to have given him a psychological mandate. "People like me who don't need to work, we make the best leaders. Entrepreneurs. We're able to treat government like a charity."

The governor says he "barely" got through college and law school at the University of Kentucky. Perhaps his gaffes come from this cursory education. Such as his remark that the university needs more business types "than . . . Aristotles and Socrateses." He has been surprised by the reaction to his statements. "Yesterday, over at the university, four thousand students showed up and were right hostile to me because of my budget cuts. When I was at school, you couldn't have gotten ten people together who cared about learnin' anything."

"Johnny hasn't read a book since *Little Black Sambo,*" says Edward Prichard, his ally and old family friend. Certainly all that time in the helicopter can mask a lack of substance. "Phyllis and I are real restless," the governor says. "We're on the go fifteen or sixteen hours a day."

The perpetual motion gives John Y. Brown the chance to do the thing that he is really good at—selling. As a young man, his father wanted Brown to earn money working on highways. John Y. sold vacuum cleaners instead, making more money in one day than he would have made in a month on the roads. He told his father he would "never work for less than I was worth." He sold encyclopedias all through law school, making twenty-five thousand dollars one year; worked in his father's congressional campaigns, stumping the state, crying himself to sleep every time his father lost. His homelife was never calm. His parents separated several times, his mother growing increasingly disenchanted about the loss of money from politics and gambling. He grew up to like gambling too, but in a state that thrives on the breeding of racehorses a gambling man is hardly scorned. Governor Brown's style is more Las Vegas—he's been known to hop on the private plane of Cliff Perlman, the chairman of Caesars Palace. During the campaign, one of Brown's opponents charged that Brown wouldn't release his IRS returns because of "gambling debts." No proof of that was ever found. The governor has a good answer when the subject is brought up. "If and when I ever did gamble, it was out of boredom." Later, he snaps, "Sure I've been to Las Vegas a few times, and so have a lot of other Americans."

He has the personality of a high roller, a deal maker. "In law school I made a deal with my professors," he says. "I could cut classes and sell encyclopedias and they would pass me. I never even wrote a contract until I got to Kentucky Fried Chicken." Brown says he went to law school because "my daddy was a lawyer." "If anybody ever told me I might have been good at sales, I could have saved myself a lot of time."

Father was very helpful to son. John Y., Sr., was a close friend of Harland Sanders in the early 1960's. The Colonel, as he was known, was selling his fried chicken out of a restaurant. He was also selling pork barbecue—his restaurant was called the Porky Pig House. The Colonel wanted to expand to two storefronts in Florida, and he asked his friend John Y., Sr., to help him with the legal work. Senior suggested Junior, then working as a criminal lawyer, for the job. When John, Jr., started working for the Porky Pig House, he noticed something: Eighty percent of the customers asked for chicken, only twenty percent for pork barbecue.

That was the beginning of Kentucky Fried Chicken. It was Brown's idea to sell chicken all over the country. Through relatives of his then-wife, Ellie, he got to a Nashville entrepreneur named Jack Massey. Massey is a visionary, an extraordinary financial manager, a venture-capitalist. He came out of retirement to buy out Harland Sanders. He once told a financial writer that he had asked the Colonel to set his own interest rate. The Colonel did: two million dollars payable over time at three percent interest. Three percent! Massey was pleased to give him five hundred thousand dollars down. He insisted John Y. Brown move to Nashville, where Kentucky Fried Chicken would have its headquarters. Brown did.

They were a good team. Brown, the salesman, opened hundreds of franchises a year, promoted the Colonel and his chicken, and then sold the franchise fast-food restaurants all over the world. Massey was the financial man; he kept the controls, the cost-efficient methods of operation, the strict standards. Brown rarely mentions Massey's name when asked about Kentucky Fried Chicken. If pressed he will say, "Massey was my partner," and that is about it. For all of Brown's talk about his ability to run Kentucky like a business, his partner, who actually ran Kentucky Fried Chicken like a business, has never been credited, even when Brown spoke to *The Wall Street Journal* this summer. Massey refuses to be interviewed about John Y. Brown, though he has told friends that he is "tired of seeing Johnny grab all the credit for KFC," but doesn't "care about getting into a fight with him."

In the late 1960's, Brown didn't fare so well in Nashville. It is a city of surprising clannishness. A businessman who knew him there described him as withdrawn at board meetings, sitting in the back row, not making an effort to fit in. He was rejected by the prestigious Belle Meade Club, a Nashville establishment so traditional that it still has a painting of Robert E. Lee in the entryway. Brown says he "hated Nashville" and "never wanted to move there," that the last years at Kentucky Fried Chicken almost ruined his life. His marriage was rocky. He was traveling constantly, opening franchises—in one year he sold 683. Massey decided to retire. There was no way Brown could handle it alone. In 1971, they agreed to sell to Heublein; Inc., a $288 million deal that made Brown and Massey and their stockholders very rich.

Massey went on to another venture-capital fortune. He started Hospital Corporation of America—a company whose

$1.5 billion assets rest on its ability to manage hospitals on a cost-efficient basis. His management of that company has made it one of the most active stocks on Wall Street.

Brown's money got him into sports. He went from the ownership of the Kentucky Colonels, in the old American Basketball Association, to the Buffalo Braves, and through his basketball teams started to meet a lot of famous people. Since he had money he was offered deals. He was able to buy a fifty-percent share of the Boston Celtics. Boston *Globe* basketball writer Bob Ryan remembers that "Brown was shallow and almost childlike in his approach to the game." This was the 1978–79 season, and the Celtics had problems, but Brown thought he could solve them by making trades. However, he never consulted the smartest man in professional basketball—his own general manager, Red Auerbach.

It was the Bob McAdoo trade that did Brown in. During the winter of that year, John Y. was in Madison Square Garden one night watching his team play the Knicks. Phyllis was with him—they were dating then. The Celtics had picked up three first-round draft choices to be determined the following spring. On the court was Bob McAdoo, a high-scoring player, not good on defense, often traded—the last sort of player the Celtics needed. But over the next thirty-six hours the team learned that McAdoo would be joining them and that their three first-round draft choices would go to the Knicks. "The effect was to ruin the team for the rest of the season," says Bob Ryan. "The theory of why Brown did it was to show off for Phyllis George."

The future governor was in over his head, untutored, yet too arrogant to consult with his coach, Dave Cowens, or Auerbach. After the McAdoo trade, the Celtics won a game in Atlanta, then went on the next day to be beaten badly in New Orleans. Brown slumped against the wall in the dressing room and confessed, "I don't understand—we looked so good last night."

All that season, one Boston sports talk show played a jingle:

"Why, Johnny Brown?" He married Phyllis in March, declared for governor, and unloaded his part of the team. When
it was announced, the players cheered in the dressing room.

Toward the end of the Richmond meeting, somebody asked
the governor if he was having a good time running Kentucky.
Brown smiled. He liked that question a lot. He said, "I sure
am. Government can work if you run it like a business.
There's nothing here I haven't run into before at Kentucky
Fried Chicken. That job was a lot tougher." He was so low
key in his answer he was positively Reaganesque. Brown
knows that he's on the long list of potential Democratic candidates for 1984. "I don't know if I'm running yet or not," he
says easily these days. "That's a long time away."

Not so far away was Phyllis George Brown, standing on the
sidewalk in front of the Richmond courthouse. A political reporter from the Louisville *Courier-Journal* asked her if her
new interest in rape and child abuse meant she was "going to
get involved with feminist issues." Phyllis took a swipe at his
arm. "Don't be so descriptive!" she said, giggling. Just then,
the trio of black women approached in their majestic prints
and plaids. They had passed by the governor and were looking
straight at the first lady as she played coy with the Louisville
writer. One of the women stared at Phyllis and then came up
to her side. She gently touched the sleeve of Phyllis's translu-
cent blouse and said to her very softly, "Bye, bye, now." As
she moved away from the first lady of Kentucky, she was still
staring, perplexed and dazzled, maybe all at the same time.

November 1981

*   *   *

J knew the piece on the Browns would be controversial,
but I didn't expect what happened: John Y. Brown denied he had ever seen me. His press officer issued a state-

ment saying, "The governor never granted *New York* an interview." It was as if I hadn't ever set foot in the state. This Pirandellian sidebar was very strange since I had spent three days traveling with the first couple of Kentucky and had the souvenir photographs to prove it.

Failing that tack, John Y. Brown's office tried another. A new statement was issued. This time, according to the press rep, I had indeed been in Kentucky and the governor had seen me, but I had "invented the entire piece." As reactions go, the Browns' was a doozy and typical of their penchant for reality-bending. The local reporters pointed out that I had been seen all over the state with the Browns at many of the locales I had supposedly invented.

Now it was time for more back-and-fill from the capital. "This is the kind of fiction you expect from Rupert Murdoch, whose similar supermarket publications, such as the National *Star,* have no credibility in journalism." That was too much for even the Lexington *Herald.* The Browns' hometown paper pointed out that yes, Murdoch did own tabloids, but he also owned those two distinguished old ladies, *The Times* and *The Sunday Times* of Great Britain, as well as *New York.* "Called again, the governor refused to respond directly," the Lexington *Herald* reported.

Norman Mailer

*A*ll of his usual rituals had been observed, the galleys recorrected, the last two pages reset, and now there was nothing to do, Norman Mailer said, but wait for the publication of his novel, *Ancient Evenings,* which he'd been working on for eleven years. Mailer was feeling very detached, he said, reading *Rabbit Is Rich* for the first time and going through unanswered mail, when he discovered the invitation from Francois Mitterand to come to Paris and be part of an intellectual conference called Culture and Development. Although he doesn't much like to travel and has too many debts to take time off from his work, Mailer agreed to go and was pleased that he did, partly because he was able to patch up a rift with William Styron that had gone on for more than twenty years. "We were like two old Turks with matted beards," Mailer said of their time in Paris together, wandering through the streets, stopping in at Hemingway's bar at the Ritz. The friendship had been strained, to put it mildly, ever since Mailer attacked Styron in *Advertisements for Myself.* There had been an additional complication having to do with Mailer's second wife, Adele. "We didn't discuss any of it," Mailer said. "It wouldn't have changed anything that happened so many years ago. What would have been the point?" Brought together by Mitterand's invitation for the weekend, it was as if, Mailer said, "Bill and I looked at one another and each decided, 'Hey, he's not so bad after all.' As we get closer to the shadow, we begin to lose a great deal of fire in our limbs."

He was discussing this quietly at Alice Mason's Valentine dinner, having landed at Kennedy that afternoon, when his dinner partner, Joan Mondale, turned to him, struggling to catch something he was saying in his, as he describes it, "black-market French." "I said to Mitterand, *'Ils veulent gagner la guerre, on doit gagner.'* " "What does that mean, Norman?" Mrs. Mondale asked. "It means that although the Russians want to win the war, we should win it," Mailer said, and then he moved on to Mitterand himself, "a stunning figure with a long face and a characteristically French nose, very much like André Gide in appearance, but his forehead is more powerful, high and prominent, almost like a phallus with the veins bulging in it, yet when he speaks his mouth is like a flower, his lips like delicate petals, opening and closing. He is extraordinary," Mailer told Mrs. Mondale, "precisely because he thinks like a novelist."

For whatever reputation he has received as an original thinker to rival André Malraux, a novelist who has often reinvented the language, a journalist who redefined style in nonfiction, a prophet of all that is subterranean in the culture, a self-styled psychic outlaw whose "disasters, failures, and booboos," as Mailer puts it, have made headlines for years, it has always been the novel, the one big novel, that has been Norman Mailer's focus in life. "Without it, what would there have been to keep swimming for?" he asks.

With the one big novel or without it, Mailer's place as the literary man of his era has been ensured. He has written definitively and provocatively on almost every large theme in contemporary life. He has been honored with two Pulitzer

Prizes, a National Book Award, membership in the American Institute of Arts and Letters, and, most recently, by the publication of a lengthy biography—a book he refused to be interviewed for—which details his every outrage and accomplishment. To imagine American letters without Norman Mailer would be like imagining America without California or New York. In *Ancient Evenings,* he has burrowed in, retreated, as he says, "into an act of pure fiction," in an attempt to re-create life three thousand years ago.

The novel is a vast departure for Mailer, a 709-page tapestry of the nineteenth and twentieth Egyptian dynasties. *Ancient Evenings* traces the peregrinations of one man, Menenhetet, through his three reincarnations—Mailer's main character changes from charioteer to general to harem master to high priest. Much of the narrative is told by a six-year-old boy "with the consciousness of Marcel Proust, but Proust at age fifteen," Mailer says. Additionally, Mailer's Egyptians are telepathic, so "you cannot be absolutely certain whether what is being told is by the living or dead." If Mailer is an unlikely Homer, *Ancient Evenings* provides an extraordinary—and often incomprehensible—panorama of the magic, mythology, and scatological practices of the pharaohs, as well as mass rapes, sodomy, scenes of battle and life at court, and the final recreation of the Egyptian land of the dead.

Mailer's immensely difficult work about ancient Egypt may not provide, as he once promised in *Advertisements for Myself,* a book "which Dostoevski and Marx, Joyce and Freud, Stendhal, Tolstoy and Proust and Spengler, Faulkner, and even old moldering Hemingway might come to read, for it would carry what they had to tell another part of the way." Twenty-four years later, Mailer says of *Ancient Evenings,* "This isn't the big book I promised, but it is a big book. I think in a literary sense it's the most ambitious novel I've ever written."

Mailer says he wrote *Ancient Evenings* "with the coach, my literary betters, over my shoulder and maybe that wasn't wise." The publishing industry, in its present depressed state, is a difficult marketplace for a difficult book. Over the winter, paperback houses showed little interest in *Ancient Evenings* and an auction fizzled when only one bid came in. But two months before publication, the bookstores had ordered a hundred thousand copies, so Mailer is not troubled by the early signs of commerce. "Look," he says, "either it's a very good book or it's not. If it's a very good book, well, fine. If it isn't, well, that will be disappointing but I'm probably not going to know for a few years anyway. I think there will be people who will think it is a great book; I think there will be people who will say it's a preposterous work. I think there will be the usual spectrum of reactions."

On the eve of publication, Mailer says he is prepared for accusations about his "pharaoh complex," and for the reviews that might invoke both Jack Abbott and the stabbing of his second wife, Adele. "It's almost impossible for anyone to review Norman's work without reviewing his life," says his wife, Norris. He is girded for the pronouncements of the Vassar grads who decry his primal urges and think his energy loathsome, the terminally smug members of the literary establishment who already say that *Ancient Evenings* is unreadable, and the academics who will devote thousands of words to analyzing his twenty-fourth book in light of his previous twenty-three. For Mailer, the worst of these will be the critics who "will accuse me of journalism" and will run around screaming I've done autobiographical work because the protagonist ends up being sixty years old. You must realize," Mailer says, "that when I started the book, I wasn't even fifty yet. Sixty seemed to me a great distance away. It never occurred to me to consider myself remotely like him. He was ancient. He was sixty."

Norman Mailer does not easily settle into patriarchy; not for him the gentle image of the elderly writer surrounded by his books and children. Mailer says his patriarchal mood "doesn't have those wonderful base chords you hear in symphonies, it becomes more like private concerns. For the first time in my life, I find that I don't spend over fifty percent of the day thinking about myself. It's all very well to be a patriarch, but my feeling is that it's an academic question. That is, if I had it in me to be the patriarch who finishes off the career with the white beard and the last three great books, we may never know. I might wind up working for George Plimpton on Atari, or maybe with *The Norman Mailer Show*. It could be like *The Blue Angel*. I might be out there scuffling."

Mailer has certain phrases he uses frequently: "Once a philosopher, twice a pervert"; "After all, Veronica, why not?" ("I stole that one from Saul Bellow"); "I'm an old club fighter—I get mad when you miss"; "The first time you hit me and I notice it, you're in trouble." He calls these his "all-purpose expressions, good for any situation in life." So, too, does Mailer have certain themes: his need to scuffle, the romance of his struggle, and, most of all, the feeling that for much of his life he has been consistently misunderstood. "Do not understand me too easily," he quoted André Gide in the first column he wrote in *The Village Voice*. Recently, he was talking about his early years. "I used to have this feeling of 'Why don't they understand? If only they would understand, they would see what they're doing to me . . .'" Studying engineering at Harvard, the sixteen-year-old Norman Mailer discovered *Studs Lonigan,* and suddenly realized the power of the novel and what he would have to do with his life to get his point across; he completed fourteen short stories and a novel in one year.

At sixty, Mailer may feel far less misunderstood, more convinced that "the iron law in life is that everyone has a certain amount of luck," but the same abhorrence of misinterpretation is still there. No matter that a torrent of print has analyzed his every move; if *Time* misstates his age, as it did recently in the international editions, Mailer fires off a curt letter of correction. If he feels he's misquoted, he rails against

the journalist, complains to the editor. "The existentialist" is
determined that his record be kept straight. "During the day,
while he was helpless, newspapermen and other assorted
bravos of the media and literary world would carve ugly pictures on the living tomb of his legend," he wrote in the *Armies
of the Night.* "Of necessity, part of Mailer's remaining funds
of sensitivity went right into the war of supporting his image
and working for it."

"You know what I don't understand?" he said recently.
"Why is it that everyone has to portray me as a fool and a
buffoon? Why am I always made to look foolish? None of my
essential irony ever comes through. Years ago, Lillian Ross
did a profile of me for the *New Yorker,* and when I read it, I
called her up and said, 'Lillian, where's the twinkle?' People
don't understand that a great deal of the time I'm just kidding.
For example, the drinking. I never really drank all that much.
I used to love to go to parties when I was younger and hold a
liquor bottle and swig from it. I was playing at being Norman
Mailer. Nobody ever gets me right, damn it."

It is Mailer's curse to live, as he says, "in an immensely re-
ductive age," an age where certain facile assumptions about
character, easy judgments and write-offs are made, especially
in the world Mailer travels in, what he calls "the intellectual
guild." Making quick assumptions about Mailer's character
has always been impossible—he is too much of a paradox to
fall into easy categories. Even as a patriarch. Just when "the
Protagonist," as he called himself in *Armies of the Night,*
seemed to be slipping into his declining years gracefully,
swamped in research on the Ramses IX period of Egypt, acting as bourgeois as a Tory, collecting his thirty-thousand-dol-
lar-a-month stipend from Little, Brown necessary to support
his five ex-wives and nine children, his edges nicely mellowed
by writing fiction again, up reared Jack Abbott, giving Mailer
another chance to be misunderstood. He did little to resist.

To review the case, briefly: Mailer and Jack Abbott had

exchanged letters while Abbott was in prison; with Mailer's help, those letters were collected in book form as Abbott's acclaimed *In the Belly of the Beast.* Abbott's association with Mailer, it was originally believed, resulted in his early release from jail, enabling him to arrive in New York, where he lived in a halfway house. On the day that *The New York Times* called Abbott "an exceptional man with an exceptional gift," he stabbed and killed a young waiter and actor, Richard Adan. Although Mailer had learned that Abbott had been released from prison because he had cooperated with the prison authorities, Mailer decided he would stick by him anyway, and in the process, he absorbed a great deal of the blame for Adan's murder.

"The Jack Abbott case was the biggest strain we've had so far in our marriage," Norris Mailer says. "It was so terrible, you have no idea. It wasn't just Abbott Norman encouraged, it was all kinds of writers. And to read in *Time* a letter saying that Norman should be tried as an accessory to the murder, or an editorial saying that they should be chained together—I don't think it's blown over yet."

A year has passed since the *New York Post* ran the headline MAILER: I WOULD RISK FREEING KILLER; the Mailers still get hate mail and some fairly serious threats, but now Mailer takes a larger view. "During the business with Jack Abbott, much of the outrage at me was, in effect, 'He has no acumen.' Acumen is the ability to read situations, to make judgments that are effective. Probably there is no virtue that those of us in the intellectual trades in New York aspire to more. I think the thing that infuriates people about me is that I keep violating their acumen."

The Abbott case was a special violation. "The feeling was that my judgment was so naive. The common thing that was said was that I had no right to help this man to get out because I wasn't paying the price, society was. It is not a judgment that you can brush away. Part of the outrage was simple horror, part of the outrage was unfounded, part of the outrage was absolutely legitimate. The part of the outrage which I thought was comic—although deadly—was that people were saying, 'You see, there it is, Norman Mailer has no acumen. Not only does he not know how to behave, he doesn't know how other people behave; which is worse?

"People still come up to me on the street and say, 'What about Abbott?' The last time it happened, I said, 'Hey, did you read the book?' and the man said, 'Yeah, yeah, he sure had his head together in the book, that's what I can't understand.' " This encounter seems definitive for Mailer. "Jack had such a command of the states of emotion that, in a way, it was my confidence that he would be all right on the outside too. Usually, anyone who understands anything that well is through with it," Mailer says. "When he first started saying to me, 'Will you help me get out?' I thought about it and I thought, 'Yeah, it's fair. He's helped me. I owe it to him.' "

But he was surprised, Mailer says, when Abbott got out so fast. "I thought it would be a year or two, if at all. It was his bad luck that he got out so quickly." Although Abbott told Mailer's biographer, Hilary Mills, that "Norman and I are enemies, we're class enemies," Mailer is still defending his motives, unwilling to admit he might have been naive. "We correspond still. I don't know, he has talent. I think it will be hard for him to become a writer, but if he can do it, it's the only thing that can save something out of it. Miller wrote *After the Fall.* This is After the Bomb Went Off." From prison, Abbott told Mills that Mailer "doesn't know this other world, but he always wants to do it in such a way that he pulls [us] into his world. In existential terms, Norman is a philistine."

Norman Mailer has not always been a philistine, hostile to the culture of his own world. Although he now says that "it is always deer-hunting season where I am concerned" and likens his position in the intellectual guild to that of "an extra added starter," there was a time in the 1950's when he was an accepted part of the guild—an editor of *Dissent,* a contributor to *Partisan Review,* a parishioner in good standing in the intellectual world, friendly with Norman Podhoretz and Irving Howe. "I was a special part of that group," Mailer says. "If I had been a girl, I would have been like our cousin Suzy who is very fragile and gets dizzy spells and she really has a very unhappy life, if only we could find a husband for her because she plays the violin so beautifully. . . . I was even friends with Philip Roth for a while, perish the mark," Mailer says with a laugh.

"When you're young and you have a certain amount of young arrogance," Mailer says, "you're above being accepted by the literary establishment. On the other hand, you want to be accepted. You remember at the end of *Lenny,* when Lenny Bruce says, 'All I really want is for America to love me'? I found that particularly moving. It's so true. Under all of it is the cry of the immigrant heart," Mailer says. "I came here, I really love America, please endure me. I secretly worship you. No matter how sophisticated you get, it's almost primitive in immigrants. You do want recognition. You can also see that if you take certain courses, you're not going to get it."

A literary celebrity by the age of twenty-five, when *The Naked and the Dead* was at the top of the best-seller lists, it took Mailer years to understand "the vacuity of a life without struggle," as Tennessee Williams wrote. Mailer calls the years after *The Naked and the Dead,* while he was working on *The Deer Park,* a time when "my self-pity was the worst." "I was just bewildered," he says. Money was not a problem yet; he was only on his second marriage and had "endless leisure"; he had written *Barbary Shore,* which had been savaged by the critics, moved to Mexico, got heavily involved with drugs, returned to New York, and published *The Deer Park.* He was not pleased with what he considered that book's middling success—it settled at number six on the best-seller list and sold fifty thousand copies. Mailer felt he was floundering; he was throwing enormous parties, occupying himself with, among other things, being one of the founders of *The Village Voice.* But, if his life seemed chaotic, his radar was onto something, picking up "clues," as he would say, in the culture that led to his eventual publication of *The White Negro,* which defined the notion of hip for the first time, at the end of the decade; and *Advertisements for Myself,* in which he invented a style of personal journalism, but which went unappreciated at the time. Mailer used *Advertisements* as a forum to attack some of his fellows in the intellectual guild: Gore Vidal, James Jones, Jack Kerouac, William Styron, Truman Capote, to mention a few. Whatever his motives, Mailer had created an entire new set of struggles, necessary to fuel him, since his primary struggle, achieving fame as a writer, was no longer a concern.

In *Advertisements,* he retreated into his ego. "I have been running for President these last ten years in the privacy of my mind," he wrote, and from then on, the psychic outlaw took off on a brilliant and original course, filtering his perceptions through his own experience, flinging himself into the world again and again, often with disastrous results. He does not regret this. "It takes a toll if you don't do anything, too," Mailer says. "As many people die from an excess of timidity as from bravery. Nobody ever measures that."

The inevitable end of his acceptance, even as strange cousin Suzy, by the ingrown, polemics-ridden *Partisan Review* crowd, came, says Mailer, "when I stabbed Adele." Locked into a confrontational marriage with Adele Morales, Mailer, drunk and stoned at the end of a long party, took a penknife and stabbed his wife. That was in 1959. Adele was badly injured, but she refused to press charges; Mailer was taken to Bellevue for observation. "A week or two after I got out of the coop," Mailer says, "I remember that Norman Podhoretz and Midge

Decter took me to a party and everyone was shocked that they would take me there, but still they all closed ranks behind me." Twenty-four years later, the evening is still vivid to Mailer. "I walked into the room and the reactions were subtle as hell," he said. Five degrees less warmth than I was accustomed to. Not fifteen degrees less—five. I guess that once you bring a violent man to a party, people are generally polite to him.

"Looking back on it, the stabbing was not altogether the turning point. I mean, it was terribly shocking and things could never quite be the same; if any of us does something like that, people just don't look at them in quite the same way. I think ten years went by before people forgot about it. Once in a while they would get a reminder and they would say, 'Oh my God, yes.' I think the real separation came after Adele and I split up and Jean and I—Lady Jean Campbell—started going around together because then, I started travelling in another world.

"Once in a while, I do long for a sense of community and it just isn't there. I don't take pride in it. Sometimes I'm rueful about it. I am the odd man out. Look, you tack through your life. Particularly if you're heading upwind, you tack."

Norman Mailer lives in Brooklyn Heights where he was reared. His mother, Fanny Mailer, lives a few blocks away, and although Mailer visits her often, "She's at that point now where much of her day is just spent looking out the window." Mailer takes a great deal of pleasure showing visitors how his neighborhood has changed—the high rise that has replaced the Italianate mansions, the paved road to the water that was once a footpath, the alterations at 20 Remsen Street, where he wrote *The Naked and the Dead.*

"I can't begin to tell you how different it looks," he says. "When I rented a room on the top floor there was a mansard roof and ornamentation on the windows. Now it's all stripped."

Each day he passes that building and the house down the street where he lived in a small apartment with his first wife, Beatrice Silverman. "I don't think much about it. No metaphors. They're all used up. The problem with being a writer," Mailer says, "is that you use up everything in your work and after a while, you go dead inside. You have no inner life. I've flattened out completely."

The day is crisp, and Mailer wears a blue ski parka, khaki trousers and jogging shoes. As he walks to lunch, he is recognized several times, and strangers beseech him for small favors. "Hey, Norman," says a man in a navy jacket whom Mailer has never met. "Is your friend———in town? I sent him a letter. I need him to help me get a job." "Well," says Mailer, "he was in the country, but he's back in the city now. I'm sure he'll receive it." Mailer sees "nothing peculiar" in these semi-intimate encounters. "The interesting thing that happens if you live in a neighborhood long enough, is that you get to be a lot like a small-town politician, able to confer minor favors on the local populace."

The small-town politician image is enhanced by the ease with which Mailer pulls out his wallet and shows off pictures of his nine children or, on another day, having just returned from the dentist where he had one more tooth extracted, takes it out of his shirt pocket to amuse his three-year-old, John Buffalo. Although this seems a different Norman Mailer from the one who drove Rip Torn to attack him with a hammer during the shooting of *Maidstone,* Mailer's daughters Danielle and Betsy insist that their father has always been quite gentle. "The outrage is gone, no question," says Mailer. "There's a simple reason: nine kids, nine kids."

A few months before John Buffalo was born, the Mailers were in Paris. "There was Norris with a great big belly and we were talking about having a baby and this and that and all the kids, when suddenly I turned to her and said, 'You know, all I ever wanted was to be free and alone and in Paris,' "

Mailer said. "So Norris said, 'Well, gee, honey, look. Let's suppose you were free and alone and in Paris. What would have happened? You would have run into some girl, and you would have started living together, and then she would have gotten pregnant, and then you wouldn't have been free and alone.' And I thought, 'Well, I can't win that argument anymore.' "

"Inside each patriarch is a closet matriarch," Mailer says. He puts in two four-hour work shifts a day, five days a week, and one on Saturday, in a small, undecorated room down the block from his apartment. Mailer says he allows no one to take a look at his spare writing quarters. "It would be bad luck. Once I had a really fancy office with a lot of pictures on the walls and photographs. I couldn't write a decent page there. I just stared at the pictures all day." At one time, Mailer owned the entire building he lives in and, in those years, his writing studio was in the house. Different floors of the building were sold off, Mailer said, "as my debts got worse." The Mailer's now occupy only the fourth floor. Mailer's yearly expenses, his alimony to three ex-wives, the tuition for six children, run $325,000 a year, so the Mailers rarely travel and Norris buys her clothes from the $13,000 a year she earns as a painter. "Thank heavens Oscar de la Renta is a friend," Norris says. "He sells me his runway samples for something like a hundred fifty dollars each. It makes me mad sometimes, all of Norman's responsibilities. Supporting his ex-wives. Sometimes I think, 'What are they going to do if Norman drops dead?' "
"I can't complain because I had it easy for so long," Mailer says. "Thank God for beliefs in karma. It all gets very casual, believe it or not."

The Mailer apartment has a large living room that looks out to Wall Street and the Statue of Liberty; in it are an antique velvet sofa and several Victorian chairs, nautical clocks that chime with ships' bells on the hour, and two walls that are lined with rosewood bookcases. Several of Norris's stylish paintings are on display, as are dozens of photographs of Mailer's children, parents, friends—Pat Lawford, Dotson Rader, Jan Cushing Olympitas, Buzz Farber, Amy and Milton Green. Mailer's City of the Future, constructed by him out of Lego blocks, which adorned the cover of *Cannibals and Christians,* his collected criticism, shares space at one end of the apartment with the dining-room table and its view of the water; at the other end are several small bedrooms and a galley kitchen that looks up to an A-frame Mailer designed with a series of lofts to accommodate children.

There is no clutter. "Norman is very neat," says Norris. "He drapes his clothes neatly over a chair, and when he takes his socks off he puts them in his shoes. Every few days I go through all the shoes and throw the socks in the laundry." Norris Mailer paints in her studio all day—until recently she shared space with Kurt Vonnegut's daughter, Edie—but is back in the late afternoon. "When Norman comes in at eight, close to dinnertime, I know not to talk to him," Norris Mailer says. "I let him come down from what he's working on. Norman will usually eat a half a grapefruit and play a game of solitaire in order to relax, or he'll read the papers. I don't badger him at that time about all the things that might have happened to me that day."

Mailer's daughters by Adele, Danielle and Betsy, both in their mid-twenties, come often for dinner. Betsy, who teaches at a nearby school, lives on the third floor of the house in a small studio Mailer retained from the sale. Danielle, a layout artist, lives in Manhattan. "Those two girls are the center of the family," Mailer says. "But of all my nine children, the one who reminds me of myself the most is Buffy, John Buffalo, especially at this age. Like me, he's both stubborn and proud."

Suppertime, Brooklyn Heights: Norris has made pot roast. Danielle and Betsy help in the kitchen. Norris's son, Matthew, is doing homework. Dinner is served. "What is it?" John Buffalo asks. "Pot roast," says his mother. "Yech," says John

Buffalo. "You love pot roast," his mother says. "I hate pot roast," John Buffalo says. After some debate, Mailer says, "You'll eat pot roast or you'll go to your room." John Buffalo flings himself under his father's chair and starts to wail. "Go to your room, John Buffalo. Now." There is a moment of tense anticipation, then quiet descends. "Fierce pride," says Mailer. "He'll stay in his room all night to show us we can't win."

Although the Mailers seem ubiquitous in the fashion press, Mailer says they "try to keep going out down to about three nights a week. The look on the kid's face is getting to us." Going to dinner parties is "sort of the last of my very small gifts to have been developed," he says. "It's sort of like finding a new sport, the kind of sport you could never play when you were young. I find now there is almost a certain pleasure in a half-difficult dinner partner, to see if you can warm her up. If I have one quarrel, it's that a great dinner has to have a faint touch of the sinister about it, and people are as kind to one another in the social community as they are in a small town. No one dares to start something with someone because there is no telling where it will end."

But not always. Last spring, Mailer was "struck by something that occurred at a dinner." That night, Gloria Vanderbilt was on his left, Barbara Walters on his right. In the afternoon, Barbara Walters had taped her first interview with Claus von Bulow, and as she told her impressions of him at the table, she did not notice that Gloria Vanderbilt's face had glazed over with distaste. "What do you think of the case, Gloria?" Barbara Walters asked pleasantly. "I don't want to discuss it," Gloria Vanderbilt said. "None of you knows what you're talking about." Her expression was as haughty as it was angry, her teeth clenched. There was some attempt made by Barbara Walters to politely back and fill. "I said, I will not discuss it," Gloria Vanderbilt said. Dinner resumed. Sometime during dessert, Mailer turned to her. "Don't you ever change your mind about anything?" he asked. Vanderbilt, who was acting as hostess of the table, excused herself before coffee. "I was struck by it," Mailer said, "because it was one of the few times I'd seen such a clear example of the clash between social prominence and media celebrity. Gloria loves cracking the whip over people. It was almost as if she was enjoying grinding Barbara down, as if she was saying to us, 'You're nothing but media . . . and trash.' "

Leon Edel describes a year in Henry James's life, a year in which "he dined out 140 times." "To have had the stamina to face so many evenings of talk—not all of it good talk by any means—so much stuffy Victorian formality, was some kind of test of endurance. . . . Henry endured, he more than endured. He thrived on it." So, too, does Mailer. Social encounters are an arena for Mailer; they provide a great deal of the spontaneity that patriarchy has effaced from his life. And they are material: "Rich people interest me," he says. "How they live. I have a dinner party that goes on for a hundred pages in the new book." The kindness of the community, as Mailer puts it, is important, too. Mailer is the resident genius of the social world, as generous with his opinions and conversation as Hemingway was in his day.

Often, Mailer takes refuge in the bosom of the well-mannered. On the night *60 Minutes* devoted a segment to Mailer and Abbott, Mailer arrived early at a dinner at the home of TV producer Mark Goodson. He had arrived after 7:00. "How did I come out? I didn't want to see it," Mailer said to friends who were there, knowing they would shield him from harsh verities. On the circuit, he can be continuously surprised, as he was when he ran into Frank Sinatra at a recent dinner at William Paley's. "I said to him, 'It's nice to meet you, Mr. Sinatra. I've hated you for forty years because I've always thought you could always get any girl that you ever wanted.' " "I think a novelist just has to get out," Mailer says. "There's many a night when we come home and I say, 'Oh, what are we doing? This is ridiculous. What a boring evening.' But if you stay home, it can be boring too."

They are a familiar sight on the Upper East Side, Norman

and Norris arriving for dinner: Norris, tall, elegant, her pre-Raphaelite features set off by stunning red hair; Norman in his black velvet dinner jacket, shorter, rounder, grayer, taking obvious pride in being at her side. Mailer loves to repeat the story of being so taken with her beauty the first time they met "that I had to leave the room." "When Norman met Norris," says Mailer's oldest friend, Mickey Knox, an actor who lives in Rome, "it was as if he had finally met his Marilyn Monroe."

Mailer had married a variety of women: Beatrice Silverman, a New York intellectual; Adele Morales, a Peruvian Catholic artist; Lady Jean Campbell, the daughter of the English press lord Beaverbook; Beverly Bentley, an actress with whom he had a daughter, Kate, before they married; Carol Stevens, another actress. None of them was quite right. "There was a seven-year period in my life," Mailer says, "where each time I took a woman to bed I was dead drunk. I'm not proud of that." "Each of Norman's previous wives had elements of what he was always searching for," says Mickey Knox. "But it was only when Norman met Norris that he found the one woman who had everything: beauty, grace, intelligence, talent, and a very strong will."

Barbara Norris, as she was called before she changed her name to Norris Church for her modeling career, had never even been on a plane until she met Norman Mailer. They have the same birthday, but would not seem to have much else in common. As an art teacher from Russellville, Arkansas, the daughter of a beautician and a man who drove heavy farming equipment, Norris's world was too special and isolated for her to have been intimidated by Mailer's. She had grown up wearing mouton coats and being a football sweetheart; she'd married young, had Matthew, then divorced her husband, Larry Norris, "a strange and private person," sometime after he'd come home from Vietnam. "I wasn't insecure and anxious when I first got up here because in all the parties we went to, I didn't know anybody or who they were. In that way, southerners and New Yorkers are very similar. They both think their worlds are complete. So if I would meet people at parties, to me they were just friends of Norman's and I was glad they liked me and were nice to me. Also, Norman made a point to bring me in. He still does. He'll say to me in the middle of a party, 'Norris, you're the most beautiful woman here.' "

The story of their meeting has been told often; Mailer was visiting an old army friend, Francis Gwaltney, a writer who lived in Russellville. Norris had collaborated on a children's book with him. "I hear you're having a cocktail party for Norman Mailer," Norris said to Gwaltney. "Well, I'm going to come." Norris walked in wearing "blue jeans and bear-trap sandals that made me about seven feet tall" and "there was Norman sitting in the window, and when I walked in, there was a kind of halo around him, the way the light was coming in." They were introduced and "Norman just walked away from me. I thought, 'Maybe this guy has a problem with tall women.' " But she was invited to dinner, and after dinner, as they sat on the porch of a local professor's house, "Norman kept coming on to me, telling me how beautiful I was, and I said to him, 'Gee, I always went for a good line if it's presented well,' and Norman really presented it well."

But, says Norris, "After that first dinner, I thought, 'What a nice man; that's it.' I didn't think of anything else. I never thought he would write to me." He did. "The only book I'd ever read of Norman's was *Marilyn*. And the only reason I read that was because I forgot to send the card back to the Book-of-the-Month Club saying I didn't want the book; it was too expensive. The Russellville library didn't have any of Norman's books. Finally, I found a torn-up copy of *The Naked and the Dead* at a secondhand bookstore. But just after I met Norman for the first time, a huge box arrived. He sent me a crate with all his books in them, every single one. In hardcover. I made this terrible mistake, which was I sat down and read them all at once. It was a really dumb thing to do. I was just overwhelmed."

Soon after, Barbara Norris arrived in New York and moved into Fanny Mailer's building. The two became close friends, but "Norman's mother never intruded in our romance," Norris says, "except that she would tell me that she never liked any of Norman's other wives." Mailer's domestic situation was complicated. He was still legally married to Beverly Bentley and also involved with Carol Stevens. "I never pressured him," says Norris. "I had my own apartment, that was a help. I was modeling. I didn't have to." "When Norman met Norris," says Mickey Knox, "that was it. A lot of his past craziness just disappeared."

It isn't unusual in the middle of dinner to see Norman Mailer turn his attention momentarily away from his dinner partner to search out Norris, even if it creates a social frisson. "Someone took us to Claus von Bulow's," Mailer says, "and Von Bulow put Norris next to him and me two tables away. What he didn't realize was that he was directly in my line of vision, so as he flirted with Norris, I fixed him with an intense stare. The next night, we were at Bill Paley's and the same thing happened, except that Paley is much smarter. He placed me so that my back was to him and to Norris and I couldn't see a damn thing that was going on."

"Norris has had an immense effect on me, a softening," Mailer says. He once told an interviewer, "You definitely don't want to be loved for your literary fame. Literary fame has nothing to do with your daily habits. I mean, finally, you're an animal that goes around and finally you have to be liked or disliked as an animal first."

The beautiful young girl just out of Princeton is awed to be seated next to Norman Mailer at dinner and isn't quite sure how to make conversation with him, so, in full innocence, she asks whether he's read a recent interview with William Styron in *The Times Book Review*. Mailer says that he missed it, "I don't read much of anything when I'm working," but he begins to reminisce and gives her something quite marvelous to take away. "When Bill and I were young, fiction was everything. The novel, the big novel, the driving force. We all wanted to be Hemingway; he was the clear influence." Mailer pauses and his voice becomes sad. "I don't think the same thing can be said anymore. I don't think my work has inspired any writer, not the way Hemingway inspired me."

Mailer believes that he might be an anachronism, a throwback to a time "when I was at Harvard and the publication of a new novel was an exciting event that everyone anticipated." He says the young men and women he might have inspired had he been born twenty years earlier are now wanting to be screenwriters or reporters; they are children of TV, products of the Cancer Gulch, a generation whose friendships "break up over movies." "I haven't heard two people getting angry at each other because one likes one writer and one another in ten years," Mailer says. He says he is one of the last men who grew up believing "that the most exciting thing I could do with my life is write novels," a passion he shared with other men of his era, Saul Bellow, James Jones, John Cheever, Truman Capote, and a few somewhat younger, such as John Updike and Philip Roth.

So the promise "to cause a revolution in the consciousness of our times" that Mailer made in *Advertisements for Myself* is a promise that he will not back away from; he likens his quest to his infant son's scampering across a room in search of an ineffable goal, "perhaps China." "I think it can be dangerous for a young writer to be modest when they're young," he says. "I've known a number of truly talented writers who did less than they could have done because they weren't vain and unpleasant enough about their talent. You have to take it seriously."

"As this well-weathered veteran, my feeling now is much more that it's silly to start deciding what your major achievement is because after you've been running for enough years you just don't feel like that. A man who's been practicing dentistry for forty years doesn't say to himself, 'Today I've done the finest extraction I've ever performed.' All he would say is, 'This was a pretty good extraction.' "

With age has come the realization that he must be "professional, rather than Faustian" and that no matter what he does "history is even more treacherous and generous and quirky than one's own news, so it's absurd to try to decide what your place in literature is or even if you have a place." Mailer feels his place will be determined by "what happens in the world. I think the world is sickening and we're going into terrible times, and to the degree to which my prophecies bear fruit— of course I'm caught in the unhappy position of hoping that I'm wrong—that is, I hope plastic is not as bad as I think it is, or TV, or modern architecture. To the degree I'm wrong about these things my work will have less importance, it will be more of a curiosity."

The test will come, says Mailer, in "the secondary work." "That is what is so important for a writer's reputation. Does the secondary work last or doesn't it? To the degree that my work becomes prophetic, my reputation will be fortified—it will disappear if I'm not."

The same test will make "Saul Bellow's virtues and the virtues of a writer like Updike appear larger. They are writing about substantial matters that tend to change less from generation to generation. Updike is almost not concerned with history; he is always looking for those elements in history that are constant. Saul Bellow sees the world deteriorating, but he really fulminates against it from a position of more or less fixed values. Bellow, I would guess, feels that European culture is perhaps the finest achievement of mankind and it is this that we're destroying. I agree with him. Two thousand years of European history, that's the family heirloom. But for all of the richness of Bellow's work, this is where I find him lacking intellectually; Bellow has no concept of why it is happening. He is just finky about it. He thinks it's awful and that people are stupid, they're degenerating. He just doesn't see the vast engines of destruction. He doesn't understand that totalitarianism is a matter of automatic buttons on TV sets. It's not just a matter of Hitler and the camps of extermination. I think Saul Bellow may be marooned too much in the idea of 'Is this good for the Jews?' I think that can destroy a good mind more than anything."

Of all the great themes Mailer has written about, the one he has avoided is the one closest to him, his childhood, growing up as Fanny and Barney Mailer's son. "I'm saving it," he says. "My last book. You have to save something for the end. And if I never get to write that book, think how annoyed everybody will be."

"I am not a typical Jew," Mailer says, although like most Jewish intellectuals his age, his childhood was spent "rejecting Jewishness at a great rate." But he was typical in that he had a strong mother to whom he gives a great deal of credit. "There have been two writers, Truman Capote and myself, who have had a very special development; we were both famous very early. Capote is wrecked now, but he didn't have a good Jewish mother and that's half of it."

Mailer's biographer sketched his parents in stereotypical terms: Fanny Mailer, primeval force, who doted on her son; Barney Mailer, a weak, scholarly *Luftmensch*. "There were no shadings to it," Mailer said. "And there was an assumption that I make pilgrimages to my mother in order to keep my sanity; it's not like that at all." In fact, he says, "My father was an elegant impoverished figure out of Chekhov." He was "a dapper gentleman in a bewildering world, a man of such sentimentality that phrases like 'the passing parade' would al-

ways bring tears to his eyes. He was marvelously involved in
himself. So involved that when he would write me a letter in
college it would be fourteen pages long, but the first ten would
be concerned with the curious sentiments he felt in himself
starting to write a letter to his son. He was always analyzing
his own emotions at all times. He played a shell game. What
he talked about never had anything to do with what he was
really feeling."

Mailer's voice, with its undertone of Oxbridge, is a direct
legacy from Barney Mailer's South African accent, as is what
he calls "that baroque element in my style, the sidewinder in
me. That all comes from my father in some funny way." Barney Mailer had moved from Lithuania to South Africa as a
young man, trained as an accountant, served in the British
Army, arrived in America for a visit and fell in love. The
Mailers were married for life. "But they couldn't pass a bowl
of soup to one another without spilling it," their son says.
"My mother is fierce, she's loyal, but if I didn't mind her, I
would have argued with her every day of my life. She's got a
mind that could send you climbing up the wall. She is absolutely literal. She doesn't have a teaspoon of metaphysics in
her, not a gnat's wing of mysticism."

An incident occurred when Mailer was thirteen: "I was to
be bar mitzvahed at the best temple my parents could aspire
to, which was hardly a number-one temple, even for Brooklyn; Congregation Sharei Zedek. I had a marvelous old Hebrew School teacher; he was a Marxist. Looking back on it, he
was probably a Communist; I didn't know at the time. We
were immensely poor, although my family was nothing if they
didn't have middle-class pretensions. They just weren't able to
exercise them much. A relative had to come through with the
gift so I was able to have the bar mitzvah party; it was all
pretty desperate stuff. So nobody ever paid attention to the
speech I was giving. It was taken for granted that I would give
one of those pious, wonderful speeches that boys of thirteen

give. But my Hebrew teacher smuggled in a terrific line. I stood up and I said, 'May I follow in the footsteps of Moses, Maimonides, and Karl Marx.' There were all my wealthy relatives in their fur boas, and I saw this sort of shift in the animals, and the rabbi looked very pale. Well, I didn't know. I'd heard of Moses, the other two were somewhat strange to me. Years later, when I asked my mother about the incident, she gave me one of her odd little smiles which means she's not going to tell me anything, but I knew what it was. She didn't care what the guy ended up doing. If he was famous and Jewish, that was good enough for her.

Fanny Mailer's determination kept the family going when "we were dead broke," Mailer says. After his father lost his job, it was his mother who took over, running an oil-delivery business. "My mother had a way of driving my father," Mailer says. "He'd go out looking for work and when he came home, we'd throw our arms around him—I was about six and my sister two—and my mother would say, 'Ask Daddy if he got a job today.' He would shake his head sadly night after night."

Her redemption came later. "When I published *The Naked and the Dead*," Mailer says, "my mother hit the stratospheres of motherly pride and hasn't come down since. The joke I always make to my mother's face is that, if I took a tommy gun and shot up hundreds of people in a shopping mall, my mother would say, 'They must have said something truly awful to him.' "

Ancient Evenings began as the saga of the Mailer family, specifically, "back in Russia with my grandfather as I imagined him." Mailer studied Hebrew for a year and was set to write about life in the ghetto when he came upon the writings of Isaac Bashevis Singer. "I thought, 'Oh, lord, there is absolutely no need for this book.' " Meanwhile, the rumors had already started—Mailer, it was said, would be writing about a

Jewish family in the time of the pyramids, the Mailer family.
"That was all factoidal and to an advanced degree," Mailer
says.

Inspired by André Schwartz-Bart's *The Last of the Just,*
Mailer's plan had been to telescope centuries of history. "I'd
read a chapter of H. G. Wells on ancient Egypt, and I was
kind of taken with it, and my idea was I would start in Egypt
and then go on to the Greeks and the Romans and acquire all
that classical culture and have a marvelous time, taking it right
up to the Middle Ages and on to the present. I know that
sounds unhinged."

Mailer buried himself in research, read a hundred books,
inhaled *The Book of the Dead,* a classic work of Egyptology,
and "didn't come up for air for a year." But when he finally
did, he understood he would have to forget his plan to telescope history, that it would be Egypt and only Egypt that
would concern him, however long it took. It has taken eleven
years. During those years Mailer completed three other
books, including *The Executioner's Song.* "I must say there was
one bit of amusement that gave pleasure to many a day,"
Mailer says. "I thought, my literary betters are really going to
have a tough time showing how I'm a journalist on this one."

For centuries, the behemoth of ancient Egypt has attracted,
and often confounded, great writers from Shakespeare to
Lawrence Durrell. Flaubert's Egyptian diaries were a classic
of the form, but his attempt to fictionalize his travels in *Sa-
lammbo* was so disastrous that his friend Louis Bouilhet, after
reading his manuscript, advised him, "Burn it." The inscruta-
ble gods of the Nile did not deter Mailer. He was determined
"to try to recapture the past in a certain way that hasn't been
done, not even by historical novelists. I wanted everyone to
lose the sense that they were reading about the past; I wanted
it to be as palpable as our own present."

Mailer visited Egypt only once, in 1974, on his way to
Zaire for the Ali-Foreman fight. The trip was unsuccessful:

The Israeli-Egyptian war was just over, and Cairo was a war zone, the Nile closed to barge traffic. Mailer's only route to the pyramids was by car. "We arrived at the Mena House, where Churchill used to stay, and I discovered that now it was a goddamn motel they had redone with a huge swimming pool and people staying there who looked like rejects from the Mudd Club."

Worse, climbing the pyramids was forbidden, so Mailer's only course of action was "to bribe a guide. At six o'clock in the morning, there we were racing up these pyramids trying to beat the cops before they came and clubbed this poor guide to death. That meant we had to run up steps that were twenty-four to forty-eight inches high; it was the fastest trail climbing I'd ever done, all of it at top speed. I always thought when I got up to the top of the pyramids, I would have an epiphany, but just as I got to the top, heaving and panting, my vision blurred. There were the smoke plumes of the police coming through the desert, so we had to race down just as the cops got around the bend."

"That was all of Egypt," Mailer says. "I thought, I've got to get out of here or I'll never write this book."

All his life, Norman Mailer has functioned best when he was convinced he was struggling: to pay his debts, to assuage his unconscious, as he puts it, or to solve a demanding problem of craft. *Ancient Evenings* was particularly hard for Mailer because during the writing of it he was afflicted with all three troubles—a desperate need for money, unrequited inspiration, and a technical problem. "I never was certain I would finish *Ancient Evenings* until I did. It was so difficult, the most difficult book I ever tackled. The choices were so many. That's why I never take Tom Wolfe seriously when he talks about the New Journalism as a higher form than the novel, because finally, in the New Journalism, your plot is handed to you, and once it is, you can concentrate on the writing. Plot is what drives me up the wall. The choices your characters have, the wrong choices they can make. I've had that experience in *The Deer Park* and in *Barbary Shore* and it frightened me for life."

Some years ago, Mailer was interviewed by the editors of the *Paris Review.* "Whenever you get into real trouble," he said, "the thing that can save you as a novelist is to have enough craft to be able to keep warm long enough to be rescued. . . . Craft protects one from facing those endlessly expanding realities of deterioration and responsibility." "Deterioration in what sense?" the interviewer asked him. "The terror, let's say, of being reborn as something much less noble or something much more ignoble. I think this sort of thing depresses us profoundly." A few years later, Mailer would be working on his eleventh book, *Armies of the Night,* for which he would win both a Pulitzer Prize and a National Book Award, but still he had to dwell in the abyss, to act as he had in his early years, "enormously paranoid . . . as if the apocalypse was coming in a year or two."

Mailer says his apocalyptic attitude might have something to do with his early fame; in any event, his problems have always been rarefied. "Being a professional writer and being successful are the same to me. If you arrive at age thirty or thirty-five or forty, you can say, 'Before success' and 'After success,' but the only book I wrote before I became successful was *The Naked and the Dead,* and I would have been in trouble even if it hadn't been successful because I put everything I knew about life into that book. I had to start over for the next. As a farmer, I would have been dreadful. I would have just scourged the fields. Each book was an attempt to throw a brickbat into the face of the enemy, whoever the enemy was.

"It's only been in recent years that I've begun to think of pacing myself and having a literary career," he says. "I've been thinking a lot about John Updike in the past few months because his history is the exact opposite of mine. If ever there was a career where a man knew he had a fine talent and he had to protect it and work at it carefully, his is it. I think one of the reasons for his vast popularity now is because he's a lonely example of someone who had a fine talent and nurtured it. He was wise enough to hone it. In this time of immense distraction, anyone who can truly exercise craft is to be admired."

But John Updike's fastidious example does not make Norman Mailer feel he has "lived the wrong life, that I should have stayed married to one woman. That would be like saying I should have been a WASP. Updike's life is just another life; he might as well have been a French writer as far as I'm concerned. I don't say to myself that García Márquez lived a more sensible life than I did because he stayed close to the people. He had a people to stay close to. I don't."

It is late in Brooklyn Heights and everyone is tired: Norman Mailer is just back from Paris and Mitterand's conference; Norris Mailer has spent the day moving out of her studio; John Buffalo is fighting sleep; Danielle and Betsy load the dishwasher. For Mailer, the day has brought an unpleasant advance review of *Ancient Evenings* in Kirkus, a book-trade publication. Norris is worried about being able to afford a new work space, and Danielle and Betsy complain about finding decent men to go out with. Mailer is hovering around the kitchen, taking various photographs off the walls, reminiscing about certain special times, when his glance falls upon a collage he'd made years before. His assemblage features a photograph of Hemingway, bearded and gray, as round as a stevedore, posed beneath a moose head with an enormous antler span. Just under the moose, Mailer had glued a picture of himself, age twenty-five, a skinny kid with a frizzy pompadour and ears out to Brooklyn, snapped at the very moment in 1948 he had come back from Paris, a celebrity-to-be, his accolades, criticism, awards, brawls, drinking, drugs, wives, children, excess, and immense discipline all ahead of him. "Look at that picture," Mailer says. "God, how thin I was. Isn't it strange? I've grown into Hemingway's body. I think he was sixty in that photograph, too. How strange, how damn strange."

March 1983

At Home with
Ron and Doria Reagan

I t had been a quiet Sunday night for the two young
New Yorkers. After dinner, they had retired to their
mattress on the floor. Entertainment was called for.
The boy reached for their TV—held together by a coat
hanger. The girl curled up underneath their quilt—a gift from
her mother-in-law-to-be. The voices of David Susskind and
Gore Vidal filled their tiny apartment on the top floor of a
Village brownstone. A presidential campaign was in progress,
and Susskind and Vidal had a lot to talk about.

This night, their topic was the boy's father's "cut-rate dye
job." For fourteen years, the boy had followed his father's
peregrinations through headlines and talk shows, but somehow this Sunday evening in New York something in him
snapped. He couldn't listen anymore. "Gore Vidal was like a
parody of himself," Ron Reagan, the dancer, remembers. "So
snide, it was just disgusting. I couldn't believe what I was
hearing. He was drooling all over David Susskind, going on
and on about this so-called cut-rate dye job of my father's
when my father has *never* dyed his hair. It just pissed me off
unbelievably. The next day I fired off a telegram to Gore
Vidal that said something like, IF YOU'RE TALKING ABOUT

CUT-RATE-DYE JOBS, WHY DON'T YOU TALK ABOUT YOUR
CUT-RATE LOBOTOMY? I just figured, fuck 'em. Did I sign my
name? You bet. RON REAGAN."

A pause. Ron Reagan's eyes flash and he looks even more
like his mother. "If something pisses me off, I do something
about it," he says. His bride smiles and looks adoringly at
her husband. For that moment, she looks just like Ron's
mother too.

New York life is not luxurious for the President-elect's son
and his bride. Chemical Bank won't cash their paychecks
without debate. They fret about their rent. They brood about
the cost of their apartment and debate moving to Harlem,
where they could afford six rooms. He eats tuna salad from the
deli for his lunches. He stammers with admiration when
Anthony Dowell appears in class. Chinatown is where they
take their dinners out. Mostly they take their dinners in.
Sometimes they get free tickets to the American Ballet Theatre. Though they don't skimp on food—Doria shops at Bal-
ducci's and turns out pesto in her Cuisinart—they are so low
on china that dinner guests have to bring their own plates.
They have one advantage over most other New Yorkers,
however: two Secret Service men installed on the ground floor
of their building.

Ron Reagan and Doria Palmieri Reagan are trying to lead
the low-key urban life. No sign of a trust fund in this fourth-
floor walk-up. No sign that Nancy has been successful in
getting them out of the isn't-poverty-romantic school of
decorating or that she's even tried. Dance magazines abound.
So do Japanese paper shades and posters. A black kimono
hangs from the living-room wall. That was a gift: from Doria,
with love, to Ron. Their bathroom is larger than their kitchen.
Their toilet seat is red. So are the baseboards—in patent-
leather gloss enamel—which provide just the right *Apartment
Life* accent for their peeling gray walls. Half of the dining-

room seating is the radiator, topped with unmatched cushions. Their records are stacked in cartons. Al Jarreau and Keith Jarrett are the favorites of the house.

Four years ago in Los Angeles Ron was working behind the desk at the Stanley Holden Dance Center. As a scholarship student, his job was to make sure everybody signed in for class. One day Doria strolled in. Ron saw the piercing black eyes, the mass of curly Linda Ronstadt hair, the tiny dancer's body—she weighs ninety-eight pounds—on the medium-tall frame. "I thought she was very attractive," Ron says. *"Very* attractive." He was too preoccupied to notice that she had already signed his sheet. Their first words were angry: Why hadn't she signed in? "I thought he was an asshole," Doria says. He was eighteen, she was twenty-five. On their first date they went to a movie, the horror film *Halloween.*

Remembering this, Ron smiles. So does Doria. "I found his presence in class so intimidating," she says. "He was so much more advanced than everybody else. I guess I was jealous." "It wasn't that I was better," Ron says, "it's just that I was put in a beginners' class when I was already very serious about my work—more serious, perhaps, than others in the class."

After a childhood of mansions, limos, an Adolfo-clad mother, Frank Sinatra, and Le Bistro, the hard life of a dancer appealed to the governor's son. So did the philosophy major from the San Fernando Valley. "Ron was always his own person," his childhood friend Cindy Wick recalls. "He was always unbelievably strong-minded, intellectual, with a quirky sense of humor, and direct." At the time Ron, who always was, as he says, "in all kinds of trouble at school," met Doria, he had had enough of formal education. He'd left Yale after one semester, studied dance, moved back to Los Angeles, and supported himself through odd jobs, most of which he despised, such as selling menswear at I. Magnin. "I got the job because my mother knew the president of the store," Ron says. "They had the lousiest selection. A guy would come in and ask for a navy blazer in a forty regular—the most common size—and Magnin's wouldn't have it. Then these customers would get abusive like it was my fault. I couldn't take it. I would just turn my back on them and say, 'Later.' I didn't care about making the sale. And I'd wear what I wanted. No suit. Jeans, with maybe a coat and a tie. All of the buyers treated the salesmen like pricks. If someone wanted to buy something, I would think, 'Okay, fine,' and just write it up. Finally I got fired."

Perhaps Ron's parents thought that his pretty dancer-girl friend was just more of Ron's show of temperament, a phase he would grow out of. Doria was never invited to the Palisades. But one night Ron got them together. The brush fires were sweeping the Santa Monica canyons, and Ron's mother was worried. Embers were flying into her backyard. "My mom called me up and said, 'Come over, we're loading up the station wagon. We need your help.' " Into a VW piled Ron, Doria, and another friend. "I was nervous," Doria remembers. "Ron went off to fight the fire, and I was just left there alone. But Ron's dad was so great. Really friendly. He sat me down on the patio and told me all kinds of Hollywood stories and then took out these maps so we could study the route of the fire. He was wonderful."

What about Ron's mother? A silence. "We've only met two or three times," Doria answers carefully. Ron interrupts. "They've really just said hello." And they've had few enough chances for that. When Ron's parents came to town before the inaugural, Doria did not go to lunch with them (she had the flu), and Ron and Doria were not invited to Brooke Astor's party in their honor.

It's all very delicate. Doria, warm-spirited as she is, may not be the wife Nancy would have chosen for her son. Nancy Reagan's fantasy would have been something else: a Chandler daughter certainly, a scion of the Los Angeles Country Club, a little artsy to interest Ron, but not so artsy she didn't know to register at Tiffany's for Shell & Thread—somebody who would not wear black Orlon ankle socks and thrift-shop sweaters to visit the Darts or the Bloomingdales, or when a writer comes to call.

After the wedding, Ron's mother was terse: "The main thing is that Ron is happy." Just when Patty, Ron's older sister, seemed to be toeing the mark, being measured for Adolfo's red chiffon ruffles, basking in being a President's daughter, looking more and more the buffed-nails-and-Chanel-pumps image of her mother, there went Ron down to City Hall in a sweatshirt and sneakers, with a Secret Service man as a witness, in a rush to tie the knot.

The wedding was not the result of Reagan-family pressure. Friends say this is pure Ron, doing just what he's done all his life, making up his own mind, standing up for what he wants. What he wanted was to cut loose. How better to prove to your family you're finally grown up than to marry? "I just knew with all the places we would be going and the people we would be seeing, it would be a lot easier for us if we married," he says. "Besides, marriage is nothing romantic to me. That's not where our romance comes from. What is a wedding anyway but a seven-dollar license and somebody asking you if you have the clap?"

Doria's parents were relieved. "They're traditional Italians," she says. "My father came from Genoa. From the moment he met Ron, he adored him. Ron is such a polite person." Doria's father used to be a painting contractor. The family had moved from the San Fernando valley to Brooklyn and then back to California, where her father was a scenic designer for Twentieth Century-Fox. Doria warms to the subject of her mother. "My mother is a real mother," Doria says. "She loves to stay home and cook, and always took care of us." She pauses, noticing a fine line of tension beginning to cross Ron's face; her voice drops and her words trail off. "She's just great," she says.

They are trying to carve out a New York City life, but the joys of the city are not so joyous on a tight budget. It helps that Ron is as motivated as any twenty-two-year-old could be, highly disciplined, strict with himself, in class and rehearsals eight or nine hours a day. Doria is mysterious about her employer, a neighborhood publisher for whom she works as a girl Friday. Someday, she says, she'll go back to school to learn how to work with the handicapped. Or she'd like to be a food consultant. Right now, though, there are no more dance classes. "If I took classes, I'd have to take them at night, and then I wouldn't be home for Ron."

"My best friend," Doria calls Ron, and there are few other friends here for Doria. No network of women—nobody, she complains, to go shopping with. "You can always go shopping with our friend Cindy," Ron tells her. "I don't have the time or money to shop," his wife says. Their nights are the sweet little dinners of chicken on a bed of spinach or pesto that Doria—"a fabulous cook," Ron says—somehow manages to whip together in the closet-size kitchen, which looks onto an air shaft. "We never go to discos," Ron says. "I dance all day. Why would I want to dance all night?"

After dinner, he reads novels—*Loon Lake* at the moment—and all the news he can. "I have to keep up," he says. "For obvious reasons."

Starting out in New York is tough enough for any newly married couple, but tougher still when one of them is the President-elect's son. Pose doing a jeté and people say, "He looks like a fag." Give an interview to Andy Warhol and the chorus grows. Even in his work, the pressure is terrifying. "You realize very fast that you could become another Margaret Truman," Ron says, "unless you're very, very good. She could have had a decent singing career except that the hot white light of the media shone on her, and that was that."

The young dancer knows too well he dances in that same white light. Reporters clog the halls at the Joffrey Ballet School. For a few weeks after the election, he couldn't leave his house without stumbling over photographers camped at his brownstone's door. "There was one guy who slept in his station wagon—literally—for three nights," Ron says. "I kind of felt sorry for him after a while, because he was a real klutz. Every time he would come trailing after me, he would say in this unbelievable English accent, 'Ronnie, Ronnie, just one,' and then he would drop his camera, and the parts would roll all over the sidewalk."

And there is the larger media pressure he has to live with: the not-so-veiled suggestions that he's gay. "Its laughable, isn't it?" Ron says. "I mean, I just can't believe the level of stupidity of reporters in this town. Until people brought the subject up—and believe me, at least they have the sense to seem embarrassed about it when they do—I never even thought about it. The idea that anyone would think dancing is effeminate. I'll tell you this: It's a lot more athletic than playing baseball."

But Ron is learning that New Yorkers are snide, as snide as Gore Vidal. They love to sneer at the situation on West Tenth Street. They love to joke about it: Boy marries mother. Ron's photographs do not flatter. In them, he looks dreamy-eyed, Baudelairean, a little sad. Ron is not the wimpy prince waiting to dance *The Nutcracker*. He admires boxer Roberto Duran for his "savagery" and "primal energy," and says that his own dancing helps him to express a lot of anger. A lot of that anger might come from having had an isolated childhood at the mercy of campaigns. Right now, it's directed at those who have attacked someone who means a great deal to him, the President-elect of the United States.

One of those is Jimmy Carter. "I'm not going to shake his hand at the inauguration," Ron snaps. "There is no way I'll be able to." Doria nods. Ron says, "I don't want to. I will never forgive the way he called my father a racist and a warmonger over and over again. Carter would have sold his mother to get reelected. He has the morals of a snake."

This apple has not fallen far from the Reagan tree. He may

be living in an un-Nancy-like apartment with an un-Nancy-like wife, but there is no debate about the point at which Ron Reagan's quirkiness stops. "He worships his father," his friend Cindy Wick says. Ron says, "I'll tell you this: My father is the most honorable man who has ever been elected President. I don't want to take anything away from Abraham Lincoln, but my father has the potential to be the greatest President there ever was." At times, his father's behavior astonishes him. "The man says anything he believes. Sometimes I just can't believe the things he comes out with. The man just never lies."

And his mother? Ron hesitates. "My mother is much cannier about sizing up people. She is incredible about knowing exactly what someone wants."

What Ron and Doria want is what all newlyweds want: to be happy. Ron would also like to be able to dance with the precision and perfection of Anthony Dowell. He dreams about the day—and can't imagine it—when he and his wife might bring in fifty-thousand dollars a year. And he knows he wants no part of his mother's style of New York social life—the lunches at Le Cirque, the evenings at Doubles, the private club. "I despise people who do nothing but go to lunches and dinners and take their jets to Bogotá," he says, although he likes his mother's chum Jerry Zipkin, the socialites' favorite escort and gossip hound. Jerry, he says, has promised to take the newlyweds to the Soho Charcuterie, but so far he hasn't called. And that's about as social as Ron and Doria get. Don't look for them at dinners on Upper East Side; don't expect to see them dancing with the Nine O'Clocks at that yearly dinner dance. So far none of the Reagan family friends have tossed a party in their honor, and no wedding presents have come in from Rodeo Drive—just a promise from Ron's parents that, come Christmas, they will fly them west.

And then, Doria hopes, the two sets of parents will finally get to meet. What's clear is that the arctic winds blowing from the Pacific Palisades don't seem to affect Doria Palmieri Reagan the slightest bit. Or maybe, after a year of living with Ron Reagan, she's learned to hide her feelings. She's certainly learned to hide a lot of information. Her employer? "I'd rather not say." Where she comes from in the valley? "I would prefer that my family not be harassed." Who was her boyfriend before Ron? "Someone else." She smiles a queenly smile, the veil stays in place.

Folie des grandeurs? Doria may be a little nervous that she's in over her head. Columnists run stories saying the newlyweds won't be invited to the inauguration because Mummy does not approve. There's the age difference to think about and the not-so-great family background. The punk makeup can be corrected. But something else might be making Doria tense. It wouldn't be easy for even the steeliest of debs to get a marriage going on an inauguration eve. A few nights ago, Ron's sister Patty came to dinner, and the two girls talked inauguration dresses. Doria has hers—an off-the-shoulder black angora sweater with long black-and-gray culottes. Over Christmas, Nancy might tell her daughter-in-law that that won't photograph well, and urge her to stick with Nixon pink.

So Ron and Doria settle in, living only for themselves, their quietude, and the dance, it seems. Ron is lucky. He is occupied by his Joffrey II performance schedules, dancing in a number called *Ladies Lingerie.* Doria accompanies him to rehearsals.

Ron protects their privacy, and does it well. He knows all about being protected. His mother had to stay in bed for three months and take hormone shots when she was carrying him, to make sure she wouldn't lose her son. "Every time I moved . . . ," she wrote in her autobiography *Nancy,* "I thought I might lose him." And as a child in Sacramento, he says, "I was never shoved in front of the cameras like John-John or Caroline to show what a perfect corny family we had."

So now it is his turn to protect his family, or at least his wife. They are young, they are broke, and they have a lot of foreign turf to navigate. But one thing is certain. New York is theirs for the taking, if only they could afford it. Elaine will give them a good table. "I know this is the opportunity of a lifetime," Ron says. "I don't want to exploit it, but it sure would be nice to meet some of the people I admire." When Doria first arrived in town, she spent hours looking through the Manhattan phone book, trying to spot the famous names.

So whom would they like to meet? Tom Wolfe, for one. And Carl Sagan. And Ron has a special request: Henry Kissinger. "I'd ask him what really goes on in the world," the President-elect's son explains. And then he sighs. "But you know what? If I don't know now, I guess I'll never find out."

December 1980

George Steinbrenner

A tense and awful silence has fallen on his baseball
field. No balls slapping into gloves, no baseball
babble from the dugout, no batters taking their
licks in the cage. A dozen of his players are frozen, watching
him and waiting in a kind of ominous quiet. Harry Reasoner
and the crew from *60 Minutes* wait for him too. And more TV
people from the networks, and the cable sports group from
ESPN. All eyes are on the scene in front of the dugout, where
the real star of the New York Yankees is posed behind silver
light reflectors beaming the sun back at the morning Florida
sky. The only sound is the wind whipping through the stadium flags and the whirs, clicks, snaps, growls, and commands
of George Steinbrenner at work.

An art director is trying to instruct him. "Let's have a little
snarl on that, George." The star of this commercial for Yankee radio broadcasts on New York's WABC is posed in his
Rotarian-on-holiday finest: a red brushed-denim sport jacket,
navy polyester slacks, and tasseled white patent-leather tropi-
cal shufflers almost imperceptibly stained with grass. Lights
. . . time for the star to play himself. Dutifully, George Steinbrenner, the man whose closest friends call him "the U-boat

Commander," juts out his lip, contorts his childlike features into his fiercest don't-put-me-in-a-corner face, and chills the eye of the camera with his growl. "They better play better than they sing."

No good. The art director wants to convey the Steinbrenner essence: erraticness, zealotry, accomplishment, and God knows winning, but, mostly, his extraordinary ability to strike fear. But he doesn't want to scare people away from the ball park. "Put a little smile under that snarl, George," he says. "Why don't you try, 'They can play better than they sing'?" "I don't like that," George says. George knows what sells in New York. He knows the rich tough guy at the top and the rich tough guys in the clubhouse are what fill his stadium, win ball games, and break American League attendance records at home and on the road. He knows how to control the act. He has raised his sour demeanor, the when-will-he-explode lunacy, to a kind of art form, established enough to sustain self-parody, sustain insult, sustain the theater of itself.

A few more takes. George fidgets. His gestures are those of a nervous man. He knots his hands, drums his fingers, whips the tiny Ace comb from his pocket, and for the fifth time this session rearranges his hair. The wind off the Florida Keys almost knocks down the foil light reflectors. And still there's not a peep from Ron Guidry, Goose Gossage, or Tommy John.

"Roll and record!" the director yells. Suddenly, in the middle of the take, Rick Cerone saunters out, oblivious. "Hey . . . what the heck is going on here?" Cerone cries. The catcher takes in everything all at once: the hush, the rolling camera, Harry Reasoner, the owner performing his lines. One beat. Two beats. Then Cerone mumbles, "Jeesus . . ."

Perhaps that was putting it a bit strong.

In a city that reveres flamboyance as much as success, George Steinbrenner flashes so much money and temperament that he has practically reinvented the national pastime.

In service to his baseball-as-show-business philosophy, he bullies, he whines, he punishes those who betray. He came out of Cleveland, an almost-nobody with some cash and a bullyboy personality, and gave back to the New York Yankees the power and the glamour that once made them myth. He reacts to every clubhouse controversy that he doesn't create by getting into the middle of the feud. If his salaries are fabulous—the players average $240,000 a year—his profits are even more so. In 1980, 2.6 million New Yorkers turned out to watch Steinbrenner's boys. The faltering ball club George bought in 1973 for ten million dollars is now worth three times that price.

George understands that New Yorkers turn out to watch and worship wherever, as he says, "the style and excitement is." In the spring and the summer, that means the Bronx. If one of his players refers to him as "a twenty-four-karat asshole," there is no question that George has elevated himself into the biggest Yankee name of all. He gets the top table all over town. His every tantrum is headline material. He hobnobs with Roy Cohn, Barbara Walters, Lee Iacocca, Bill Fugazy, and Cardinal Cooke. Elaine makes him special sundaes when he comes to call. New Yorkers know all about his horse farm in Ocala and his shipyard in Tampa Bay. He is the one owner in baseball who has overshadowed his players.

The commercial is finished now, and, off camera, George is agitated, having just learned that his company, American Ship Building, has lost a thirty-six-million-dollar contract from United States Steel. The contract could have taken care of eighteen months of Yankee Stadium overhead. A Cleveland paper has run an editorial saying, "Not even George Steinbrenner may be able to pull this one out." On top of that, George is trying to keep out of the papers the fact that one of his top players got into a spring-training barroom fight.

And there is Reggie Jackson. There is always Reggie. This

day in Fort Lauderdale, George and Reggie are not speaking. Harry Reasoner and George stand in the sunshine when number 44 walks out of the clubhouse. "Hi, Reggie," Harry says. "Hi, Harry," says Reggie. Silence from George. "I'd like to interview you about George, Reggie," Harry says. "Well, he isn't talking to me," Reggie says, smiling. "I smiled at you," George sniffs. Reggie stalks off. George is too busy to think about Reggie this day. Ted Kennedy is looking for him, and George Plimpton, and on his desk in the trailer is a special eight-page horizontal chart of phone calls and messages in just the past twenty-four hours.

The governor is expecting him at a baseball dinner in Tampa. He is scheduled to conduct "Stars and Stripes Forever" at a benefit concert. Friends are due over the weekend in Ocala at his horse farm. His kids are arriving for spring vacation. He has to line up the helicopter to take him to a special National Invitational Tournament basketball game tomorrow. He has to organize tickets for the Braves game for Anna-Marie, the waitress at the local Stouffer's. And all those plans are subject to cancellation, to change, as George makes ready to rush to the airport, flee the *60 Minutes* crew that is following him, strap himself into his first-class seat, headed for his most crucial shipbuilding negotiation of the year.

Sixty-five million dollars is at stake. That sixty-five million could make his thirty-six-million-dollar loss so trivial it would be funny. There is only one problem. American Ship Building has made no attempt to put in a bid. And George has just learned the bids are due in four days.

Not to worry. George doesn't. He always gets what he wants. He's the perfect symbol for these Republican times. George Steinbrenner III, born, as his publicity constantly reminds us, on the Fourth of July, has skated through eight years of sniping New York liberals and sportswriters to triumph in this new era. His peer group rules. Memory dims. George's felony conviction for campaign-contribution shenanigans in the Nixon years has been forgiven or practically forgotten. The hysteria over Martin-Lemon-Howser is a chapter of the past. His firings and rehirings and tantrums have become part of Yankee lore. To hear him tell it, forward motion is all. He sees that the little people of the city—as he calls them—respect him. His people, he says, are the cabdrivers, the construction workers, the doormen, the fans. Like him, they are keyed up, they are battlers; all they want is to win. The method, however mad, is no longer questioned. The means, to George and his little people, are just a way to the end.

The ship crisis festers. Minutes before the Yankees meet the Texas Rangers, Steinbrenner sits in a tiny trailer hunched over a telephone. One imagines the terrified executives huddled in Cleveland at the other end of this conference call. Figures and schedules of shipbuilding are demanded; George must go into his meeting armed. "You're going to convert those to sixty-six feet? Are you cutting off the bow and stern? What about the deck crane? Give me the figures!" He pounds the table in the Florida trailer that has nothing but an American League calendar on the wall. "So just add a million a ship for that. . . . Come on, Gavin, get with it!" he explodes once again. "I'm in a hurry. I don't have all day."

The lineup on the PA system floats back like a foul ball: "Batting second . . . Elliott Maddox. Batting third . . . Dave Winfield." George ignores the loud applause. The mayor of Fort Lauderdale waits; the president of the American League waits. George runs down his calls: Get Tommy John's agent; do something about a Phil Rizzuto day; and "make sure Pete Axthelm's daughter gets to meet Bucky Dent."

Another flick of the Ace comb. George is out of the trailer and he runs into Gunnie Corbett, wife of the former Texas Rangers owner, the other Young Turk of the New Baseball. Gunnie Corbett's diamond throws sparklers into George's eyes. "How's the family, George?" she drawls.

"The kids are all fine," he says quickly. There's no mention of his wife.

A crumpled Bud can blocks George's path. He stops, scoops it up, and fumes. "Why the hell does nobody except me pick up a goddamn thing around here?" And then, ever fastidious, George dusts a nonexistent piece of lint from his pants.

The egrets circle in the Florida sky. The pinstripes shimmer on the field. Next to this bucolic baseball setting is an executive landing strip. This is where the pastoral becomes prosaic. Cessnas descend as Lou Piniella pops up. George massages his hands. "Oh, Lou, don't be so anxious," he says, sounding very sad.

Third inning: Four to one. The Yankees stink. The sliders look like balloons. George is cheered by the parade of young matrons with infants who insistently shove their babies and souvenir books into his arms. Like most bullies, George is a sucker for kids. He is visibly hurt that each infant he's handed for a proud parent's photo opportunity reacts by breaking into an earsplitting bawl. Behind him a kid unfurls an elaborate banner: GEORGE STEINBRENNER IS CHARLIE O. FINLEY IN DISGUISE.

At sunset, George is on a flight to New York. He travels with his ball-club treasurer and grills him on every single Yankee debit. Nautilus equipment. ASCAP fees.

"Thirty-six thousand dollars? That's ridiculous!" George's voice carries across aisles. He turns to his other companion. "You wouldn't believe the waste I have to put up with. How many balls do you think the Yankees use every season?" George takes a breath. "Seventeen hundred and fifty. Do you know what each ball happens to cost?"

George's thrift is legend. In the early days of the Steinbrenner regime, Yankee department heads were routinely called in to George's office after each game to go over the comp list, the free tickets given out. Often, says a former employee, the meetings would go on till dawn.

Over the Manhattan skyline, George grabs the bowl of hot fudge from the stewardess, then buries himself in *Sport.* He makes a few grabs at the toddlers practicing sprints in the aisles, and advises one nine-year-old Yankee fan, "Don't get into any fights unless you have to. I wouldn't like it." He takes down names, addresses, requests for hats, balls, tickets. He will follow through on every single one. About twenty passengers have accosted him on a two-hour flight, and George has advice to dispense to everyone, including the stew. "You better drop a little suggestion in your suggestion box. Tell your boss that Eastern is giving a movie on this flight. You better get movies on Delta too."

At Kennedy, George's driver—a retired cop—waits with his car, a navy sedan with NYY plates and a Yankee seal on the side. George always sits in the front. On his seat is a stack of bulging folders, his daily mail. They are sorted by his secretary: invitations, general, commissioner's office, look over, requests, and thank you. It is the thank-you folder that George turns to first and that he displays when a visitor comes to call. "Thank you for the tickets; for the T-shirts; for saving my little girl's life." A thank-you from the child who's still alive because Daddy Warbucks stopped NYY on the Long Island Expressway and made a phone call offering to pay for an operation after reading about her case in the *New York Post*. Dear Mr. Steinbrenner. Dear.

His life is filled with these private works, sometimes carried out from the plain sedan with the disco tapes provided by Patrick Shields, the director of Le Club. In these acts of charity he is no more Mr. Tough Guy. Even bullies need to be loved. That thank-you pile compensates for a lot of private hurts. In the thank-you folder, George is appreciated for "all the good things I do that nobody finds out about." In the thank-you file, nobody snipes at him for being a lunatic, a Boss Steinbrenner. Nobody accuses him of being cruel.

In the beginning, there was no cruelty. In the beginning, in Cleveland during the Depression, there was only the egg.

Rather, there was the egg company created for George by the Teutonic demigod Steinbrenner still deferentially calls Dad. George Steinbrenner II, who owned five ships on the Great Lakes, told his son early on, "No allowance." Instead, he bought young George chickens. Out of those chickens came the eggs that George sold to buy baseball cards and James Fenimore Cooper novels.

James Fenimore Cooper was one of the few pleasures in George's grim early life. His father insisted that his school uniform be an impeccably maintained coat and tie. He was told never to forget that his dad had been an MIT hurdles champ and to "always work harder than anybody else." Of course he was sent to military school—Culver, in far-off Indiana. Father's dictums about working hard took time to sink in. For most of George's Culver years, he was in the lowest quarter of his class, and he "used to complain about how he was pushed to excel," Jack Beardsley, a classmate, recalls. "He seemed to be under his father's domination." But he was never a bully, his classmates remember. "At Culver that wouldn't have been allowed."

In athletics, George could be his own man. He felt free on the football field, and George remembers happily that, "When the track coach got sick, he asked me to take over the team and keep it together." But, says George, he was hurt when his team didn't elect him captain.

He was also hurt by his parents' lack of affection. But if he didn't get their love, George decided, then he would get their respect. In the last year, he knew he had "to pull something together, so I brought my grades up to the top quarter." Even so, the Culver dean had to beg Williams College to let young Steinbrenner in.

He began to blossom at Williams. If his grades were mediocre, he was a study in motion—sports editor, elected to Gargoyle for leadership and the Purple Key for sports. He jumped the requisite hurdles and developed a passion for General Patton and the French and Indian War. As an adult, Steinbrenner still says, "You can be goddam sure that I would rather follow Patton into war than Ike."

His father made him learn the boat business from the bottom up. George's task was to spend hours crawling through the underdecks on ships, counting rivets, checking out what needed replacing in the tight and filthy space. At Steinbrenner's shop, Kinsman Transit, the rules were unbreakable. But George, like Reggie Jackson later, knew how to bend the dictates of an autocrat. When the Kinsman employees were denied desk phones, George hid one in his drawer.

For a time, he had a reprieve from the family business. The military took him for three years, but George wasn't about to relax. He spent his service years setting up a coffee-cart franchise that served sixteen thousand soldiers and office workers. And then came what he calls "my happiest time." Those were the football years, the years he spent as an assistant coach, first at a high school, then at Northwestern and Purdue.

He was out of his father's control. There was romance with one of the Kettering girls—as in Sloan-Kettering—but it broke up because, as George says now somewhat wistfully, "She didn't want to be married to a football coach." Steinbrenner's detractors like to say that the years George spent coaching college ball were consumed with, among other duties, securing tickets for rich alumni.

Whatever he was doing there, the happy times didn't last. There was no way Hank Steinbrenner was going to allow his son to remain assistant coach of a college team. George was pulled back to Cleveland and by the late fifties had settled down with his wife, Joan, a blond Junior Leaguer who pronounces her name Jo-ann.

The first years in Cleveland were not easy. The Steinbrenners had five ships working the Great Lakes and had to scramble to fill them. The independent operators like Kinsman had dwindled from thirty to eight. In 1960, besides

George's business problems, there was trouble in his marriage and talk of divorce.

Perhaps it's a coincidence that in the same year George chose to deal with his problems by throwing himself back into sports. He got the money together to buy his first team as a young hotshot, a pro-basketball franchise called the Cleveland Pipers. The team took two years to sink, but George's marriage survived. He emerged from the Pipers a quarter of a million dollars in debt.

Those who have known Steinbrenner longest theorize that it was at this time that his personality began to change. He took a gamble, he issued orders—he would not declare bankruptcy; he would pay off his debts and take control of the family's five fading ships. Nobody in Cleveland would lend him a dime. George went to New York and sold, sold, sold. Before he left, his father told him, "The fleet has no future."

George had other ideas. He reasoned, if the family's ships are losing money hauling iron and ore, why don't we forget the ore and concentrate on something cheaper but more plentiful, like grain? He was able to convince a New York bank that the Kinsman ships could transport grain more economically than freight trains could. He got his loan. *His* company went into the black. And nobody was ever able to tell George Steinbrenner how to do anything again.

George's next target was American Ship Building. He started buying hundreds of thousands of shares. The shareholders were pleased to name him president of the company, in order to avoid a proxy fight. And then George was able to resolve his Oedipal problems at a stroke. George III brought George II out of retirement to run the subsidiary. His father reported to him.

In Washington, Steinbrenner met Ted Kennedy, who urged him to chair Democratic fund-raising dinners. At last he was getting close to real power and glamour. His dinners broke all records for fund-raising. He was able to call Kennedy "one of my good friends." But he wanted more. He was rich, but he was nowhere, a chamber-of-commerce tycoon stuck in the Midwest. In control of his destiny now, his thoughts turned back to sports.

George Steinbrenner has told the story about the little boy who loved the Yankees so many times he has perfected it into a set piece. The litle boy didn't have much of a childhood. His father was one tough son of a gun. He didn't get an allowance, but sometimes, if he was really good, he would get to escape to the ball game, especially when the Yankees came to town. The little boy knew that, win or lose, the boys in pinstripes were special. They had Lou Gehrig and Joe DiMaggio. They were part of the American metaphor. When this American metaphor checked into the Hotel Cleveland, it was a holiday, as special as the little boy's birthday, the Fourth of July.

By the time the little boy turned forty-two, he had taken over the New York Yankees, now fallen on hard times. It was more than a business. It was a chance for him to bring back what he called "a major symbol of the American way of life." He was able to buy his piece of New York for ten million dollars. But what George Steinbrenner never counted on was an extraordinary piece of luck called the free agency. A year after he had gotten his bargain, a court ruling enabled him to buy and sell any player he desired who qualified under the rule.

Steinbrenner has given New York a team of personalities, and New York rewards him by treating him as a man of power—scribbling down his opinions on politics or on the rankings in the American League East. Here is George Steinbrenner on foreign policy: "Believe me, I'm no isolationist, but I admire Taft. Take this El Salvador situation. In these countries that shoot at our embassies, if I were President, I would say, 'I'm cutting your ass right off. From now on, you get nothing. Not even a smile.' "

On the trade gap: "The situation in this country is a disgrace. Twenty-six percent of our cars are foreign imports. If I were running things, I would say to Japan, 'Now look here. We can't afford to keep your economy working overtime. You either stop this twenty-four-hour overtime production or we're going to throw a helluva quota on you.' I'm sick and tired of hearing how American steel is being crippled."

On his Type A personality: "On a scale of one to ten, how tense is George Steinbrenner? You can say that I would rank myself a nine."

The chopper waits in St. Petersburg as Steinbrenner beams from the dais of the annual Spring Training Baseball Dinner. Behind him are a few national symbols: Stan Musial, Bob Feller, Al Lopez, Buck Leonard, and a row of unfurled American flags. Next to George sits his friend Bob Graham, the governor of Florida, who insisted George make the introductory speech. In front of them are a thousand male baseball lovers in full polyester-and-plaid kit.

A moment of reverence. Steve Garvey, Mr. Nice Guy, accepts the Roberto Clemente Award. "I only wish my dad could have been here tonight. My dad is a bus driver and he couldn't get off. But from him I got the desire to make this country the number-one democracy in the world."

Moments later, George is hurtling across the parking lot toward the waiting helicopter. "You know," he says, "I don't understand it. None of the guys like Garvey. They think he's a goody-goody. But I happen to really love what he said about his dad."

Fathers and sons: The theme recurs constantly in George's life. Theories abound. Billy Martin didn't have a father, so he couldn't deal with a strong authority figure like George. Bob Lemon couldn't manage because he was heartsick over the death of his son. George's father was so hard-driving he could only pass on how to command, not how to love. Reggie and *his* father were so intimate, number 44 demands the closeness of a love bond. Lou Piniella was George's first new player, so he will always be treated like the adored oldest son. "George is misunderstood," Tommy John says. "All he really wants is a father-son relationship. He wants us to be able to feel we can come to him at any time."

But what kind of father is subject to these childish fits of temper? His outbursts paralyze: *"Rick Cerone is disloyal! Reggie? A child! Executive vice-president Cedric Tallis is a goddamn dumbbell! Dick Howser has nothing to complain about—I set him up in business, didn't I? Didn't I take care of my own?"* It seems that at the ball park and in his life George has made a full psychological circle. He has become the father who must always be in control.

Reggie Jackson is the one Yankee he cannot control. George gives Reggie and then takes away. He made him a star and now seems to resent the one player more famous than he is. "A lot of this fight with Reggie is theater," George admitted. "I wish he could tell *me* that," Reggie sighed later. "If he would be able to talk to me and say he wanted some headlines, then I would put on a tuxedo and take a plane and land on the first-base line. But he just talks *at* me and can't look me in the eye. His behavior wears me down. After all these years, he knows I'm not the type to follow his rules."

George's need to be on top of things extends everywhere: the ball park, the shipyards, his home. Asking about what goes on in his household can move him to rage. No interviews with his family are allowed. No matter that his children are good-looking and intelligent—one daughter is a Phi Beta Kappa. George, like his friend the senator, is worried about death threats. He will admit his homelife is "not happy." End of subject. His friends say the problem is the classic dilemma of the executive husband and wife: She stayed home raising children while he grew famous, acquired power, traveled, and outgrew her. For a while, the columnists gossiped about George Steinbrenner and his friend Barbara Walters. George says they are just "very good friends. We have a lot of fun," he says. "We used to go to P. J. Clarke's, and after dinner we'd walk down the street and see who got recognized more, me or her. I swear, we went one-to-one."

Life is fun at the top. But George's metamorphosis took time. When he first got to New York, he used to be seen having dinner at six, at Sardi's, with his one friend, Jimmy Nederlander, the Broadway producer. In those early days in New York, George was just considered a guy to get free tickets from. Now his best friends are one limo king, one fur king, and two brothers who build shiny glass boxes on Park Avenue. The cronies, like Cohn and Iacocca, Cardinal Cooke and Bill Fugazy, fill Box 332. George's box is stocked with ice cream from Tom Carvel. Every night that he is in New York, his pals keep him surrounded at restaurant tables.

"I'm not big for entertaining at home," George says. (Home in New York, once a townhouse, is now a suite at the Carlyle.) Crowds he's big on. Also jokes, funny stories, and keeping things light. That's how his friends describe what happens when the boys go out at night. They all say that they barely know his wife. But don't think that just because George is out with his intimates he's not in control. "George never likes us to invite anyone to join the gang unless it's his idea to bring them along," says Mike Forrest, the fur king.

George relies on his friends. His shipbuilding crisis turned into triumph when George called in a favor and another "good friend" awarded him the sixty-five-million-dollar contract. George is even able to use the word *coasting*—and he's not kidding—as he describes how he feels about his business interests now. What next? There's talk that he's approached yet another good friend, Sonny Werblin, about taking Madison Square Garden off his hands. Perhaps George and former Yankee head Mike Burke will be back under the same roof.

A final moment: We are cruising in a helicopter over Tampa Harbor toward a college basketball game. Underneath us, George's new hometown twinkles. For a moment, George's face looks almost placid. "What are you thinking about right now?" I ask. He looks startled. "Nothing," he barks. "Absolutely nothing." He is so uncomfortable with the introspective, he can't even invent a response. Not winning, not the lights of the harbor, or Winfield and Reggie, or what's happening at home. He's got everything he wants now. Almost the last thing George tells me is that he never dreams.

April 1981

The Latter Days of
Ethel Scull

S he was called Spike, he was Bob. Spike's clothing was
by Courreges, her hair by Kenneth, her lunches by
Grenouille. Bob came from the Bronx and was a
high-school dropout who liked to identify himself as an art
collector. In fact, taxis were his line. For a time, not so long
ago, Spike and Bob—Ethel and Robert Scull—were social ar-
biters or maybe social climbers. In those days—the mid-
sixties—it was hard to tell the difference. But it wasn't hard to
tell that Spike and Bob were very, very rich.

Their world was Madison Avenue and its galleries; their
personal fiefdoms were the styles of pop and op. When those
styles mattered, Spike and Bob were the collectors who mattered most. The art crowd thought that Spike had taste. What
they didn't know was that Spike also had the money.

Spike and Bob grew famous acquiring Jasper Johns's tar-
gets, flags, and beer cans. George Segal dipped Spike and Bob
in plaster, and Spike lost a Courreges boot to his cast. They
were a metaphorical couple of our crazy days. Frank Stella
worked his stripes on their living-room wall. The Robert and
Ethel Scull collection toured the country; their names popped
up in art-history books.

Their joy was not to be forever. The press sniped at Spike

and Bob. Tom Wolfe immortalized them as "the folk heroes of every social climber who ever hit New York." Their excesses were sneered at, such as the James Rosenquist mural they hung on the bedroom ceiling. We took comfort in Bob's Bronx accent and brash manner, and rejoiced in Ethel's snubs from Alfred Barr. We were jealous. Many a schemer schemed to get invited *chez* Scull at 1010 Fifth Avenue to check out the all-white setting Ethel had designed "just for the art." We sniggered at them, and we went to eat their canapes and to trade remarks with Larry Poons and Jasper Johns. We knew the Sculls would go on and on.

They didn't. Spike is now called Ethel again. She lives in a one-bedroom apartment way east on Sixty-eighth Street. On her walls hang just two lithographs—gifts from her old friends Robert Rauschenberg and Jasper Johns. Her paintings—the hundreds of canvases—have been sold at auction or are in a warehouse. Like so many modern romances, the Sculls' will end in court.

Pathos surrounds Ethel like a noose. From the flamboyance of her pineapple-color-hair days, Ethel Scull exudes that watchword of the seventies: *vulnerability*. To hear her story is to think "a woman wronged." Perhaps her story is not much different from those of other women of her time. Perhaps Ethel was a victim of her own dependence: It may have taken her too much time to realize that her marriage wasn't very solid all along.

A broken back finally broke her marriage. Spike and Bob had been in Barbados in early 1973. Spike suffered a bad fall. After months of hospitals, tests, and false diagnoses, she learned the damage was severe. There were more hospitals and operations. The parties stopped. For nine months, she was confined to bed. "Our life was so glittery, so intellectually stimulating, that I was blinded by all the activity," Ethel said recently. "I couldn't see what our situation really was until I was flat on my back for a year."

What she saw shocked her. Bob was urging her, she says,

to dismantle the Robert and Ethel Scull collection. He demanded, says Ethel, that they auction off dozens of their acquisitions—some fifty paintings, most of them mural-size—in one enormous sale at Sotheby Parke Bernet. Ethel, doped up on painkillers, was in no condition to argue. "He said he wanted to sell things at the top of the market. He said this was the right time to sell. There were paintings that he was insisting he wanted to get rid of, even some that were personal gifts to me. I tried to stop the auction, but I had no strength left to fight."

The sale was scheduled for the fall of 1973. Weeks before the auction, the catalog arrived from Sotheby's. The cover read, FROM THE COLLECTION OF ROBERT C. SCULL. Ethel's name was nowhere to be found. "It was shocking," she said recently. "He said he had done it for tax purposes. I didn't believe him, but I was in such terrible physical agony there was nothing I could do about it."

Scull had negotiated well. Before the sale was held, Sotheby's had advanced him almost two million dollars, Ethel says. "He showed me the checks as they came in," she says. "And he would always say the same thing: 'Now we are safe for the rest of our lives.'"

As it turned out, that safety did not extend to Ethel. Shortly after the Scull sale, the eleven rooms at 1010 Fifth Avenue were scheduled to be repainted. Ethel remembers Bob prompting her, "Why don't we put the thirty-five canvases that are in the apartment in a warehouse?" The sale had proved how valuable they were and Bob told Ethel to think of the harm that could be done to a Larry Rivers by a splatter of eggshell white.

Off went the canvases to a Manhattan warehouse. They were registered in the name of Robert Scull, says Ethel, and that was the last she ever saw of them. Soon after, Robert Scull told his wife their marriage was over.

And that is when Ethel's real problems began. Her daily

physiotherapy was hardly covered by her temporary alimony—$350 a week. "I had to learn how to beg," she says.
"I had to go to the butcher and tell him, 'Listen, I've been a
good client of yours for all these years, please could I have
eight months of credit?' " First, she had to deal with her depression, then her rage. "I had to stop feeling sorry for myself. I had to learn that you're born alone and that you die
alone, and that you better make the most of it. That you have
to be productive and keep yourself away from bad or evil."

Her temporary alimony was raised to around forty thousand dollars a year. That figure seems generous enough until
one realizes that her medical bills took almost half. And
through the daily bouts with Empirin and therapy, Ethel decided she had to fight. "The legal situation was extremely
complicated," says Ethel's attorney, Liz Searle. There were
delays, postponements, stallings: It took six years to bring the
case to trial.

Ethel Scull hasn't lost her sense of humor. "I should have
listened to my mother," she says. "She never forgave me for
marrying Robert Scull." Ethel had been the taxi princess of
Riverside Drive. Her father had owned taxis, hundreds of
taxis—his company was called Cabol Cabs. Ethel had been
sent to Calhoun School, to Parsons School of Design, to dancing lessons with all the other nice girls at Viola Wolf's. She
started collecting art when she was a teen-ager; her first ac-
quisition was a poster by Ben Shahn.

At Parsons, she was friendly with Robert Scull's cousin.
The match was made. At that time, during the war, Scull, who
was 4F, had an office on West Fifty-third Street, where he
designed clocks and laid out department-store ads. Ethel
brought him home to meet her parents. Her mother said,
"How could you do this to me?" Ethel remembers her mother
calling up her ex-boyfriends before her wedding and begging,
"Please take Ethel out again!"

It didn't work. Ethel and Bob married and moved into a

studio apartment at the Parc Vendome. Ethel enrolled in classes at the Art Students League. Bob's company went out of business. Ethel's father decided that he didn't like the way his daughter was living—he gave in to Bob's request, Ethel says, to go to work for Cabol Cabs. Scull's first job was gassing the cars and working for the dispatcher.

He was on his way. Ethel's father still controlled the company, but bit by bit he gave them some taxis—half to Ethel, half to Bob. By the late sixties, Scull's Angels were all over the city.

Ethel is philosophical. "When Bob started getting interviewed about art collecting, I wanted to stay in the background. Bob would beg me not to tell people it was my father's cab company. He'd say, 'I've been poor all my life, and this is the first time I've felt like I owned anything.' "

Incredibly, she agreed. Marriages were different then. It was important to Ethel to be what she called "a good Jewish wife." She says, "I felt it would make Robert feel more secure if I let him have his illusions about owning everything and having power."

Perhaps she made him feel too secure. She says that Robert was color-blind and that she had to explain to him "what a Rothko looked like." She had to point out the colors in a color field painting. She acquiesced when he asked her to tell their new social crowd that his occupation was art collector. If Ethel ever questioned any of this, she kept her doubts inside.

Her doubts are no longer inside. Ethel Scull is older now, and one hopes, wiser. The pineapple-color hair has given way to a becoming frost. The skin is still flawless, the figure still lean; only her eyes betray the betrayal. She gives lectures on modern painting and works as an art consultant. She and Scull do not speak. What she wants is what she calls "what is rightfully mine." That means exactly half. Robert Scull has refused to talk about the case.

"I've learned a lot from this experience," says Ethel now.

"I've learned that without your health you are nowhere. That kindness and goodness are what count. That all the glitter and the parties and the intellectual stimulation cannot make up for the human things." She has spent the last six years rehabilitating her vertebrae and her psyche. "The irony of it all is that had we divorced after July 19, 1980, when the divorce laws changed, right now I wouldn't be going through any of this at all."

April 1981

*   *   *

Ethel Scull changed lawyers and in the summer of 1983, the court finally ruled in her favor. She had always claimed that the taxi company was a gift from her father; the court agreed, and declared it a joint asset. The court also ruled that the art collection was "a joint effort." "Curiously enough, defendant admitted he was color-blind," the ruling said. The total award could come to $15 million. Robert Scull intended to appeal, *The New York Times* reported.

Reggie Jackson

*A*long weekend loomed, a weekend without his friends or his profession, without much but humidity and the noise of exploding rockets assaulting him when he stood on his tiny terrace, twenty floors above Central Park. It would be Reggie Jackson's first Independence Day without baseball in a city where his body clock is timed only to the game. The Yankees—and every other team—were out on strike. He wasn't sure whether to stay or to flee. He didn't look forward to spending the weekend at Oren & Aretsky's talking about how far apart both sides were. He didn't want to risk the danger of another headline duel with his boss. Too much was at stake now.

He stood on his terrace, with its cushionless chairs and rusty hibachi, staring down at the emerald carpet of the park, the silvery skeleton of the Metropolitan Museum of Art. "I just don't feel comfortable when I'm here," he said. "All this time, I've never even walked into the Met."

Taking off would mean ten hours of red-eyes and airport traffic jams on the Van Wyck, but staying, he said, would mean loneliness. His psychological life was out west. His ambivalence was nothing new. "Sometimes I get all the way out to Kennedy, and then I turn around and come right back here," he said. He was aware of the paradox of his isolation. Indecision filled the air. Perhaps the notion of having to decide where to spend a summer weekend overwhelmed him. For Reggie Jackson's entire life, every summer evening has been planned at least two seasons in advance.

He had been back in New York for three days, and predictably the headlines had been filled with him. REGGIE WANTS OUT. REGGIE IN AN UPROAR. GEORGE IS A THORN IN REGGIE'S SIDE. JACKSON: STRIKE TALKS ARE A FARCE. A columnist accused him of menopause. His boss said he was in the "twilight of his career." The headlines made him sound as bombastic as ever, but the anger seemed hollow, synthetic, shot with holes. The remarks about his depression, his menopause, and his twilight didn't seem to bother him. Perhaps he was numb as a result of not playing summer ball. Anyway, he's had a lot of time to think. "I don't care what they write about me anymore," he said. "I really don't. Finally, it has nothing to do with my insides . . . with where I live."

Where he actually lives comes as a surprise. A Persian rug—"Well, a modern one," Reggie says—warms his living-room floor. A reproduction antique armoire hides a sterling Georgian coffee service and Crown Derby cups. Nearby, a candid photo, Reggie's favorite, shows him bandaging Thurman Munson's arm. Needlepoint pillows and Cartier clocks, bookshelves crammed with Solzhenitsyn, Adelle Davis, and vintage Irwin Shaw. Very cozy. It could be any rich New Yorker's apartment except, of course, for all the trophies and the porcelain whatnots from the fans.

More eclectia in Reggie's bedroom: the reproduction furniture he picked out himself and a lovely marble-top desk cluttered with poetry books, calendars, ledgers, and a bag of pistachio nuts. He ignores the memo instructing him to sign this "To Rita" and that "To Frank." On his floor is a box from Ellesse—a company he now swings for—loaded with

monogrammed Windbreakers for his California friends. The
closets are flung open in preparation for the trip. One just for
shirts. Another with cashmere sweaters stacked like Necco
wafers, yards of pressed denims, and casual pants. "They just
deliver all that stuff here," Reggie says. "I get almost all of it
for free." The windows are jammed with an odd combination
of batting trophies and flowering plants.

Here he is serene. He folds jeans into his suitcase and says,
"I know I'm in a transition period now. That is the reality.
And I know myself well enough to know there isn't anything
wrong with that." His litany is familiar to anyone who reads
the sports page. The sigh: "I may just about have had enough
of the game." An easy silence is in the room. "Do you feel as
if you're defined by baseball?" he is asked. "Absolutely," he
says. "And in every way. Mentally. Physically. Spiritually. Intellectually."

"Then how can you say you've had enough?"

A scene, two days earlier: The sadness took about an hour
to creep in. There was lunch, a shake-hands-with-Reggie
event, the kind of lunch he's had a thousand of. This one was
held so that Reggie, tranquil after two weeks in Carmel, could
shake hands with a few dozen Jeep dealers in his new role as
spokesman for the Jeep Scrambler. He was pleased to do this.
"They're paying me," he said later, laughing. "I guess I better give 'em what they want."

A 258-pounder named Ricky ("Ever have a problem in
Jersey, call me") Crosta wanted his money's worth. It was
Ricky, so Ricky said, who had signed Reggie to six figures
with Jeep, and this, Ricky figured, made him and number 44
the best of friends. "Listen to me," he told Reggie Jackson
halfway through his meal. "Your problem is simple. Anybody
can see it. Forget how paranoid you are. Forget your pride.
You gotta start thinkin' positive. Just get your battin' average
up and your problems with George will be solved. Work on
your hittin', Reg. I've been around a long time, a long time.
Let me be your PR man. You'll see I'm right."

By dessert, the California mellow-cool was gone. Finally, Reggie Jackson snapped. "Are you now going to start telling me how to hit? Do you think, do you really think, I'm not going to hit again? Well, let me tell you something. If I was eighty-four years old or forty, I would hold my neck and grit my teeth one more time. I would shove it up their fucking asses. No matter where I am."

Ricky pressed on. "You wouldn't be happy anywhere else, Reg. I know. Listen to me, will ya?"

"Well, I'd sure like to try it and fail," Reggie said, fast and cold.

The sudden anger caused him to withdraw, and then the melancholy swept over him like a tide. His features seemed to blue. His lucid analysis of the strike stopped. He asked for coffee and then stared at two boxes of balls Ricky expected him to sign. Just a moment earlier, he had been carrying on about the "idiosyncrasies, ramifications, and annoyances the owners were prepared to endure to shut the season down."

Reggie Jackson is too bright to be oblivious to insults, yet not secure enough to rise above them. And he knows it. "As soon as I get into a rut like everyone else does, then I become human and then I'm vulnerable." And when an overweight Jeep dealer or a front office pressures him, his rut becomes a pit.

A few days later, back in his home, just before his flight, Reggie is asked to analyze what had happened at the lunch. "You know why I let that lunch get to me? Because after two weeks of being away, suddenly I was reminded of what it really means to be a baseball player. How everyone has their opinions about me. How everyone says, do this or that. I was reminded of the pressure of being me."

He pads through the apartment to the kitchen, toward the sound of radio station WINS and a dryer going around and around. Reggie Jackson is out of uniform. On a normal July night he'd be sitting in the dugout, deadened to the anthem. Now he stands in front of the dryer, damning its lint filter, which has come apart in his hands. Out tumble his sweatshirts and Jockey shorts, crew socks and Yankee warm-ups, filled with snowy flecks and just dry enough to make it west.

The exile is self-imposed, of course, as are his pressures in the batting cage. These days he tends to link those pressures with the city, and, whether or not he is worrying about his contract or his .199 average, New York life is very much on his mind. He says that the city is not for him. He has had it with the Reggie machine, the hustlers of New York, the frenzy, the pressure to endorse, the ringing phone, the agents, the requests for the electric baseball player to sign balls and shake hands. "Look, I'm grateful for all the money I've made. That is extremely important to me. But there is no difference now in my making nine hundred thousand dollars or one point four million. How much does anyone need?" Now he is looking out from the bell jar and watching how we behave. "Everyone has such a compulsion to be busy here. Everyone always has so much to do. Lunches, dinners, deals, dates, opera, movies, symphony, ballet. Connections. Travel. I hate all that. I just like . . . to be.

"I don't have the same desires as the people here. I don't want to go to the Hamptons. I don't want to go to nightclubs or to chase women, read best-sellers, learn to speak Italian, or make more friends. Damn it! I don't want to go to Athens. I don't want to learn anything more. I don't want to meet anybody else." He bangs his hand on the wall. "I don't want to feel like I *have* to go into the Met."

He is thinking about what will happen to him when he finally takes his leave of that special isolation that is a baseball player's life. He has a lot to think about. Were he to stay in New York as a broadcaster, he would have to hold his own with others who are as accomplished in their fields as he is in his. He would have to move on to new realms of achievement. That might give him pause. "If I'm lucky," he says, "I'll have three good seasons left." And after that, Hall of Fame or not, nobody could logically cast Reggie Jackson, then thirty-eight, in the role of front-office man.

He casts himself in California on his six-and-a-half-acre spread. "I have a house I'm fixing up," he says. "It has plank floors all the way through it and a big door in front that swings open like a barn's. I'm building another wing on it with a library and a guest room, then maybe later I'll add tennis courts and a pool."

He produces a dozen hand-braided horse bits from a shopping bag on his bed. He works on them in the afternoons. It's a nice picture: Reggie Jackson propped up on his needlepoint pillows in front of his windows, spending long hours listening to his telephone ring and ring, plaiting leather thongs for his mares.

He reveres his quiet moments. "Very late at night, I love to take my car into the park when it's closed—they know me and let me in—and just drive around and around on the drives, usually alone, sometimes with a few beers or a friend. The park is completely still then. It's another world."

The car waits for him downstairs, but he lingers on the chair where he braids his horses' reins. A Christopher Cross ballad floats over the speakers. Reggie Jackson closes his eyes and very gently starts to sing, "I got to ride, ride like the wind, to be free again."

July 1981

Lena Horne in Rehearsal

*L*ena Horne is not quite sure what she is doing in this dusty room. In black cashmere and modified diamonds, she straddles a rickety chair in a Broadway rehearsal hall. Homesick in California, she had wanted to spend the summer touring in *Pal Joey*. Jimmy Nederlander had other ideas. Why not a one-woman show? He had some persuading to do. Lena Horne has always been ambivalent about her career. At sixty-three she is surprised that her vocal range is still the same. Her top note remains C. She doesn't have to use any Sinatra tricks to get through Cole Porter. If her vibrato isn't quite as steady, her energy is still astonishing, her body lithe, her face young enough so that, as she says, "When I get myself gussied up, there's still a semblance of that flash chick everybody used to make such a fuss about. I wonder, 'Am I going to get away with it one more time?' "

She's always gotten away with just about everything. For years, she was the white man's symbol of black glamour and sex. Her voice sent smoke through the Copa and the Cotton Club. Her mocha color made her approachable. She carried herself like Brenda Frazier. On screen, she refused to play maids or whores. She was promoted as the Jackie Robinson of singers, the black entertainer white enough to break color lines. She was a reluctant pioneer. The NAACP made her go to Hollywood. Count Basie told her that she would be "letting down the Negro race" if she didn't "go out there and show them Negroes can sing."

She did. Louis B. Mayer cast her as an exotic chanteuse in a series of movies; then she endured seeing her song segments cut when her pictures played the South. It wasn't until she was fifty that she realized she didn't want to be a representative, to be just "useful" to her race, that all she had ever done was to "camouflage" what she was really about. Her one-woman show, *Lena Horne: The Lady and Her Music,* at the Nederlander Theater, is called "autobiographical" by its promoters; but it really isn't. Lena explains, "My life has been so schizoid you would have needed Eugene O'Neill to write the book for it."

Several years ago, she announced her retirement from nightclubs. She had had enough. In a one-year period, she has lost her husband, music arranger Lennie Hayton; her son, Teddy; and her father. At the time, she said that all she wanted to do was play grandmother to Teddy's twins and to the children of her daughter, Gail Lumet. She gave up her rambling apartment in the Apthorp on New York's Upper West Side, filled with vintage 78s, and moved to Santa Barbara. After a time, life by the ocean no longer satisfied. "I guess I thought if I was going to end it all, I'd better do my own swan dive or have my own swan song. . . ." Her voice wanders like a gulf breeze. "You know what it really is? When I get out there all nervous and tense and scared and then I smell it's going to come out all right—well, then you don't think about your troubles. You kinda lose yourself."

On the surface of it, one wouldn't think Lena Horne had anything to be nervous about. Her closest friends are theatrical royalty. In her childhood, she was shielded from the realities of race prejudice by her middle-class origins. Her grandmother was an early member of the Urban League. She was born in a four-story house in a mixed neighborhood in Brooklyn. But her mother, an actress and "the real beauty of the family," Lena says, was ambitious. She abandoned Lena to tour the country with black tent shows. Her father, a numbers runner, disappeared, and Lena was sent to a series of foster homes in the South. She once told an interviewer that she learned "never to get too comfortable or too attached. After the first few wrenches, it's hello, good-bye."

Her dream life centered on New York and her family. Finally, she was sent back as a teen-ager to live with her grandmother, who taught her that she should be "bright, well read, independent . . . and to survive at any cost." Her grandmother's common sense took the place of affection. "She was never sentimental," Lena recalls. "She never touched me. I wanted to live with my mother. But she married a Cuban and I was already a teen-ager and there were a lot of problems."

The only thing she could do was dance. Her mother's solution to her daughter's loneliness was to sign her, at sixteen, to a lifetime contract at the Cotton Club. Her audience was mostly white. The gangster-owners controlled the stars. Lena's mother sat in her dressing room to protect her. "Nobody really knows what went on in that place," Lena says. "I tired to escape once and the gangster boys came and beat up my stepfather and then smashed his head in the toilet."

She fled the Cotton Club by marrying the son of a Baptist minister. Her husband struggled to make a living and raged against white society. When her children, Gail and Teddy, were infants, a B-picture producer offered Lena a lot of money to go to Hollywood. She went. Her husband felt emasculated. He wanted to control her career. The marriage became impossible. Lena was allowed a divorce under the condition that she give up custody of her son.

She continued to struggle. Billie Holiday urged her to accept a job with a white band, saying, "You gotta feed your kid, don't you?" She became a permanent fixture at the Café

Society nightclub, in the Village. Those were her happiest days. Her best friend was Paul Robeson. Teddy Wilson and Duke Ellington were her musical mentors. With classic ambivalence, again she agreed to go to Hollywood, because she felt pressured to be a symbol of her race. When she arrived, she was miserable. "Over and over, I kept saying to everybody, 'I hate this fucking place.' "

At MGM, the muscial director was Lennie Hayton. He heard her rehearsing "Honeysuckle Rose." "They'll never put that up on the screen," he told her. "Who is this conceited ass?" she wondered.

Lena says it was Lennie who taught her how to sing. He told her she was "strong on drama and weak on vocals." In the process, they fell in love, and their interracial marriage caused a scandal. They continued to work together, and the scandal died. Her career soared. "We worked dead ahead on trying to build up my weak little voice."

Her early recordings belie her modesty. Her phrasing was always intelligent, her voice warm. The sex-bomb tag haunted her and surprised her. "It was crazy. I was never thinking sex on that stage. I was always furious. I would be thinking when I got up there I was going to show them a remote, grand black woman. I wasn't sharing anything. I was singing in. Later, I'd ask white men why they read that as sex, and they'd say, 'Because you were safe to admire. We knew you were black, but we always fantasized you were Polynesian.' "

In the 1950's and 1960's, she was never allowed to forget her place. Her friendship with Paul Robeson caused her to be blacklisted. For years, she couldn't work. She became more and more active in the civil-rights movement, marching on every picket line. Times changed. Harold Arlen wrote a show for her, *Jamaica*, which was a black musical with an interracial cast. When the show closed, her life went into crisis. She realized that she was the only black performer in the cast who would be able to find work again.

Her personal tensions reflected the tensions of the time.

When Malcolm X was killed, her rage knew no bounds. She turned on everyone close to her. "Even poor Lennie had to be tested. I thought because he wasn't black he couldn't understand me. All he had ever done was just to love me. I was literally alone. Lennie was blind to color. All he ever cared about was music."

Somehow she began to soften. "I began to see a common cause. I felt like I didn't have to be a soapbox. I stopped thinking, 'Hey, I'm different,' and started to think, 'Well, I'm just Lena.' "

Her family life began to obsess her. She pulled closer to her daughter. "I'd always been so overprotective with Gail. I tried to compensate for the fact that my own mother ignored me. When Gail's marriage (to director Sidney Lumet) broke up, I took it harder than she did. I was like the Jewish mother, thinking that my daughter had to have the perfect husband to take care of her. It really hurt me, and it took me a few years to realize that Gail had never been on her own. She had always been Lena Horne's daughter or Sidney Lumet's wife."

Lena Horne was already a grandmother before she decided she had to do something about her own mother-daughter problem. "The love-hate thing I had with my mother just kept me going. Gail kept telling me, 'You have to understand, you've never had a mother.' I knew she was right, but I had to confront my mother. It happened just a few years before she died, which wasn't so long ago. I went to see her and I said, 'Mommy, do you love me?' and she said, 'No.' I just broke down. 'Lena, I wanted a career,' she told me. 'I wanted what you have. I wanted to be glamorous. To be famous.' I asked her, 'Why did you have me?' and she said, 'I only married your father because he was the best-looking guy in our set. We wanted a boy and we got you and you got my career.' "

Telling this story in her rehearsal hall at the Broadway Arts Studios, she seems transported, reliving all her feelings of that time. " 'Mommy,' I told her, 'I didn't want the career. I never wanted to be a singer. I only wanted you to love me. I would give you every bit of it if I could. You could have had all of it, if only I thought you cared about me.' My mother looked at me and said, 'It's over now, Lena. Just forget about it.' "

In her mother's last days, there was some sort of resolution. "I went to the hospital and she asked me to help her move to a better room. When I walked in, she said, 'Lena's here. Now I know things will be all right.' I felt good because she let me make a fuss over her. I thought it meant that maybe she did care about me after all."

She sighs. "You know, if they ever make a movie of my life, I sure hope somebody else plays it."

Her rehearsal break is almost over. For a moment, she looks at herself in the mirror and tries to imagine how her career would have been different if she had been white. "I would have probably done muscial comedy," she says. "That's what I always wanted to be . . . a Broadway star."

She'll be alone onstage at the Nederlander. "Some days I think to myself, 'Lena, what are you trying to prove at your age?' I don't know. Maybe it's ego, maybe it's masochism. Maybe what I'm thinking is that if Liz Taylor can have a show and Lauren Bacall can have a show—well, why can't I?"

May 1981

Social Notes

The Royal Wedding:
The Wedding of the Century

*T*hey were frozen there in a kind of eternal tableau, posed on the sweeping rear lawn of Buckingham Palace on this very special party afternoon, just before the wedding of the century. Instinctively, all the guests gathered understood their parts in the collective ritual of a palace garden party, one of thousands of complicated collective rituals that make English life at once so rarefied, so moving, and, often, so absurd. The queen's garden-party guests—her seven thousand Tongan diplomats and Tory MPs, her children's-charity workers and the mayor of South Ribble, her managers of Sainsbury's and British Shell—arranged themselves into the requisite three paths, neat as primrose borders, where the royals promenaded, stopping only to greet various presented guests. It was assumed that the queen, as was her custom, would take the middle path, where the crowd was densest. No velvet rope was needed to contain it. No beefeaters needed pikes to hold the unruly back. Brixton aside, the rule of civility in England still holds sway.

Even the weather knew how to behave during the half-hour wait for the royal party. A strong wind blew top hats and boaters toward the delphiniums, providing the necessary light-

heartedness of the afternoon. The skies were gray enough not
to outshine the queen, and, as if orchestrated, one shaft of
sunlight pierced the gloom and managed to illuminate the
copper dome of the massive, golden stone palace, with its family snaps by Vandyck and Winterhalter, its alabaster statues of
nymphs and nobles, this monument the Windsor-Mountbat-
ten family calls its London home.

And then there was quiet. High on the terrace, Prince Philip, tanned and elegantly erect, led the promenade with his
wife, Her Majesty, the queen. They moved slowly, solemnly,
with all the pomp the occasion called for, at last turning to face
the crowd. There wasn't a hint of a smile or a wave. There
wasn't a cough or a fidget. Another moment. Tears came to
eyes, lumps to throats. After a thousand years, the monarchy,
however pointless, still thrived. What was more, the astonishing poetry of this moment was italicized by everyone's aware-
ness of the coming festivities at St. Paul's.

At some point during the final trumpet run, the crowd
began to notice the turquoise dot. The turquoise dot was a hat,
a different kind of hat from the one the Windsor women wear.
This was a Cecil Beaton-type fantasy of silk flowers and yards
of aqua net. It was the kind of hat that showed that its wearer
just might have a sense of style and an understanding of the
kind of flair that will be required of a royal in a more demanding, electronic-media age. "God Save the Queen" evaporated
from the horns and cymbals, and the rumor spread: "Lady
Diana is here. Is Lady Diana here? Is that Lady Diana in the
turquoise hat?"

She was, it was. The future Princess of Wales was at her
first official engagement with the queen. Soon, Diana's blond
hair came into view. She had swept the Sassoon fringe under
her brim, but her face was camouflaged by the netting, a piece
of brilliant fashion theater that separated her from the dowdy
Windsors, stealing all the attention from her sour sister-in-
law-to-be, Princess Anne, and her future mother-in-law.

Diana's presence electrified the Tongan diplomats and the charity workers. Suddenly all was frenzy, as if they had spotted Elton John. There was a stampede from the queen's middle lane. The seven thousand subjects raced across the lawn in their haste to get to Diana's path. But the question was: Which path would she take? The north route toward the royal tea tent and the herbaceous border? The south route, toward the gray-and-green-striped tent? The crowd, as if possessed, surged toward the right, then pushed toward the left, straining, shoving, jumping, fighting to see which way Lady Diana and her fiancé—the fellow who used to attract all the attention—would head. All the collective ritual broke down. Manners vanished. Not a "sorry" to be heard. And when Diana floated eastward toward the gazebo and the delphiniums in a cloud of turquoise-and-mauve chiffon, the guests in their droopy dresses and morning suits got even more frantic to grab a spot in the right-hand path to get a really good look at their next queen.

Girl of the Moment

It's like that in London this royal wedding summer. Diana's coy smile and Charles's somewhat wary smirk hang in every chemist's window, in every Barclays Bank. Everyone knows his part in this royal wedding ritual too. The anti-monarchist M.P., Willie Hamilton of Fife, made the predictable declaration about the six months of mush. The bricks fly in Toxteth and Moss-side, but everywhere else it is the bunting and not the bullets that is on English minds. But the bullets—or at least the BBC coverage—are on some minds. The hotels are only half-full. The tourists haven't arrived. Flights are empty. Still, tourists or not, for the moment, unemployment and the disintegrating pound are off the front page, and Diana's family link to Humphrey Bogart has come on. For the moment.

Collectors are out trying to scrounge for the sixty-six kinds

of Charles-and-Diana mugs before the ceremony. Diana's face
will wash your hands, dry your dishes, pour you a drink, warm
a teapot, hold a pan. You can have her with your tea, on your
biscuit, and as an after-dinner mint. A hundred million dollars'
worth of wedding kitsch has cheered up Carnaby Street vendors and the price of Royal Worcester shares.

Gossip abounds—another proper wedding ritual. At upper-
class tables, people wonder what will happen to Lady Tryon
and Camilla Parker-Bowles, Charles's two blond, married lady
friends, whom *Daily Mail* columnist Nigel Dempster inevitably refers to as HRH's closest confidantes. The aristos wonder
if Charles's real friends—shooting types such as the Butter
family, or his groomsman, Nicholas Soames—will ever accept
Lady Diana as the real thing; they haven't seemed to yet. The
public adores her; the private friends adhere to the English
tradition of holding back. Oh, all very polite, of course, but, so
far, a little too polite.

Anyway, Charles's grandmother is thrilled. Diana was the
candidate she had been pushing all along. The queen mother,
according to the aristos, had been competing with Lord
Mountbatten, whom Charles called HGF—honorary grandfather. Mountbatten's candidates had been his granddaughters,
the Knatchbull girls, and the queen mum had been pushing
the granddaughter of her lady-in-waiting, Lady Fermoy.
The surprise was that after Mountbatten's death, the queen
mother won.

Mothers and grandmothers know how to push here too.
Charles, for his part, seems charmed with his bride-to-be. Apparently, he fell in love with her during those weeks he was in
Australia alone. He saw this glamour girl in the press every
day and, according to a friend, realized that he had been
pushed into marrying one cute cookie.

Meanwhile, the cute cookie has blossomed, having har-
pooned Wales. She's dropped a good stone. She's thrown out
the middy blouses, and shops every day for strapless, backless

beaded gowns. She's said she doesn't want to wear the same dress twice. Who's paying the bills, even at discount? The theory is that it's Diana's mother, the wife of a wallpaper heir. In London, people realize that both the prince and Diana's father are land-rich but cash-poor. You need more than the prince's half-million-dollar yearly income to keep up appearances.

Mrs. Shand Kydd, Diana's mother, has obviously taught her to stay glamourous if she wants to keep her man. Frances Shand Kydd did what was impermissible in English upper-class life: She left her husband and her children and married, God help her, a man whom she loved. And the kids got a step-mother, Raine. She's nobody's favorite. In fact, just before the wedding, with all those souvenir tea towels to sell at Althorp, her stately home, Raine has lost her butler. But there are larger concerns. Lloyds of London has insured the gewgaw makers in case Charles, not the world's greatest polo player, takes another tumble from his horse.

Tongues wag, often viciously. The talk is that Barbara Cartland was not invited to St. Paul's. One hears that the queen worried about what form of pink Diana's step-grand-mother would wear, and that Cartland's announcement that she had given her invitation to her son was merely an attempt to save face. And royal hostesses, such as Liz Shakerley, the third cousin to the queen, and Serena Balfour (as in the declaration), are being hounded by old friends to allow them to bring their sudden houseguests to their balls.

There's worry too, of course, a sense of dread about a possible terrorist attack on Prince Charles. It's a kind of undercurrent, rarely discussed, except obliquely—like the way Princess Margaret's manicurist, a redhead named Pauline, frets openly about the IRA in her Mayfair shop while applying some deb's gloss. It isn't in the papers, though. But the American papers seem keyed up that something might happen—they are said to be sending street reporters as well as society editors here. At ABC, they've already planned where

they will have special cameras, just in case an attempt is made.
The security will be massive. The English papers are using
ambulances to get their wedding film back to Fleet Street—all
of two miles. That's how blocked off the route of the procession will be.

That kind of tension somehow heightens the suspense—
and the excitement. So does the scale of the public spectacle,
the 750 million wedding guests who will be linked by the
BBC. Once again, the subjects of the Commonwealth will be
united. In Calcutta and Kenya, they will watch Diana not
promising to obey, with proper tears in ex-colonial eyes and
Pimm's No. 1 Cup gripped in ruddy hands. Incredibly, the
prince, always somewhat lonely and naive, seems oblivious to
most of these goings-on. His life has always been like this.
Friends say he's somewhat confused by all the attention.

Charles doesn't seem to have thought about the ramifications of the Archbishop of Canterbury's advice about his future sex life: a good thing given by God that, nevertheless,
like all God's gifts, need to be directed aright. Nor does he
protest the two miles of TV cables that will be in St. Paul's.
Charles is the first media prince. For him this is normal, and
it's kind of sweet how sheltered he is in the midst of the circus
that surrounds him. He's told his friends—and he means it—
that he considers what will go on on July 29 an absolutely private event.

His bride, who was called Two Amp when she was at
school, in this matter is not so dumb. She comes from the real
world, the world of media events and divorces, where sisters
get anorectic and fathers almost go bankrupt—as hers did—
and then suffer near-fatal strokes. Lady Diana escaped into
fairy tales as a child—one likes to think that *Cinderella* was her
special favorite—but on the matter of her wedding she har-
bors no two-amp illusions. She understands that this service is
pure spectacle, her spectacle. She knows that well enough to
have brought in the makeup woman who did *A Clockwork Or-*

ange and *Barry Lyndon* to make sure that she will be the perfect TV bride.

For Diana Spencer, the ceremony on the morning of the twenty-ninth will represent the moment when she will finally get the ultimate security, a security never provided by the real world. Her future life will be defined by royal ribbon cuttings and court circulars in *The Times*, by summers at Balmoral and winters at Sandringham, by weekends at Windsor and weekdays at Highgrove. Her life will be without divorce or deviations from protocol, without ambivalence or being able to escape the obligation of having to attend a Royal Air Force show. After Wednesday noon, this twenty-year-old will never again be allowed out on the street alone.

The Garden Party

At the moment, Diana trembles on the brink. Her chin juts out when she speaks, her hip sinks into her leg, her arm flails, her eyes drop. The giggle pierces the air. None of that matters to her future subjects. It certainly didn't matter to the Maynards from Maidenhead who had come in their brand-new polyesters to possibly be presented to their future queen. They stood there in Siberia, on the farthest reaches of the lawn, looking more than a little tense. Mr. Maynard, a legal cashier, was as flushed as he was bald. His walrus mustache clumped in spikes, so often did he lick his lips. He had no idea why he had been invited to this royal affair. "I suspect someone has to recommend you," Mrs. Maynard preened.

Somewhere in the middle distance, the prince and Lady Diana were a good hour's promenade away. Just then, a man in a morning suit approached us: "Are you being presented today, Mr. Maynard?" he asked. "I am." "Very good," said the retired colonel. "If you will just stay right here, I believe the prince and Lady Diana will come this way."

The chance of being next to a loyal subject being presented

is somewhere between slim and none. Soon our little patch of
Siberian sod became the only place to be. By now, I had lashed
myself to the Maynards' side. The prince and Lady Diana
swam into view. Charles paid little attention to her and seemed
somewhat sad, lonely, and very, very small on a sea of lawn.
Diana was the star: radiant, perfectly dressed in her Pierrot
collar and pale, pale hose, in a sexy drift of a suit that parodied
the Hardy Amies armor her new family always wears.

Closer in, one noticed other things. Diana's glamour began
to crack a bit. The adolescent gait lingered. Her nerves
showed. It was Charles who threw the sparks as they both
drew near. His eyes pierced. His posture made him look spin-
dly and somewhat tentative, but his face told another tale:
There was warmth and wit, as well as a sense of the absurd.
Like anyone who is truly regal, he seemed not particularly
grand.

He stood inches away. Mrs. Maynard dropped to one knee.
"Are you retired now, Mr. Maynard?" HRH politely asked.
"Yes, sir," Mr. Maynard mumbled, "I am." "Well, I hope
you're not having too hard a time keeping up appearances."
The prince turned to more fertile conversational ground.
"And Mrs. Maynard, you're a writer, then, are you?" "Yes,
sir. Gardening books."

"Tell me, Mrs. Maynard, do you write under your maiden
name in Maidenhead?" "No sir." Mrs. Maynard hesitated. "I
write under my married name, which is Maynard, in Maidenhead."

"Do you mean to say that you write under your married
name of Maynard in Maidenhead and not your maiden name,
which isn't Maynard?"

"Indeed, sir."

"Oh, I see."

Another pause. "You know," HRH, the Prince of Wales,
said, "I wrote this silly little book for my younger brother
that's in the shops now, and it's terribly embarrassing, but, do

you know, the thing has gone and sold a hundred ninety thousand copies?" He paused a moment. "Isn't that extraordinary? They've even gone and translated it into Japanese."

This was too much for Nan Maynard of Maidenhead. "Well, sir, that won't happen to me." "No," said the proud author, "I suppose it won't." And still the prince lingered. "You know, sir, I once stopped to watch you play polo. . . ."

"How terribly brash of you, Mrs. Maynard. I do say, that was brave." Almost as an afterthought, Wales turned to a matron by Mrs. Maynard's side: "And what have you done with your husband today?" he asked cheerfully.

The woman looked stricken. "We're separated, sir, I'm sorry to say." The prince registered nothing, not a flicker of sympathy or chagrin. "I see," he said, and then he was gone, without saying good-bye.

Meanwhile, Lady Diana was ten steps behind him, greeting another couple slightly down the line. The woman pulled a Lee Annenberg and wrongly dropped dramatically to one knee. Diana's response was to cough nervously in her face. "Oh," she said, "excuse me. I have such a sore throat. All the excitement."

Clearly, Diana didn't go far enough with her Clarence House instructions. Someone will have to teach this twenty-year-old that queens are not allowed to cough and complain within the public eye.

But she was trying. "Have you been to many of these garden parties before?" she asked gamely. The matron looked confused. "Oh, no, ma'am. This is my first." Diana giggled. "This is my first too. I'm awfully nervous."

Everyone was charmed. The woman grew brave. "Are you enjoying your engagement, Lady Diana?" An explosion. "Oh, no! I absolutely hate the engagement. But I shall adore being married to Charles." Off she wobbled like a marvelous duckling, fast on its way to becoming a royal swan.

She will have role models to help her. Princess Michael of Kent, with her upsweep of blond hair, her Givenchied presence, might be able to teach her a few things—about appearance, anyway. The Windsor women are not Princess Michael fans. They call her "the poor relation" and snigger about how her stipend of twenty thousand dollars a year forces her to have to ask for a royal discount on those nice Bottega Veneta bags in Knightsbridge shops.

The family is not amused. One could see that at the garden party, during the final promenade. From out of the royal tea tent first strolled the queen, looking surprisingly strained and irritable in her ivory Hardy Amies and midwinter black kid gloves, accented with matching shoes. To loud clapping, Princess Michael in her cream Givenchy smiled and dazzled the glamour lovers in the crowd. Just to Princess Michael's right, making her way past the beefeaters, was Princess Petulance, the unlovely Anne. Her hat for the occasion appeared to have been picked up on a beach at Mustique. Loosely woven raffia, in a cone shape, held down by a chiffon scarf. Anne had added a touch of color to the brim—a cluster of miniature plastic fruit—so as she stared viciously at Princess Michael gathering all that applause, her rage was so intense that the banana bobbed against the cherry, which crashed against the plum. "You would have thought Anne could have come up with something a bit smarter for her head, now, wouldn't you?" one onlooker said.

But there's another lesson to be drawn here. Perhaps Lady Diana should think of what happens to those who try to steal any thunder from the Windsor women. Maybe she should forget about the fancy hats and Bally shoes and act more as if she wants to fit in.

What to Buy the Bride

The secrets are just north of Sloane Square, in black plastic notebooks, as hard to get into as the pre-wedding ball at

Buckingham Palace. Even the bride's closest friends won't tell you what's in those little books. One slip about the black leather trash cans at fifty dollars each could sever a relationship, bring the Highgrove shutter down. Diana and Charles's imperious command, "No decanters," which is boldly printed throughout their register, could have Engligh glassmakers in a fury that they don't want a crystal camouflage for the not-so-vintage port.

Diana has registered herself at the General Trading Company, an eclectic bazaar in Chelsea that carries a royal appointment but is eccentric enough to stock both the Mel Calman T-shirt ("What wedding?") and those upper-class leather bins. Also, Paddington Bear dolls, avocado shells, Mexican *tchotchkies,* and, for the royals and their friends, Royal Worcester, George III three-tier mahogany whatnots, and heavy, heavy Royal Brierley glass.

One has to mount an undercover mission to get into those notebooks. You can't wear jeans and a rugby shirt. On came the droopy silk and the garden-party hat, white cotton gloves. "My mother and I have just arrived from America for the festivities," I whispered.

The trash bins were first on a seventeen-page typed list of requests ranging from antiques to salad crescents to Bloomingdale's country china. Most of the requests have been filled—Lady Porchester, the wife of the queen's racing manager, is giving her the two dozen champagne glasses at fourteen dollars per. You mustn't linger too long in those lists, though. For God's sake, don't have a pen in hand. A Knightsbridge blue-hair came bustling over. "You mustn't write anything down," she said. "Are you sure you're a family friend?"

I swept up to the antiques department with all the indignation that I imagine Barbara Cartland shows on such occasions, only to be greeted pleasantly by a very bored salesman who was a double for *My Fair Lady*'s Freddy Eynsford-Hill. This time I did not make a mistake. I commanded Freddy to write down what I wanted. In England, everyone responds if you just treat him like a clerk. Freddy not only made notes about their special-request Regency toilet mirror with candle sconces and chinoiserie decoration—you can have it for £750—he rushed to drag out the three-tier whatnots and the Georgian tufted stools, to try to explain their request for two Chippendale-design sofas at £470 each. The second one was so that Diana's decorator could paint the Chippendale base to look like bamboo. "I can't imagine why," said Freddy Eynsford-Hill. One item intrigued—the Chinese procelain vase, with a floral-and-snake design, circa 1870, converted to a lamp. Price, eighty-five pounds. It had been reserved for Mrs. Callaghan. The wife of the ex-prime minister? Indeed. Freddy and I looked at each other in the same way: You would think a pol would know better than to spend only eighty-five quid on a man who will be king.

On to china and glass, then. Diana's choice of porcelains reveals she is still stuck somewhere in her teens. She's picked Royal Worcester's Evesham—a white background spotted with corncobs, asparagus, and blackberries. Very like Anne's hat. Oh, well, she'll have time to learn about Mason's Ware.

Her glass pattern, Apollo by Royal Brierley, is much more regal. It's heavy, anyway. Move away from the apple-dotted marmite jars—at £32 per—and choose the two dozen salad crescents with beveled bottoms, £12.90, for those Highgrove dinners. But the breakfast guests won't be so lucky. No one has bought her an Evesham breakfast cup or saucer, much less the £32.70 *pot de crème*. She's registered for six.

Party Time

The big one is at the palace, of course; sixteen hundred people Monday night. This dance is "for all the people who have known each other forever," according to a peer. He means the English upper class. Diana's hairdresser won't be at the Buckingham Palace affair, nor will the ministers from Sri Lanka who will have gotten the invite to St. Paul's. But the musical trio—Placido Domingo, Colin Davis, and Charles Groves—will. That same night is the Berkeley Square Ball, usually a highlight, as they say, of the London summer season.

Not this year. This year, anyone who shows up at Berkeley Square will simply be announcing that he was not included in the gala for Diana and Charles. The organizers expect Lynne Sellers and David Frost. Just about as exclusive will be the next night's fireworks display in Hyde Park, which the tabloids say will be the biggest ever. A million people are expected to see Buckingham Palace re-created with rockets in the sky. The other night at dinner, Barbara Walters joked, "Well, I do have one exclusive. To the fireworks in the park."

On Tuesday night, Serena Balfour will have a gala of her own—a ball in her house in the Little Boltons, off Fulham Road. Charles and Lady Diana won't be there—it is the night before the wedding, after all—but what people still call, somehow without laughing, the "international set" will. Carolina Herrera, staying at Kensington Palace with Princess Margaret, will be there. So will Betsy Bloomingdale, Lord Snowdon, the *Women's Wear Daily* crowd.

No one will be short of things to talk about. Two days earlier Charles will have played polo for the last time before his wedding. They will all have been there. And that same night, the polo night, the new American ambassador, John Louis, is throwing a do for Nancy Reagan. The Balfour guests will have been there, more interested, to be sure, in Mrs. Reagan's Galanos than in the paintings on loan from the Wildenstein that hang in the ambassador's new home—one of those nice little perks of his job. That party will be a very big deal, the American equivalent of the palace ball. Nancy Reagan will be kept busy—she'll have two hot dinners at Buckingham Palace and two lunches with Prime Minister Thatcher. Drue Heinz is throwing her a ball. She'll watch Charles play polo at Windsor and have drinks with Lord Carrington. Presumably, she'll have her Beverly Hills matron chums in tow.

The day of the wedding, the proles will be celebrating too.

The Roof Garden, formerly Regine's, has sent out a flier advertising "our large video screen" and, for the children, a Punch-and-Judy show. Dai Llewellyn, Roddy's brother, is throwing a Charles-and-Diana disco party at his new nightclub, Tokyo Joe's. That party will attract the same group who will have shown at the Berkeley Square Ball.

The night of the wedding, there will be only one place to be, if your ambitions run to hanging out with the royal crowd. That will be Liz Shakerley's ball at Claridge's. She's Patrick Lichfield's sister and a third cousin to the queen, who is supposedly showing up at this one. But Liz is a little controversial. Not always so discreet. One editor asked her if he could send a photographer to the party. "God, no," cried Liz. "The queen is expected. But, of course, if you want to have your photographer outside snapping color photos for your next issue, I wouldn't mind at all."

Then there are the gatherings that no one ever hears about: they don't make the William Hickey column or "Nigel Dempster's Diary," in the *Daily Mail.* These are the parties for the closest friends, the quiet little pre-wedding get-togethers in some fancy Mayfair spot. Like the dinner for twenty-four people that Nicholas Soames threw last week in a private suite at Claridge's—in the Royal Suite, of course. Nicholas Soames is Winston Churchill's grandson. A lot of his own success is based on his relationship with Charles, people say. And Soames knows how to please his prince. For this dinner, he'd invited Wales's real friends, such as the horsey-racy crowd, the Van Cutsems, and the Halifaxes, as in the Earl of. Charlotte Soames Hambro was there—she's Nicholas's sister and the ex-wife of the banker. Charlotte's daughter, age five, is a bridesmaid for the royal wedding; it will be her fourth bridesmaid's job this month. Then, there were the Parker-Bowleses, Andrew and Camilla. You have to wonder about them. Charles's relationship with Camilla is as close as it is publicized—those sly mentions in the tabloids, the proper mentions in Anthony Holden's book, *Their Royal Highnesses: The Prince and Princess of Wales.* Yet Andrew Parker-Bowles and Charles are the best of friends, and Charles is a favorite Parker-Bowles houseguest. They have a lot of time alone to talk on those grouse shoots.

All of this makes sense, of course. There's a lot of prestige in European upper-class circles attached to having one's wife enjoying the kind of friendship that Charles and Camilla—as well as Lady Tryon—supposedly had. Charles even has a pet name for Dale Tryon. He calls her Kanga. She's Australian, naturally, and Charles met her at a sock hop when he was at school at Treetops, in Australia.

Everyone here talks about this and writes about it too. The husbands all seem rather proud. Anthony Holden makes the point that, in this way, Charles had a lot in common with his great-uncle the Duke of Windsor. They both found "a unique security in the close friendship of married women." They didn't have to worry about rumors of marriage or "declarations of interest." Charles happily serves as god-father to the eldest children of Kanga Tryon as well as those of Camilla Parker-Bowles. Now that Charles is marrying Diana, things might have to change gears slightly. They are very civilized.

And that's the point to remember about HRH. The civility and the ritual extend to all things. Even Charles's closest friends call him sir and drop curtsies to him. On the surface, Wales may try to act almost normal: He may talk about his book sales with the Maynards from Maidenhead with the élan of a William Morris agent; he may have gone—for the first time in royal history—to school with other kids; but Charles much more than his father, who is nicknamed Phil the Greek, is very aware of who he is. He doesn't like having strangers ask him how he feels about getting married, or whether he's capped his teeth. For all those childhood pranks and skiing and scuba diving, Charles adheres, more than his predecessors, to every shred of royal decorum. If at times he seems a little priggish, one can't forget that one day he'll be a king.

Rita Regrets

It's not enough to get an invitation to Buckingham Palace and St. Paul's. Not enough to have the Claridge's footman bow to you because you've gotten the silver-bordered command to The Reception (read: "ball") given for HRH, the Prince of Wales, and his bride by HM, the queen.

So Rita Lachman worries. She sits at Claridge's amid the cabbage-rose silk wall hangings and her seven Vuitton cases of her decade-old Diors. How can she get invited to the dinner for Nancy Reagan at the American Embassy residence? How can she give those Art Deco glasses to Prince Charles and Lady Dee, as she calls her, and then put them in the catalog of her new mail-order business without it looking to her dear friend Raine as if she's cashing in? How can she allow the BBC to film her on the wedding day without the Spencers' feeling that this doesn't reflect so well on them?

Problems. Anyone who reads the columns knows more than he wants to about Rita Lachman's problems. About the thirty million-dollar lawsuit—she'll tell you it's "really my daughter's lawsuit"—against her ex-husband's widow, Jaquine. (Rita and Jaquine were both married to Charles Lachman, the man who, years ago, was the *L* in Revlon.) But never mind all that. For the moment, that crisis is not on Rita's mind. Now that Rita "has proven to all those social climbers like Joanne Herring that I stand for something in New York because of my invitation," you would think her anxieties would end.

They haven't. Take this Nancy Reagan thing. *"Dahling,"* Rita says one morning on the telephone, "I don't know what to do to get into the American Embassy party. I mean, it would be an embarrassment for the American people if I, Rita

Lachman, as the only unofficial invited guest—and a dear friend of the Spencers'—wasn't there at the dinner for Mrs. Reagan. *Dahling,* that would be terrible. So *ven* Raine dropped over to Claridge's yesterday to see the ball gowns— you *von't* believe how elegant they are; a vintage dress is always right, you know—I asked her what to do."

A pause. "So Raine suggested that I should just write a note to the embassy saying that I am 'passing through' London for the marriage of Prince Charles and Lady Dee, and just let it drop at that."

Raine and Rita understand each other. "You know," she says, "Raine is so incredible. She saved Earl Spencer's life. She's such a lady. So good with servants. The other day she called me, and she said that six hundred people had visited Althorp and she had spent the whole day picking up cigarette butts. . . . I never thought I would get invited to Lady Dee's wedding. When the invitation came, I was opening my mail in front of my building, and I saw that in the bottom corner it said, LORD CHAMBERLAIN. To tell you the truth, I thought it was the invitation to the opening of a new nightclub. When I looked at it and realized what it was, I just started screaming on the street. I fell apart.

"I am so nervous. I don't want to do anything wrong."

And so much could go wrong. "Do you know that I just learned from Raine the other day that you never say 'Queen Elizabeth' when you mean the queen. Raine told me that if you say 'Queen Elizabeth,' that means the queen mother. Can you imagine what would have happened if I had made such a mistake?"

Rita's worries occupy her day. There's the worry with the new present—she has to cancel the Art Deco glasses—and her new mail-order catalog, *Rita L.* ("a collection of *vunderful* things, my taste"). There's the worry about Betsy Bloomingdale and Lee Annenberg—"Can you imagine those two?"— and the awful realization that, while they will certainly get to

Ambassador Louis's party, she may not. With all of this, it's hard to stay calm. Somehow she does. "You know," Rita Lachman says, sighing, "since I've been invited to the wedding, nothing can be bad anymore." She stares at her Diors lined up in the Claridge closet, their ruffles grazing the closet floor. "What more could I ever want? Now . . . life is beautiful."

August 1981

Scenes from a Marriage

O ne of them was out very early. His Mini sped down the Mall. It was odd to see this dark-green Mini hurtling toward the Admiralty and the cathedral at that hour of the day. Not that lots of people weren't already gathered by 7 A.M. in St. James Park—a quarter of a million massed and each with a hand-painted sign of some kind of eccentric and typically English display. GOD LOVE YOU, CHARLES, FROM THE WILKINSONS. An entire family wearing hand-crocheted red-white-and-blue doilies on their heads. Police were everywhere. But they were smiling. So were the royal trash collectors, who were clearing the Mall of the breakfast leavings of the tens of thousands of overnight guests.

And then came Mark Phillips, rushing in his green Mini, hours before the first notes of Elgar, the first glimpse of the veil. Before the visiting royals arrived for eggs and brioche, before Jane Pauley got to the *Today* trailer and stuck the hot rollers in her hair. That 7 A.M. safari must remain one of the minor unsolved mysteries of this extraordinary royal-wedding day. Could Fog, as he is known in *Private Eye,* the English satirical magazine, have left something in the church during

the rehearsal? Been fetching something for Princess Anne?
Out to get the *Daily Mail*? Early on, the day was like a diamond—make that a sapphire surrounded by diamonds. Any
newcomer on the Mall got a tremendous ovation, whether it
was a passing sweeper or a pigeon touching down. Just behind
the geraniums fronting the queen's London house were the
TV people en masse. The networks' platforms hugged one
another. They were all there, of course—ABC, BBC, NBC,
ITV, CBS. The world's most expensive talent thrust on the
narrow, pebbled paths. Their raised stages were small, just
large enough to hold up the tiny sets, a few cameras, several
staff members, and a guest. There was no way the palace was
going to let the technology upstage the spectacle.

Garry Trudeau stood on the NBC platform in his jeans
taking photos of his wife, Jane Pauley. "Are you having a
good time, Mr. Trudeau?" she called out to him, very gay. A
Goodyear blimp floated overhead. Tom Brokaw smirked into
the camera, getting his *Today* face on. Moments before the
red light flashed, someone rushed up the ladder of the platform with a sketch of the wedding dress. Was it the same as
Women's Wear's early guess? It was not. And, down below,
over near the flower beds, the police carried out a stretcher
with a body. A boy had fainted from it all.

From somewhere over near Victoria, the horns, the drums.
It had begun. And then, the approach of the Irish Guards with
their wolfhound and band. The sun glanced off brass, flashed
in eyes. And then, more sounds: the clatter of horses, the roar
of the crowd. The shared knowledge that very soon the car-
riages would come out. And the irony that the NBC team—
Tom and Jane; the queen's biographer, Robert Lacey; and
Tatler editor Tina Brown—would have to stay fixed on their
cameras. They were the only ones who couldn't turn around.

What they had to miss, in service to their craft: Another
drumroll, then the first view of those coaches. "God Save the
Queen." The horses blurred. Those dowdy hats bobbed up

and down in front of us; and smiles were appropriately re-strained, as were the waves. And still the *Today* stars couldn't turn around. The royals rushed by us, the symbols of a civili-zation, the most powerful litmus of how this society feels about itself. Their display dazzled. The horses all behaved. And the queen mother beamed and beamed. Her family was on its way to another grand occasion of perpetuation, to watch history being made.

But before the wild bells could ring out, the family had things to do. The day before the wedding, Lady Sarah Arm-strong-Jones was in Mayfair being worked over with a curling iron. A few blocks away, two Daimlers waited threateningly outside Asprey's for some shoppers with titles to come out. A crowd formed. No one dared to walk inside. The class system extends even to a public place. Everyone prayed it would be Lady Diana picking up some last-minute sterling. It wasn't.

Inside, the king of Norway browsed with his son, Crown Prince Harald, and daughter-in-law. The king laughed a lot. The Asprey's help, so used to fawning over titles, fawned over this jolly Robert Morley of a king. The crown princess wor-ried about whether the brass corkscrews could be made up in gilt. Like all royals, they dawdled with their errands, pleased to have something worthwhile to do. They wandered into the five hundred-pound-handbag department. The king of Nor-way boomed, "So tomorrow we'll see you at ten. That's what is written in that little book. Can you imagine how they do things in this country? Isn't that so like the British?" His laugh reverberated around the room.

The saleswoman approached, carrying a bulging plastic bag, but the king of Norway still had business. "Now, you're absolutely sure that the bill won't get sent with the gift?" The saleswoman became very correct. "Of course not, sir. We're well used to this sort of thing." The king walked to the door and peered out at the crowd. "Oh, my God," he said. "What-ever are we to do?"

He didn't have to worry. Outside, the police held the Diana-watchers back. Police were everywhere in London that week, looking very tense.

The groom didn't. For once, he looked happy. He ate cheese soufflé with his bachelor friends. He took Lucia Santa Cruz, his first love, to *Don Giovanni.* They were not joined by Lady Diana. On the polo field he scored the eighth goal for England against Spain, and when another player fell from his horse, Charles jumped to his aid and was rewarded by getting blood all over his polo pants. "Well," the ITV commentator reassured the viewers, "we've had news on the ponies. They're going to be all right."

Never mind. Charles's family knew its priorities. Princess Margaret and the Duchess of Kent spent a lot of time at David and Josef, the Mayfair hairdresser, hidden behind the shop's venetian-blind stall, which passes for a temporary royal enclosure when the Windsors are on the premises. On one occasion, Princess Margaret took twenty minutes to have her hair shampooed. On another, one could see the Duchess of Kent dimly through the slats, her waist-length blond tresses being teased into a threatening piece of artillery something like a medieval ponytail. And then Nancy Reagan came to town with five hatboxes, two presents, and Betsy Blooming-dale. Nobody knew what to make of them.

Mrs. Reagan didn't care. She has finally got something that probably matters to her as much as her Washington address: the affection of the Prince of Wales. This feeling of accep-tance is a new development. Charles's friends say that he had sneered at her when he first met her in Washington, finding her, as most of the English do, stiff and rather cold.

Then came his June visit to New York for the Royal Ballet, and his heavy security, his run-ins with Mayor Koch and the IRA. Charles has told one friend that all he ever saw in New York was a phalanx of police and the first lady. She really comforted him, the friend said, confiding in him her fears about her husband's being shot.

Unlikely as it seems, there is a natural affinity between the Reagans and the royals. They share a solidly provincial, aristocratic view of life—the adulation of the family, the middle-class values of the Moral Majority. Both families are long on physical accomplishments, short on intellectual prowess. Both believe in the preservation of class. Cuture is not their métier, neither is the urbane, live-and-let-live sophisticated city life. They observe decorum; they understand tradition and propriety.

Diana Spencer and Nancy Davis Reagan have a lot in common too. They share broken homes, odd childhoods among the upper class, isolation, and the need for security. Each found the powerful male figure to dominate her life. Diana says her first priority after her marriage will be to be a good wife. The first lady could teach her a great deal.

At Windsor, the sun came out for one glorious afternoon. Twenty thousand people gathered in the hush of the English countryside to watch Charles mount his polo steed. Diana hid inside the royal box, looking somewhat nervous, chatting with the queen. Sometime during the second chukker of the first match, I decided to take a stroll through the Windsor back roads. I paused at a small pond by a narrow lane. Suddenly, the birch trees rustled. I could hear nothing but the sound of galloping horses, the clattering of hooves. An Edwardian carriage was approaching. The carriage drew closer. Its driver was in green tweed and a brown bowler and had two attendants by his side. It was Prince Philip out in his landaulet—a page from Thomas Hardy slipped into modern life.

I continued my stroll. Past the Pimm's chukker bar and the ice-cream trucks, down to the entrance of the park, where the estate keepers live. In quite Berkshire, sirens suddenly rang out. Lights flahsed. Limos and staff cars and motorcycles shot by. Inside her limo, Nancy Reagan waved to the gathered masses, all of six. "Who was that?" one of the gatemen asked.

"The first lady of the United States."

"Oh, dear me. Why is she making so much fuss?"

Indeed, Nancy was making as much fuss as a deb in her first season. That night, she threw on another scarlet frock and swept down the stairs of Winfield House to greet 150 British lords and nobs. David Frost was there too, with Lynne. So were Barbara Walters, Tom Brokaw, and Princess Grace. Another princess, Alexandra, was preoccupied with the trials of her brother, Prince Michael of Kent.

"Isn't it a terrible pity that the house is haunted?" she was overheard to say in the loo. "I'm so worried. After all they've been through, and now the other day Prince Michael was followed by a plank."

The party was a smash. The guests dined on *veau princier* and *cassoulet feuilleté de langoustines.* Ned Sherrin played songs by Stephen Sondheim after dinner. Mrs. Bloomingdale hovered by her friend Nancy's side. Perhaps she was feeling socially insecure. The talk is beginning here about her run-in at the airport some years back. It seems that Mrs. Bloomingdale changed some prices on her made-in-Paris togs. Worse, she got caught by Customs. "To cut the tags off is one thing," said a guest. "Everybody does that. But to pretend that you paid something else—why would she do that?"

At the ambassador's house, the worry among the press was intense: Just who was the Duchess of Grafton? Whoever she was, she was there. Barbara Walters seemed obsessed with finding out, according to a guest. It became a kind of running joke. *Tatler* editor Tina Brown saved the day—mistress of the robes.

The Duchess of Grafton, of course, was the least of it. Wednesday morning was a celebration of conventions, order, and majesty. Certainly, it was a celebration of love. Diana's choice of hymn said it all: "I vow to thee, my country, the service of my love." Though that sounded solemn, Diana wasn't. She giggled, poked her veil, and fluffed one of her lines. Charles added an extra one. His whispered "Well done" had to be, for the rest of the world, the ultimate eavesdrop.

There was so much to reflect on during the actual event. The appearance of Diana's mother, for example. Frances Shand Kydd looked elegant, well preserved, and very, very rich. Diana's marriage is her mother's triumph too. The Princess of Wales is a further victory for Mrs. Shand Kydd over her own mother, Lady Fermoy, who had cut her daughter off when she left her husband to marry a walllpaper heir. Frances's daughter remained loyal, however, and now this daughter will be a queen.

So those final trumpets must have sounded incredibly sweet to Frances Shand Kydd. She and the queen mother seemed to stare at each other with understanding of the emotion of the event. The queen could show nothing, of course. In fact, she looked rather glum, except at that second that everyone had waited for, when Charles and Diana began their final procession down the aisle. Charles paused and looked at his mother, who offered only a wry smile. Charles bowed. Diana bobbed. That exchange was a metaphor for the entire royal role. It was at once as professional as it was personal, irrational, and preordained. Neither a mother's kisses nor exclamations can ever be offered in public. And so Charles and Diana bowed and curtsied to their queen.

And then began their long, long walk. They will have a life of this kind of ritual and pageant, of pomp and circumstance. The color will be trooped, the Welsh Guards inspected, the duchy of Cornwall tended, but now, while waiting to act out his destiny, the Prince of Wales will no longer be alone.

August 1981

RSVP
The White House

*J*t was the first anniversary of the inaugural, a huge, dull
political dinner, and all through the Vice-President's
speech at the Washington hotel the ladies gossiped into
one another's ears. They leaned in and laughed and looked
very pretty, feminine, rich, oblivious, and so predictably os-
tentatious that it seemed nothing had changed in the Reagan
circle for a year. The mandatory diamonds were on their
hands, and on one of the hands was an enormous emerald in a
lasso of shiny stones. There were earrings to match it. The
woman who wore the emeralds and diamonds was named
Betty Adams, and she looked very much like her close friend
the first lady. Betty Adams came from Los Angeles too. She
sat and chatted with a New York socialite. Betty was "exhausted," the friend reported. She had "flown all night to sit
at the President's table, because Nancy had asked her to," and
then discovered the tables had been switched for security reasons.

So now here sat Betty Adams, halfway to the kitchen, past
David Stockman and author Anna Chennault, but not quite as
far out as Clare Boothe Luce, who shivered through dinner in
her blond mink. The New York socialite had her own prob-

lems: Another blizzard was on the way, and she had her ballet benefit the next night in New York, and a friend might have to send in his jet to rescue her. "I can't bear being on the boards of eighteen things at once anymore," she said. "It's just too tiring." She had arrived alone. "Jerry Zipkin called me as I was going out the door. He said, '*Chérie,* why didn't you tell me you were going? I would have come too.'" The socialite sighed. "I wouldn't have brought him," she said. "Jerry is always so critical of everything."

The socialites and the politicians and the second-city millionaires and the corporate leaders had all come to celebrate, or maybe just to mark, the first year in office of their President. The dinner was moderately exclusive: A donation of ten thousand dollars a year to the Republican cause ensured an invitation as well as membership in a group called the Eagles. This night in Washington, twenty-four hundred Eagles turned out. A few close friends of the Reagans' were noticeably absent. But the Washington best friends like Charles and Mary Jane Wick were there, and so were Nancy Dickerson; Mr. Quaker Oats, Max Fisher; John Connally; Elliot Richardson; George and Barbara Bush; and the two social couples in the President's Cabinet, the William French Smiths and the Caspar Weinbergers. The other, less social Cabinet officers were there too. Everyone kept saying it was just like the inauguration: a lot of rich out-of-towners wearing new-money stones and tired ball gowns.

Except that it wasn't at all like the inauguration. A lot had gone on in the past year. The President had been shot outside this very hotel, the Washington Hilton. This night the ballroom was filled with Secret Service. The day's *Washington Post* had been full of the President's press-conference gaffes and "clarifications." His popularity had slumped in the polls. A lot of the best friends stayed away from the dinner. There was no sign of the Bloomingdales or the king of the car salesmen, Holmes Tuttle, or the drugstore millionaire Justin Dart.

The Walter Annenbergs were in Rancho Mirage, and Jerry Zipkin, the First Walker, had stayed in New York. Maybe the friends no longer thought Washington was so much fun.

"Are you as confident as you were a year ago?" the chairman of the Republican National Committee asked the crowd. There was a pause and a smattering of applause. The President was introduced and he smiled and looked as pleasant as ever. "We're in a recession," he said. "But it didn't start this year. . . . The loudest cries of pain come from the people who did the worst." As he spoke, Betty Adams and the New York socialite nodded almost imperceptibly, their chins hard, their jaws set. Jars of jelly-bean party favors sat in front of them.

"Nancy and I are happy in our work," the President told the dinner. As proof, Nancy stood up and gave everyone in the Hilton ballroom an opportunity to see her dress—presumably on its way to a museum—a one-shoulder black Galanos with a foot-high rhinestone star on the bodice. Thousands of rhinestones reflected the lights of the TV cameras, almost blinding the Eagles with the first lady's message.

The Reagan's new-money style had caused a lot of comment. Nancy's china policy had gotten more attention than her husband's foreign policy. As do all her amusements: her White House redo, her grudges, her Georgetown lunches, her field-flower arrangements, her friendship with Frank Sinatra (her friends say it's a crush she has had since childhood), those borrowed ball gowns and Bulgaris, and her frequent telephone conversations with her best friends, Jerry Zipkin and Betsy Bloomingdale.

The Reagan defenders have called this "a return to glamour." They say it's about time a sophisticated couple represented the country. They say the Reagans are the epitome of the American success story. This group thought it was a relief when the Carters checked out of Washington. The Carters were so tacky, they say, congressmen used to have to pay for their breakfast when they came to the White House. The defenders are proud: The Reagans continue to live just the way they did in California.

A lot of other people feel different. They see the same new-money style, only they see it as a kind of let-them-eat-mousse myopia, an indulgence in conspicuous consumption without social conscience that rivals Versailles: social blindness and everything that's wrong with the American success story at a time when the poor line up in snowstorms for a five-pound lump of processed cheese. The criticism transcends politics. Even people who like the President and don't want to be churlish—after all, why shouldn't he be able to relax?—wonder if the Reagans understand what goes on outside their preserve. The critics believe the social side of Reagan's Washington is of a piece with his politics: well-meaning but limited, filled with dubious judgments, as if the President isn't always quite sure what is going on.

The fact is that the Reagans' social world has changed since his first year in office. A lot of Californians have gone home. The novelty has worn off. The Reagans don't go out as much anymore. Security is a big problem. Washington has hardly embraced them, socially or philosophically. The forays they made at first into Georgetown didn't work so very well. Snide, old-money, inbred, establishment Washington has gotten tired of the Reagans too.

In an odd way, the Reagans have become almost as isolated as the Carters were, protected by staff, prisoners of circumstance. This happens to every President, of course; all part of the game. John and Jackie Kennedy, the last stylish presidential couple, used to invite the Ben Bradlees over to hear Joey Dee records. The Reagans break the monotony in their own way: They invite friends to the White House screening room for a movie every few weeks.

In the beginning, it was different. Everybody remembers the beginning. All those California millionaires camped out at the Watergate and the Fairfax. The Annenbergs rented a place in the Watergate. So did the Bloomingdales and the Wicks. It was hard to tell the millionaires' wives apart. "Can you really tell the difference between Mrs. French Smith and Lee Annenberg?" a hostess asked at the time. At Maison Blanche, the lunchroom of favor, the maître d' hid a chart of photographs under his reservation book. Washington called them The Group—the Darts, the Deutsches, the Bloomingdales, the Wicks, the Wrathers, the Tuttles, the Prices, the Annenbergs. They all gave lunches and dinners for one another—they didn't know anybody else in town. The Wicks entertained for the Reagans. The Prices entertained for the Wicks, the Darts for the Annenbergs. There was a lot written about the his-and-hers terrycloth bathrobes and the daily *Los Angeles Times* deliveries the Watergate was lavishing on its VIPs.

In the early days, the Reagans made an effort to get around. A few days after his victory, the President-elect threw a dinner at the F Street Club for the Washington Establishment—the journalists, congressional leaders, and Georgetown matrons like Katharine Graham. "When the invitations went out for dinner, some of them responded with, 'Is this a kind of joke?,' " Bob Gray says. Bob Gray is a PR man, a Republican, influential in the Reagan era. He organized the F Street Club dinner and was cochairman of the inaugural with Reagan's best friend, Charles Wick.

Bob Gray says that the Reagans were determined not to make the same mistake that the Carters had: to view Washington as an enemy camp. Even before the inaugural, the Reagans were at Katharine Graham's house for dinner. During the inauguration there were a hundred parties in four days. Then the President turned seventy. The Group was back, and so was Frank Sinatra, and the state dinners started to get less diplomatic and more like American Film Institute film-tribute nights.

Like most husbands, Ronald Reagan stood back and let his

wife organize his social life. Only there was a problem: Nancy Reagan went a little overboard. Prince Charles was honored with a Zipkin-inspired "fun group," as Peter McCoy, the first lady's staff director at the time, called it: Audrey Hepburn and her boyfriend, Rob Wolders; Sammy Cahn; Bobby Short, Shelley Hack; Betsy Bloomingdale; Diana Vreeland. The next king of England upstairs at the White House with the stars of *Interview.* A classic picture was taken: Mrs. Vreeland in full regalia dropped to the floor in front of her prince as Jerry Zipkin looked on. It was as if Nancy Reagan were saying to the country, "I am going to do what I want to do." The dinner for Prince Charles came five weeks after the President was shot. Perhaps her behavior was self-protection, a retreat into the world in which she felt most secure.

She became the First Target and took off for the royal wedding in a storm of mounting abuse. In London, her response was to attend fifteen parties in five days with Betsy Bloomingdale. Her motorcade roared through the hush of the English countryside. She was excoriated by the British press. When she returned, she disappeared with the President for a month to Casa Equestria.

During the summer, she threw herself into her first lady activities. She visited orphanages and met with foster grandparents. She looked for a researcher for a book on foster grandparenting. She made statements about the drug problem, posed with retarded children, and even made time to show Mother Teresa around the family quarters. "I don't understand why the press thinks Nancy just dabbles with her activities," a close friend says. "She is genuinely concerned."

She also went to lunch, a series of lunches, organized by Tish Baldrige, who used to work for Jackie Kennedy. The idea was to get Nancy Reagan involved with the community, to introduce her to Washington's other first ladies: Evangeline Bruce, Polly Fritchey, Oatsie Charles, Susan Mary Alsop. The Georgetown ladies were thrilled when the first lady came to call. A matron was said to have been so excited that she rented plants. The lunches were small, usually six women, which presented a problem for the hostess because who wanted to offend the uninvited seventh friend? One hostess imported her ladies from out of town.

The Reagans are more isolated now. They stay home a lot. So do their friends. Betsy Bloomingdale's husband, Alfred, is ill—she stays on the West Coast with him. The Annenbergs have given up their apartment at the Watergate. "After you've been to a few state dinners, heard 'Hail to the Chief,' and then the same Hollywood stories, you realize it's not all that interesting after all," a Washington hostess says. "It's really pretty dull."

Security is a problem. The shooting in March of 1981 has quieted the Reagans, spooked them. Even Carolyn Deaver, the wife of Michael Deaver, one of Reagan's "big three" aides, tells her friends she's nervous in crowds. The curse of the Libyan hit squad had caused even the most minor events to be covered with Secret Service. At a recent going-away party for White House aide Lyn Nofziger, with only a few Cabinet officers among the crowd, the Secret Service was at every door. "The President doesn't like to go out to dinner anymore," says Peter McCoy. "The entire neighborhood is blocked off, traffic is diverted, special phones have to be installed."

Security is not the only reason for the isolation. Washington has changed too. In the past, the White House has always set the tone for social Washington. A dinner was a disaster unless you had a certain mix: a senator, a coungressman, an influential journalist, maybe a TV personality, someone from an embassy or the State Department, *and* someone from the White House. Until Carter and Reagan, thirty years of Presidents had come from this Washington world. Even Ike came from the Washington military. These Presidents understood Washington, thrived on its social fabric of mutual favors and temporary admirations, its power eddies and subtle vibrations. Washington dinners are always subliminally about work. The Washington-dinner-party question is, "How does it cut?" In this Washington, for decades, the President was always the leader of the country club.

Watergate began to change this. The leader of the country club might have gone to jail. Journalists became more glamorous. The Fords clearly weren't there to stay. The Carters made an effort, but it didn't work. They were considered cornballs and hostile, parochial out-of-towners who felt that anyone going to parties, as Carter once said, "wasn't working hard enough."

Meanwhile, the rest of Washington made a discovery: It didn't need the White House so very badly. The Carters vanished to Georgia; the Reagans will ultimately be back near Beverly Hills. The permanent Washington—career politicians, Georgetown dowagers, journalists, arts figures—remains. The permanent Washington is mostly liberal. "We're a very inbred little southern town, with all those idiosyncrasies," a member of permanent Washington says. The Reagans' values isolate them even more from this terrain. "I was at a huge party last week," a first-rung Georgetown hostess says, "and I never heard the Reagans' name mentioned once. It was as if they didn't exist. People are finally beginning to realize how limited they are. I mean, who wants to talk about china?"

"The first lady's Georgetown lunches didn't really work," a Georgetown-watcher says. "There was no common language. However exciting it was to have the first lady in the house, finally nobody was won over." How could they have been? The Georgetown women are readers, women who live in eccentric old houses, who favor plain hair, talk, and pearls. This draws a social line. So do the Reagan policies. "Mrs. Reagan is not exactly the type to discuss her views on abortion over lunch," a hostess says.

So much easier to stay with one's own. You can see this in the Reagans' new pattern of entertaining. They still go out to dinner once in a while—for example, to George Will's house. But the guests around them are philosophically in tune. Or at least non-threatening: Jim Palmer, the pitcher, and the basketball coach from Georgetown University were invited to the Will dinner.

The White House screenings are non-threatening too. The Reagans schedule them frequently. Sometimes guests are invited for lunch and a movie on a Sunday afternoon. Conversation is not the point. Entertainment is. The President can enjoy the kind of diversion that makes Holmby Hills bearable. These long nights in the White House screening room have become a very big deal indeed. A while back George Will and Alexander Haig appeared on *This Week with David Brinkley.* Just before they went on the air, Will turned to Haig in a classic moment of one-upmanship. "How'd you like the movie?" he said.

Recently, a few guests at a screening of *From Mao to Mozart: Isaac Stern in China* were surprised to see David Begelman arrive for dinner. These guests of the President's have no trouble explaining away his loyalty to Frank Sinatra: It's based on history, campaign favors, Nancy's affection—she calls him Francis Albert. (He still drops in about once a month for dinner, but always without fanfare.) The guests can forgive Betsy Bloomingdale her old run-in with the New York Customs officials, her changing of the prices on her Paris tags. But David Begelman? An embezzler?

Reagan is relaxed in his screening room. He puts his feet up, asks his guests if they need to use the bathroom, waits to start the movie until everybody's returned. In front of each guest is a table with a silver bowl of popcorn. The President adores popcorn. After dinner, he works his way through his bowl and then moves Nancy's over and makes it two.

The state dinners are the centerpiece. Every President has

had his own state-dinner style. The Eisenhowers used to sit together, presiding over a long table. Jackie Kennedy broke up
the tables into Georgetown-style clusters of eight and ten.
The Carters' state dinners were like benefits. The Reagans'
are brilliantly organized and relaxed.

There are eight tables for twelve. From the moment a
guest arrives, every member of the staff is able to say, "May I
take your coat, Mr.———." There are cards for the entertainment, and, a guest says, "They really know how to move you
from room to room." There's not a lot of flexibility in these
state dinners: Most of the guests are diplomats and others
whose presence is dictated by the visiting head of state. The
balance is what tells you about a President, whom he wants to
flatter or confer favor upon (the guest lists are published in the
Washington Post). The Reagans' favors go to The Group or to
the Washington "green book"—a kind of social-political register—and, inevitably, to the Hollywood stars, the ones close
in age to the President. This mix is determined by Mrs. Reagan and her social secretary, Muffie Brandon, who comes
from the green-book world. So far the prime ministers of
Japan, Israel, and Great Britain, the presidents of Egypt and
Venezuela, and the kings of Jordan and Spain, among others,
have been entertained.

The state dinners cause comment too. It's not that Nancy
Reagan doesn't know how to give a dinner. She does. "She
asks the cook to prepare three sample menus and then decides," Peter McCoy says. She knows her table arrangements
and how to place the little Madison Avenue bud vases on a
mirror and accent them with tiny votive lights. She's cut the
size of the state dinners down from 130 guests to 96. She
knows her way around a green moiré tablecloth. In other
years, the waiters stumbled over chairs. Trays would often fly
across the State Dining Room. Now the after-dinner entertainment is just as perfectly organized: Everyone gets a chair.
Now you're seated to watch Robert Goulet work the room.

This is something new at the White House. The drinks before dinner are organized, too: You can have your choice—club soda, orange juice, white wine. All of this gets a lot of points with the Reagan social defenders, like the columnist Betty Beale.

Betty Beale defends the china policy too. "There was a lunch for Sandra O'Connor," she says, "and the coffee went right through Mrs. Lewis Powell's cracked cup. Another guest turned his cup over because he didn't want coffee, and there were chips all over the bottom. *Chips.* At the White House."

At any dinner, there are subtle shifts, turnings of the head for the famous, the neck arch to the man with power, the strain to hear his words. Kissinger monopolized his table, as did Nixon. Not Reagan. He hangs back, lets others talk. When he does talk, he often tells Hollywood stories or homilies: "I talked to a bus driver today and do you know what he told me?" The guests are usually taken aback: The talk is nonpolitical, non-Washington, convivial country club.

The guests come as a surprise. Old-time Hollywood: Cary Grant, Gordon MacRae, Jimmy Stewart. "It makes an even bigger circus out of what is already a circus," a guest says. "Once when Omar Sharif didn't show up, that's what everybody talked about all night." The politicians don't like this. "In the past year," says a former Reagan associate, "very few Reagan state chairmen have been invited to the White House. These guys put him in office. He's so uninterested in politics that all he does is socialize with people who never wanted him, the elitists who wanted Bush."

The former associate blames Muffie Brandon and Nancy Reagan for this. "Nancy Reagan doesn't feel comfortable around the polyester set," he says. Muffie Brandon and Nancy Reagan make a perfect pair. The social secretary became something of a figure in Washington when she married the London *Times* man Henry Brandon. It is a marriage so

old-fashioned that Henry Brandon used to dismiss her when
the dinner-party conversation would turn to politics. Even
now, when she works late at the White House, Muffie Brandon "gets hysterical if she's not at home to cook Henry his
dinner," a friend of hers says.

She is a nanny for Nancy Reagan too. Like the first lady,
she reveres appearances. "We do not wear pants. We do not
wear clogs. We represent our country," Brandon once told
Interview. Not long ago, she said, "The White House is having a tablecloth crisis." Now she no longer gives interviews. A
few weeks before she was hired, Muffie joined the Women's
National Democratic Club. A local column reported that
Pamela Harriman had pulled a few strings to get her in. Muffie was said to have called the club and announced that she
must resign. But, she insisted, she didn't want anyone gossip-
ing about it.

Jerry Zipkin has become important too. But something
strange has happened to him since he's become known as
Nancy Reagan's closest man friend, as he describes it, and a
semihousehold word. Le Zip has started to speak a peculiar
Park Avenue style of French. *"Je suis ici,"* he says on the telephone to his friends the moment he arrives in the capital. Jerry
Zipkin has never been so busy. His mother, whom he lived
with, passed away. Now he is free to devote himself to his
rental buildings and his other ladies: They all need, they say,
his flattery, his gossip, his ministrations, his advice on clothes
and shoes and hair. He's so busy he's become very formal,
necessarily precise.

"This is Jerome Zipkin," he said the other day on the telephone. "You know, you can't imagine what I am going
through. *Au fond,* I am a businessman. I am not just a dilet-
tante with nothing to do. Everyone is pursuing me. There was
a woman from *Newsweek* who sent me orchids and on the card
wrote, HOW CAN YOU NOT SEE ME AFTER I'VE SENT YOU OR-
CHIDS? They call me, they pursue me, at seven in the morning

and at midnight. Another woman followed me to Washington and waited to ambush me in the lobby of my hotel. She waited there till eleven-forty-five for me to come home, and then she left me a nasty note that said, I HAVE WAITED FOR YOU TO COME BACK TILL 11:45, AND NOW I WILL AWAIT YOUR CALL, WHICH I KNOW MAY NEVER COME. I can assure you she was right. All of these people who are pursuing me are just so devoid of *politesse*. Can you imagine that one of the people from another news magazine called me at seven, as I was leaving for dinner, and said, 'Please go through your picture file. I need some stills.' I said, 'When do you need these stills?' She said, 'Right now. Tonight.' She knew that I took pictures at parties. So I went through my files for her, but I just don't know what's happened to manners. I never wanted this attention."

"Nobody understands how Nancy can be friends with the First Fop," a Georgetown hostess says. "Zipkin is antithetical to everything this city stands for: true knowledge, earnestness, seriousness of purpose, work."

Zipkin has his defenders. The socialities have a way of praising him. "I've known him forever." "When my mother was sick he visited her every day." Like Muffie Brandon, Jerry Zipkin is discussed in nanny terms: the first one there with the chicken soup. "The first lady goes through hell in the White House," says Peter McCoy. "Anyone who makes her laugh shouldn't be begrudged."

The Nancy hug: Jerry gets it, that's for sure. So did author-artist Fleur Cowles at a recent do. The first lady stands at the entrance to the Blue Room. "Often, at a large reception, it is impossible to avoid her on your way to the waiting punch," says a guest. Nancy steps forward, takes a breath; her arms shoot in the air. "Fleur!" she cries. Then those arms find their target, seize it. They embrace. "You never know when to pull away," a first lady friend says. "She is that warm."

So all the friends say. In Washington now, the core group remains: There are staff friends and friend friends. One of the latter is Nancy Reynolds, a tough-minded former-senator's daughter, a Bendix Corporation executive. Nancy Reynolds knows her way around Washington—during the campaign she was Nancy Reagan's press secretary. They still go to lunch. A few people in Washington think the two Nancys haven't been so close since an article in *The New York Times* in the fall connected Nancy Reynolds to the Blair House-bugging leak. "That just isn't true," Nancy Reynolds says. "Nancy Reagan doesn't hold grudges. I've made a lot of goofs. My friends tolerate these shortcomings." "If Nancy Reagan pulled away from Nancy Reynolds," another friend says, "it would be a terrible mistake. She is the only one around the first lady who has the faintest idea of what is going on."

The Deavers—Carolyn and Mike—are the other crossover friends. Nancy Reagan depends on Michael Deaver for advice. He's a PR man from Los Angeles, a smoothy. He once worked his way around the world playing the piano. He and the first lady see eye to eye. Apparently, it was Deaver who organized the White House screening of *Reds,* which had most of the right wing of the President's party up in arms. He is a man with upper-middle-class tastes, a fondness for seed catalogs, who says, without embarrassment, "I'm going back into the private sector because I can't afford to live on sixty thousand dollars a year."

One night, the friends were out partying again. That day in Washington, the Air Florida flight had crashed into the Potomac during a snowstorm and seventy-eight people had been killed. The party went on as planned. It was the going-away party for Lyn Nofziger. Black-tie, of course. Nofziger was leaving under a slight cloud. The word had been out for months that he was persona non grata with the first lady. She hated his looks, his inelegant clothes, his views. Nofziger had been passed over for the press secretary's job.

Inelegance was everywhere: The party organizer was a St.

Louis promoter named Roy Pfautch, who so honored his friend's leaving that the announcement board at the Washington Sheraton said, ROY PFAUTCH'S PARTY. It was Pfautch's moment to profit by being close to power, and, in true Washington spirit, he wasn't going to let a plane crash slow a good time.

The theme was a circus, as in "Life's a circus when you know Lyn Nofziger," and a calliope was blasting in the frigid, moribund atmosphere. Mignon the elephant came out and stood with his sweeper, clowns circulated cotton candy and peanuts, but the mood was grotesque, surreal. Mr. and Mrs. William French Smith walked into the ballroom. That week he was under special fire because of the administration's decision that colleges that discriminate against blacks could claim tax-exempt status. He seemed perfectly cheerful. Smith, Reagan's former lawyer on the West Coast, was rewarded for his friendship with the job of attorney general. He has had to appoint a commission to advise him on the law. Never mind, he's very pleasant. Everyone is pleasant around the Reagans.

Was he concerned about the college-discrimination issue? "Not at all." He laughed, reached for a drink, his eyes fixed somewhere near Mignon. Then he said he was having a wonderful time in Washington and he loved going out a lot because "I have a fatal curiosity to go to all these events we shouldn't do."

At this point, Jean Smith arrived, and as the calliope blared, she chatted amiably. She was wearing a black lace dress studded with red jewels, and she looked like Spring Byington, her own feathers-by-Julius hair neatly in place. Jean Smith is pleasant too. She was saying that *she* was loving Washington because "all of us have been friends for so many years. It gives it a good feeling." As she spoke, her ruby-and-diamond earrings dangled prettily—later, she would angrily deny to the *Washington Post* that they were real. They looked very real.

Sometime during the first hour of the party, a dark, round-faced man appeared. He looked a little like Bebe Rebozo. He went from Cabinet officer to Cabinet officer, lavishing Hollywood-hello kisses on the wives. He seemed like a William Morris agent in a Tony Curtis film. This man was Charles Wick (President Reagan's closest Washington pal). Wick comes out of Hollywood too. His name used to be Zwick—he changed it to Charles Z. Wick—and for a while he worked as an arranger for Tommy Dorsey. After that, he was an agent. His main client was the band singer Frances Langford. Frances Langford married Ralph Evinrude, as in Evinrude Motors, and Evinrude and Wick went into the nursing-home business. He made a lot of money. Wick is now head of the International Communication Agency. In a way, that's show business too: Charles Wick now oversees the Voice of America.

In Wick's first year running ICA, the Voice of America's news director quit. Wick was said to be trying to turn the Voice of America into a propaganda machine. Maybe, like Franklin Roosevelt, Wick is just "trying to try something new." Like his television project, *Let Poland Be Poland,* which Wick has described as "the biggest show in the history of the world." Wick enlisted some experts for this effort: Charlton Heston and Frank Sinatra singing in phonetic Polish, all of which prompted a reporter to remark somewhat acerbically on the evening news, "Of all the European countries, only Luxembourg agreed to show it sight unseen." In any event, the program was dismissed as dull propaganda.

The Reagans spend a lot of time with the Wicks. Nancy Reagan and Mary Jane Wick brought their children up together. The Reagans went to the Wicks' apartment on Christmas Eve. Mary Jane Wick is very blond, very proper, also perfectly dressed, with a ready smile. She lives in a tight circle too: At the Lyn Nofziger party she was complaining about the paralysis from the snowstorm in Washington. "It took me two hours today to travel from the Watergate to the

Capitol Hill Club." In Washington, that route is a metaphor, a whole world. The Watergate is the Watergate. The Capitol Hill Club is where Mary Jane Wick raises money for her pet charity, Republicans Abroad. Mary Jane Wick is very sensitive to criticism: "Everyone is always needling us in the press. During the inaugural, I was so criticized because I told reporters everyone should wear white tie to show their respect. Well, I'm sorry, but the office of the President is the highest in the land."

The night of the first-anniversary dinner of the inaugural, Wick was in high spirits. He hovered around Betty Adams and the New York socialite, singing a Jerome Kern medley. The Reagans and the Wicks share a love for great American standards. He was still singing as he made his way out of the Washington Hilton ballroom, crooning in the ear of the New York socialite. She was loaded down with her party favors: *A Great New Beginning,* a commemorative volume complete with photos of Sinatra and Johnny Carson. Her Jelly Belly jelly beans balanced precariously in front of her, propped on top of the book. The book rested against her chest. "Oh, Charles, Charles," she called out. In the ballroom Marie Osmond was still singing. "Look," the socialite giggled, "I have my jelly beans!" The director of the International Communication Agency made a half-pirouette and then hummed the ending of "Make Believe." The socialite giggled again. So did Charles Wick. The President's best friend, at any rate, was having a splendid time.

February 1982

Holy War
on Park Avenue

*T*he most fashionable service of the Episcopal Church is traditionally held at eleven o'clock on Sunday mornings, and, recently, at such a service at St. Bartholomew's, things were pretty much the same way they've been all year. A sense of foreboding and an awful tension hung in the air. The church was almost filled, but, significantly, the pews the rich people used to rent were not—in line with the rector's policies, several bag ladies had sought shelter in them. The rector's sermon this particular Sunday was based on a parable, a lesson about God's gifts, by which the rector meant real estate, the very chunk they were praying on, at the corner of Fifty-first Street and Park Avenue. The rector was a commanding presence in his snowy robes as he intoned from the pulpit, "Jesus Christ died on the cross, and if we accept that gift, we have little choice but to accept this one, the land we sit on ... our resources." Then, the Reverend Thomas Dix Bowers, the rector of St. Bartholomew's, invoked his bishop, the highest authority in the diocese. "To make a parish an end in itself is garbage and blasphemy."

For a long time now, Father Bowers's weekly message has been some variation on this theme—the admonition not to place "bricks and mortar before human needs," the exaltation of the church's "new mission," which the rector sees as attending to the city's poor and to his own TV ministry. That mission, he says, can be carried out only with the millions of dollars that will come from leasing St. Bart's real estate. If only his parish could ignore the city's "architectural idolaters," as Father Bowers calls those who disagree with him, the congregation could go forward together. Going forward with Father Bowers's mission would mean tearing down the St. Bartholomew Community House, a city landmark directly adjacent to the church, so that a fifty-nine story glass skyscraper could rise above the last open space on midtown Park Avenue.

As the rector spoke, the ushers circled, white carnations in their lapels. They eyed each other coldly, as people who despise one another tend to do. Some of these men used to be close friends—confirmed together, groomsmen at one another's weddings. No more.

Now, St. Bart's is divided into factions, and they are in the midst of a new kind of holy war. Just that morning, before the eleven o'clock service, Marc Haas, the former senior warden of the vestry and a septuagenarian multimillionaire ex-partner of Allen & Company, had been doing some nasty name-calling before the ushers took their places in the church. During the sermon, outside on the steps, one of Haas's adversaries, a young investment banker, was telling his side of the story to WNEW-TV. This man, John Chappell, had been the head of the associate vestry and a member of the church Finance Committee until the rector fired him for his opposition to the church's building plans. Up in the chancel, Father Bowers was talking skyscrapers and soup kitchens, invoking the names of Bear Bryant and Charlotte Brontë to bring in the blasphemers.

So nobody even minded that later, during the recitation of the Nicene Creed, two gum-chomping TV cameramen lumbered up the aisle and trained their lights on the church's rose window, its rector, bag ladies, blacks, singles, and matriarchs in white gloves and veiled hats. The TV lights didn't bother the rector either. After communion and the singing of the final hymn, "Ora Labora," he marched up the nave. In front of the rose window, he turned, his arms thrust toward the heavens. His Virginia Tidewater tones boomed through St. Bart's. "For the gifts of God . . . go forth in the world rejoicing in the power of His spirit!"

For this church, the gifts of God have been considerable. St. Bartholomew's is located on one of the most valuable pieces of land in Manhattan, if not the world. It fronts on a full city block between Fiftieth and Fifty-first streets on the east side of Park Avenue. To the south sits the Waldorf-Astoria. By a conservative estimate, the property is worth between fifty million and a hundred million dollars. The church, of course, has never paid any tax. If it did, at the current rate, it would be paying something like five hundred thousand dollars a year. In 1967, the St. Bartholomew's complex—with its Byzantine church built to the design of Bertram Goodhue in 1919, the Community House erected nearly a decade later, and the terraces and the garden—was designated a city landmark. That means it cannot be touched without the approval of the Landmarks Preservation Commission. Inevitably, the buildings and the garden are described in lapidary terms: a jewel, a gem, a treasure. Their old-world scale has provided a pocket of serenity in a badly overcrowded part of town. It had always been thought that the city's landmark laws would be enough to protect St. Bart's complex from the wrecking ball. This may not turn out to be the case.

A lot of complicated and subtle issues have come to a head because of the location of the church, the personality and ambitions of Father Bowers, and the vagaries of the real-estate market. The rector and his vestry, the governing body of the church, have been offered a very rich deal by an English de-

veloper, Howard Ronson. His offer would be very good for
the church's treasury. But there's a problem with Ronson—he
has a cloudy past. The rector and the vestry say the church
cannot survive without Ronson's ground rent, but few people
believe that.

Many people in the parish are opposed to the rector's plan.
So are a lot of powerful people in the city. Critics ridicule it as
Bowers Towers. The controversy is not minor. The battle
over St. Bart's is the biggest landmark struggle since Grand
Central Terminal was in peril. This time, however, the issues
are very different. The rector insists that nothing less than the
separation of church and state is involved. The questions are
complex. Do religious institutions have the right to use their
own property to fund social programs in an era of disintegrating federal support? Does the city have the right to regulate
aesthetics and the quality of urban life? Are the church's pre-
rogatives more important than the city's? It comes down to a
Rashomon-like view of needs—whose and which—a conflict
between a church and the environment, between the city's
need for open spaces and its human needs. And as in every religious war, each faction is convinced that it is absolutely right.

If St. Bartholomew's is to be successful, the church will
have to steer the building proposal through a labyrinth of legal
and municipal procedures. First, the parish has to vote on the
proposal. Then, the bishop and the Standing Committee have
to approve the plan. They will make their ruling in the first
weeks of 1982. After that, the church's proposal heads for the
Landmarks Commission, and if the Landmarks Commission
refuses to change the Community House's status, the church
will go to the courts. The court fights will go on for years, but
if the church ultimately wins, yet another series of tangles will
begin.

The proposed building will require a zoning variance, and
that alone will take the church and its developer to the City
Planning Commission, and to a ULURP—a uniform-land-

use-review procedure. Then, the Board of Estimate will have to have a say. (Already the City Council has voted against the plan, and although its vote is only an opinion, it gives an indication of how the winds will blow.) The Board of Estimate is the only city body with the power to veto the plan. The church faces the board last. The fight is already getting ugly. The rector and the parish have had several sessions in the courts.

The rector is fighting so hard because he and the vestry think it's going to be worth it. Howard Ronson's deal would give St. Bart's at least $9.5 million each year for forty years. There are initial payments that add up to eleven million dollars—small for the size of the project—plus escalators and clauses for inflation. A substantial chunk would be budgeted for disbursement by the bishop. Whatever is left over, says the rector, would go to the church's mission—to programs to help the poor and to his TV ministry.

St. Bart's is already very active. There are daily noontime services, a celebrated music series, theology classes, a kindergarten, meetings of Alcoholics Anonymous, pool and exercise classes in the gym. The church keeps clothes closets and a food pantry to aid anyone who needs help, including New York's Vietnamese refugees. The Community Club has seventeen hundred members, most of them single. And the St. Bart's Players produce new shows every couple of weeks.

The rector wants to extend the church's mission far beyond this. His plan includes an Urban Training Center for the needy people of the Grand Central area—the bag people, the homeless, and the desperate. All of this is detailed in the church's vestry report. In it the rector and the vestry are quite clear about their mission: money for disaster victims abroad through religious charities, money for the city's indigent, money to go up to the bishop for the diocese. By moving the church forward with all this money, Father Bowers will actually be turning it back to the way it was in the past. In fact, he is turning it all the way back to 1888, when David Hummell Greer was rector. He too made it his duty to administer to what he called the "dark, dirty, prayerless, and Godless City" and its overwhelming needs.

Make no mistake, the rector is not backing down. He is not interested in the city's aesthetes and their nice social questions about land use, preservation, urban space, quality of architecture, quality of life. His main interest is not the last bit of blue sky left on Park. He says he doesn't care that his few millions will be a drop in the South Bronx bucket. He doesn't care about the current state of the law—he's ready to go all the way to the Supreme Court, he says, to fight for what he calls "justice" and the "separation of church and state." He knows that tearing down a landmark is against the law. He says, "We're going to change the laws."

If the church wins, it will be erecting a 719,000-square-foot reflecting-glass tower designed by Peter Capone, the president of Edward Durrell Stone Associates, a firm that has known better days. *The New York Times* has seen fit to run an architectural appraisal of the design on page 1: "The wrong building in the wrong place." Many of the city's fine architects refused to have anything to do with the plan.

But Tom Bowers is not a man who is easily discouraged. New to New York, he doesn't yet understand its intrictate social webs, who helps whom and why—how, at the first sign of trouble, the city's powerful band together like a thousand mercury beads. The rector's populist style is new to New York too. He can be a povertician, ruthless, disingenuous, mean as hell—there's a lot of Jimmy Carter in him. He can say strange things. The other day, Father Bowers was moved to remark about two of his adversaries, Jackie Onassis and Brooke Astor, "You think those two care about poor people? They despise poor people. Do you think Mrs. Astor thinks about Harlem? Do you think Mrs. Onassis knows what it is to starve?"

Very few Episcopalian rectors talk this way—particularly about Brooke Astor, probably the most important civic and philanthropic presence in New York. But Bowers is unusual. He loves a double martini, dinner parties, lunch at "21." A very earthy man, he has a terrific sense of humor and a lot of southern charm. He's a great friend of Liza Minnelli's—the wedding scene in *Arthur* was filmed at St. Bart's. He's also a big liberal, very much in the style of the 1960's, so he's right in psychological harmony with New York City's activist Episcopal bishop, the Right Reverened Paul Moore, Jr. The bishop and the rector both spend a lot of time with the rich, but say they want to help the poor. The bishop seems to be backing the rector completely—an important fact in this battle. So is the nature of the rector's tactics. Bowers is probably the first rector in the history of his sect to file a lawsuit against some of the most loyal members of his church.

The proposed demolition of the Community House has become a flash point for the city. A lot of very important people are involved, some pro, some con. Many religious figures in the city have signed a statement backing the project. Leading the opposition are Philip Johnson, the dean of American architects, and *New Yorker* theater critic Brendan Gill, a defender of city landmarks. Along with Jackie Onassis and Brooke Astor, they have formed a committee to oppose the plan. These four may sound a little rarefied to be very effective, but they can ring up Punch Sulzberger, at *The New York Times*, governors, corporate chiefs. Before the battle was joined, Mrs. Onassis gave a luncheon at her apartment for the city's editors. The results have been visible in the attentions of the press.

That committee is one of two. The other grew out of the Municipal Art Society under the leadership of its energetic president, Ralph Menapace. Menapace, a prominent corporate lawyer, knows his way around the powerful. He will be a very tough foe, indeed. The peripheral characters are interesting, too: Walter Hoving, retired chairman of Tiffany's; Donald Trump, real-estate developer; Lewis Rudin, another real-estate man; the City Council; the rector of St. Thomas Episcopal Church on Fifth Avenue and Fifty-third Street; the community planning board.

And this is *outside* the parish. Inside, the opponents are equally strong. At the center of the opposition is J. Sinclair Armstrong, active in Episcopalian causes, a former chairman of the Securities and Exchange Commission, an early supporter of Ike's. Armstrong, an elegant figure in his mid-sixties, has a tremendous amount of energy and tastes that run to a Brigade of Guards mustache, loden fedoras, and ties of tartan plaid. Armstrong was baptized at St. Bart's. For a while, he left the parish because his good friend the bishop asked him to take charge of rebuilding the burned-out St. Mark's in the Bowery. He did. Now, he's back at St. Bart's, and he and the bishop have had a falling-out over his activities there. Armstrong is a product of Milton Academy, Harvard, Harvard Law. His grandfather was one of the founding partners of Charles Scribner's Sons, and one of the many ironies of his situation is that Charlie Scribner, Jr., now sits on the vestry and is one of "Sinc" Armstrong's most determined foes.

Helping out Armstrong are the Chappell brothers, John and Donald. These two men are one generation younger, active in business—John is in oil and gas, Donald at Fiduciary Trust Company. Before the rector arrived, the Chappells were good bets to take over the leadership of St. Bart's. Donald Chappell had been the head usher. John ran the associate vestry. The rector has seen to it that they are no longer in these roles. Within the parish there is a lot of additional opposition, some of it from famous names: Lillian Gish, Mrs. Douglas MacArthur, and old New York families—Livingston, Morris, and Bristol, as in Bristol-Myers.

What they are doing is revolutionary—and agonizing. They are going against their rector. This is not done in the

Episcopal Church. The normal practice is simply to change parishes if you disagree. Episcopalians are too well bred to make a fuss. But many of the parishioners have been part of the church for generations. They see themselves as fighting for St. Bart's very life.

Their foes, of course, are the rector and the vestry. It's unfortunate for the church that the seventeen men and women who make up its governing body are not as well connected or as urbane as those on the other side. At recent question-and-answer sessions on the issue, the vestry members have been pretty rude. Answering polite inquiries with a snap: "We don't get into that." Ignoring questions. They act like bully-boys under siege. But they've brought out their own reinforcements for this fight: lawyer John Zuccotti to represent them and Landauer Associates to do the real-estate deal. They've hired a PR firm. The former senior warden, Marc Haas, is said to be operating very much in the background. Haas is so rich that years ago he sold his stamp collection for eleven million dollars. Born Jewish, he was baptized by the last rector of St. Bart's. Now, his navy Rolls-Royce can be seen parked in front of the church each Sunday morning. He and the new rector are extremely close.

Both sides are slinging a lot of mud. Sometimes it gets silly. The rector has accused Sinclair Armstrong—among others—of being paid off by Lewis Rudin. Rudin owns the building next door. The other day, at a demonstration in front of the church, a former vestryman, Alan Sanford, started screaming that Sinclair Armstrong and the Chappells were "liars and frauds." Alan Sanford had been in John Chappell's wedding. The opposition has its innings too: Talk of megalomania, deception, maybe Swiss bank accounts. They too accuse the other side of fraud.

The tangle of personalities is very interesting, but so are the times they have chosen to tangle in. Causes have their fashionable periods too. At the moment, the needs of the underclass are less fashionable than urban preservation. The Victorian Society flourishes, the South Bronx languishes. A lot of traditional liberals and city elitists have shifted their focus from the poor to the inanimate. A certain fear of the poor, the illegitimate, the wounded city has set in. A lot of courageous people now feel stymied, powerless, overwhelmed. They have seen their causes atrophy. It is a time to burrow in, and that means trying to make sure the society's physical heritage doesn't slip away as well. With his concern for the black poor and the bag ladies, the rector is pitching a hard cause at a hard time.

There is a claustrophobia as well. The skyscrapers seem to shoot up like concrete weeds. The next decade will see twenty-five percent more people clogging the midtown streets. The powerlessness that liberals feel is italicized by the very real diminishing quality of city life. So, the paradox: The city's liberals are acting like conservatives, insisting that no money can come from skyscrapers even if the proceeds are destined for the poor. And the Episcopal Church is acting populist, even radical—its own charitable interests conveniently allied with the goals of the real-estate operators.

Like a lot of other churches, St. Bart's is having problems. It still has a large endowment—$12.5 million—but it no longer has the powerful congregation or social cachet of St. James's or St. Thomas's. Forty years ago, social status in New York meant a pew at St. Bart's and a box at the Met. The previous rector, Dr. Terence Finlay, was so traditional that he felt it would be vulgar to institute an Every Member Canvass, and the parishioners were rarely called upon to vote on anything.

So, at the behest of several members of the vestry, the bishop of New York brought in Tom Bowers. Bishop Moore wanted, so he told Sinclair Armstrong, to shake up a dying parish. Soon after Bowers arrived, he decided that the church should take a look at its property. It did. In September 1980, Father Bowers let it slip to the congregation that the church was considering a hundred-million-dollar offer to knock down everything—the church, the gardens, the Community House. That might have been an exaggeration—a former senior warden says there never was any such offer—but it was the beginning of the storm.

Before St. Bart's, the rector had been in Atlanta at St. Luke's, a downtown church for the city's rich that also had seen better days. Tom Bowers was very successful in Atlanta. He was a civil-rights crusader. Several powerful Atlantans backed him up, among them Anne Cox Chambers, director of Cox Broadcasting, the owner of the Atlanta *Constitution,* a woman of great power and prestige. Mrs. Chambers helped to launch Jimmy Carter on the national scene, and, in a way, she helped to launch Father Bowers too. In Atlanta, the rector's soup kitchens, new prayer books, communion for children, and success on TV helped to enliven a very wobbly St. Luke's. Bowers had a lot of clout in that arena. "Hell," he said in his office, "in Atlanta I could have just called up somebody with a lot of money or one of the judges and said, 'Will you intercede for me and get them off my back?' Here I can't do that. I don't have the connections."

He was an unlikely candidate to be a priest. His father sent him to Virginia Military Institute because he thought "I was a discipline problem." It was, he says, "like a prison." The shock of fighting in Korea made him take stock of himself. When he came home, he went back to school, to Sewanee, where he took a theology course that inspired him. He was on his way. He started off in Virginia and then moved to Washington, D.C., before going to St. Luke's. In Atlanta, at the height of his success, he was approached to run for mayor. Instead, he turned to television, and that same energy that could have run a city made him a religious star on TV. He hesitated about coming to New York. "I knew I would be hated here. My style is so different," Bowers said. He made a lot of demands—use the modern prayer book, abolish the rented pews, bring in black ministers, women staff.

Father Bowers feels that if St. Bart's is going to survive it has to deal with the modern world: "Take away the focus from the fuddy-duddy social prestige of the old style. It must become the true body of Christ. There's nothing wrong with rich people in the parish," he says, "but I want another world to creep in."

That world could creep in with the help of his TV ministry. At times, the rector says, he would be happy to provide an alternative to Jerry Falwell—just give him a few TV cables and a public-access station. Other times, he says, as he did at a recent party, "I want to be like Fulton Sheen." The whole notion of an Episcopalian going on television is against type enough to be seductive to the rector. One motive for everything he does is his delight in the shock of the new. "When I tell some of those bishops about the TV thing, they look at me like I am tacky, but it goes beyond tacky. They don't know what I am talking about. They don't understand that the implications of TV for the conventional religious world are staggering. They think it's something a southern Baptist would do. You know what I don't understand? Why does every Episcopalian have to be so sweet and phony all the time?"

At the moment he was asking this, we were in his office at St. Bart's. It's a plush place, appropriate for an old-style Episcopalian. The curtains are red damask. The paneling is dark. For all the rector's talk about helping the poor, it's clear he likes a little privilege too. On his desk is a picture of his daughter taken when she came out—in fact, just next door at the Waldorf—at the International Debutantes Ball.

The rector's apartment on Park Avenue is owned by the church. It's worth close to $750,000 in the same real-estate market he wants to plunge into. The maintenance alone is $3,000 a month. Father Bowers has made no attempt to sell that asset or to move to more modest rented digs. Why should he? He needs a place to entertain. He is, after all, the rector of St. Bartholomew's and must move gracefully among the rich. Father Bowers sees no irony in his stance. His solution: Mount a fierce attack.

At Jackie Onassis, for one. "The other day," says Bowers, "I got a letter which was an announcement of that committee with its four chairmen: Philip Johnson, Brendan Gill, Jackie Onassis, and Brooke Astor. The famous, the rich, the powerful. It is tragic and pathetic that these people are the heroes of our city. Well, I refuse to be crushed by them." He's started to insult them from the chancel because he feels betrayed. "This summer, when I heard about Mrs. Onassis's lunch, I wrote her a note. She came for tea. She listened to everything I said, and then I got this letter. She's a Kennedy. How can she act this way?"

A lot of people ask this same question about Father Bowers. The rector's operating style is very, very tough. At the first sign of opposition last fall, he brought a legal action against six of his parishioners, claiming their group, the Committee to Preserve St. Bartholomew's, was a trick to siphon off contributions to the church. In his complaint, the rector said that the committee members would be "personally liable" for all the church's losses. This was ridiculous. "I had no idea that a rector could sue his parishioners," Sinclair Armstrong says. "Suddenly, I had the specter of all my savings vanishing because of my stance on a building," says John Chappell.

One of the committee members was an elderly woman named Margery Brown. Mrs. Brown is a widow; her husband had been a minister. She's been a parishioner for twenty-two years. No matter. Before Christmas, Mrs. Brown was at home when she got a phone call from the law firm, Milbank, Tweed, Hadley & McCloy. "A young lawyer was on the phone and he told me that he had a subpoena for me and that he wanted to deliver it. I told him that I had to go out shopping and I live in Queens. He got very nasty. He told me that if I didn't wait there for him it would go hard on me with the judge. I was shaking when I got off the phone." Other members were served at their offices, and on the morning after his father died, Sinclair Armstrong spent a solid two days in court.

When his slate of candidates won a vestry election, the rector said of his opposition, "We blew 'em in the weeds." Paul Goldberger, *The Times*'s architecture critic, was attacked from the chancel. The day after Judge Edward Greenfield ruled against the church on a procedural question, Bowers remarked at a party, according to one of two witnesses, "He's getting paid off under the table." Bowers vehemently denies saying this, and the judge, hearing about it, said, "It's hardly worth dignifying with a remark. Obviously, this was an intemperate statement made in the heat of the moment." About the city's landmark laws, Bowers has said, "It's just like Nazi Germany here. I know I'll get in trouble for saying this, but I don't care. The laws are confiscatory."

"This building proposal is being pushed with the ruthlessness of a corporate takeover," Donald Chappell says. The voting rolls of the church, says Chappell, somehow have mysteriously shrunk from two thousand to six hundred. "Anyone who is oppposed to him he bullies out," says Chappell. Some stand up to the rector. When Donald Chappell announced his opposition, the rector phoned him. "You are fired as head usher," he said. Sinclair Armstrong called his friend Bishop Moore. He said, "Tell Father Bowers to cool it." That time Bowers did. Chappell served three more weeks, until he sent off his first letter to the parish. Then, "I received a nasty letter firing me again. He never even thanked me for my three and a half years of service."

The rector retorts, "You're darn right I got rid of him. I'm not going to have anyone at the door saying demonic things about me. He is supposed to be my representative." Donald's brother John was relieved of his duties on the Finance Committee. After twenty years, the associate vestry—which

Chappell recently headed—was abolished. "He did it in an odd way. He waited till just before summer when everyone was going away and then he just announced it. There was no reason, no discussion. We were all incredulous. He knew that as younger men we might give him a harder time. So he just knocked us out."

"Our Lord spoke very strongly too," the rector says. "Let me tell you something: I don't think I have been strong enough. I haven't been as bad as I am going to be. The committee is the one taking the under road here. Well, I am responding in kind. Look at the New Testament. It's filled with dissension."

"I don't know why everyone here is so agitated about Tom's tactics," says a friend from the South. "He's always been like this." "There are clergy and there are clegy," Bowers says. "The opposition has all bought into the politics of riches and greed. I care about the poor." Margaret Bowers, the rector's wife, was overheard in church. "You know Tom," she said with a smile. "He plays very dirty when he gets crossed." She was smiling at the time.

However Father Bowers may decide to play, he is going to have to consider his problems with the laws. Almost certainly, the Landmarks Commission will refuse to change St. Bartholomew's status—that procedure is called de-designation—and the church will have to go to court. The landmark laws are clear enough: To change a landmark's status, the owners must prove they are suffering hardship in trying to maintain it. Thus, in the case of Grand Central Terminal, it wasn't enough that the Penn Central was going bankrupt—maintaining the terminal wasn't the cause of its financial problems. Not-for-profit institutions are governed by even stricter standards.

Is St. Bartholomew's hard up? It's difficult to tell. Like most institutions these days, the church is having problems—the

most recent deficit was $325,844. But St. Bart's does have the
$12.5 million endowment, larger than that of most
churches—including the bishop's seat, the Cathedral of St.
John the Divine.

Two months ago, the vestry of St. Bart's issued a thick report that sought to explain its financial situation. The white
paper, "Securing the Future of St. Bartholomew's Church and
Its Ministry," claims that without relief the church will run
out of money sometime around 1989. But St. Bartholomew's
auditors, Main, Hurdman & Cranstoun, weren't involved in
the projections, and they aren't sure how the church arrived at
its figures. For a long time, the church refused to disclose any
of its financial data. By contrast, each year St. Thomas's pub-
lishes a statement that looks, according to a St. Thomas parishioner, "like the GM annual report." Every contributor
and every minor expense is listed.

Not so at St. Bart's. At first, Father Bowers said he could
not open the books because the accounting methods were ar-
chaic. Then the vestry said it would have the figures "re-
stated." Finally, the vestrymen released an accounting of sorts
in their white paper. Many items are lumped together—the
clergy's and the maintenance men's salaries, for example. The
vestry report does include a highly controversial schedule of
repairs claimed to be necessary for the church—seven million
dollars worth.

For example: In the report, fully one million dollars in re-
pair funds is earmarked for work to appease the fire department. The fire department says there are no violations
outstanding at the church. The city does require that a
sprinker system be installed, but an engineer retained by the
anti-Bowers faction reported that all the church needed was
that sprinkler system and it would cost about fifty thousand
dollars.

John Andrew, the rector of St. Thomas's, has talked about
the St. Bart's proposal from his chancel. He said, in effect,

"We've got a valuable piece of property too, and we've never received an offer for it. If we did, I could assure you we wouldn't take it, even if it was one hundred million dollars."

A killing in the real-estate market would provide all the things St. Bart's says it needs. His prestige ensured in the diocese, Father Bowers could take his hat out of his hand. The rector is not a man who likes to spend his time asking anybody for money. Some of his wealthiest parishioners have never been asked to help the Community House. The fund raising has been limited to the minimal Every Member Canvass.

What happened with the International Telephone and Telegraph offer may be symptomatic. A year ago, an ITT executive had several casual talks with the rector. ITT's headquarters is across the street, and its concern was to keep Park Avenue very much the same. So the executive offered—casually—to give the rector fifty thousand dollars a year for a decade and to try to get other corporations up and down the avenue to do the same. The offer wasn't made in a formal way, but the rector never pursued it. Father Bowers said, "I finally told them, 'You are asking us to mortgage our property for fifty thousand dollars.' " He preferred to do things his own way. Several months ago, St. Bart's auditors wrote to Father Bowers suggesting that he go back through the church's vestry-restricted funds and see if any of them could be freed. Bowers didn't follow up this either.

Then there was the matter of transferring the air rights over the Community House—another option gone astray. Essentially, the owner of a low building can sell the air rights to the owner of a plot immediately adjacent—permitting the buyer to erect a taller building than he otherwise could. Lew Rudin, who owns the building directly east of the Community House, says the church offered him the air rights in 1978, but the city rejected the arrangement. Then, says Rudin, Marc Haas asked him whether he would donate a three-million-dollar addition to the Community House. Rudin said no.

There has been talk that the rules might be waived to let the church transfer the air rights to a developer on, say, Lexington Avenue. One major realtor, Cross & Brown, tried to pursue this with St. Bart's but got nowhere—and John White of Landauer Associates, the church's real-estate consultant, did not try again, presumably because an air-rights deal would bring St. Bart's only a fraction of what the rector's building plans would yield.

"We have tried our own fund raising here," Father Bowers says, "but New York is tricky. Everybody is trying to set us up. The Municipal Art Society said it would raise a hundred twenty-five million dollars, but I know I'll never see that money. People come to see us and say they will give us twenty-five million dollars if we'll be good little boys. Then I ask them to sign a pledge card and they get angry and run out the door." Some of those pledges might have a few strings attached—for instance, the one from Walter Hoving. Years ago, he was senior warden of the St. Bart's vestry. Hoving told friends that he would personally give the church one million dollars and help to raise another twenty-five million dollars on one condition: Bowers would have to go. (Walter Hoving says this isn't exactly true. "The rector came to see me. Money was not discussed. I told him what my feelings were about the building. I resigned my position there because I don't agree with [the vestry's] ideas.")

Father Bowers says he has explored every possible alternative to tearing down the Community House. He uses the example of the Every Member Canvass. "Only eleven percent of our yearly income comes from tithing," he says. But the Every Member Canvass is only two years old. Already its contribution level is up forty percent—even without the help of the large section of the parish opposed to the rector's plans. A well-known New Yorker went to see Father Bowers some time ago. "I wanted to see if there was a coalition I could put together to help get them some money," he says. "I came away from that meeting with a very bad feeling. It was clear to me that the rector was not interested in my help. It seemed as if he had every intention of just knocking the building down."

Originally, the church put most emphasis on "hardship"— perhaps with an eye on the Landmarks Commission requirements. Now, the church is focusing more on its right to use its assets to further its ministry. The church says the legal issue here is embedded in the Constitution: the separation of church and state. "If they refuse to de-designate us, it's a constitutional issue of the deepest kind," the rector says.

The first legal skirmish erupted in the fall of 1981. The rector and the vestry found themselves in New York State Supreme Court, where the legality of the parish vote on the building proposal was challenged—successfully, it turned out—by Sinclair Armstrong and his committee. The vestry had argued a form of separation in this case. Justice Greenfield was very direct. "The argument of the church that 'constitutional principles of separation of church and state require this court to refrain from interfering in purely internal church affairs' is specious indeed!" he ruled. "When it comes to temporal matters, the church is obliged to 'render unto Caesar the things that are Caesar's.' Nothing could be more temporal and of this world than a proposed multimillion-dollar sale of a valuable parcel of New York realty."

The vestry report deals with the architecture of the proposed building too. "No one can be said to place greater emphasis on maintaining the architectural integrity of the church building and our landmark site than the present rector and vestry," the report reads. So concerned were Bowers and the vestry that they brought in Robert Geddes, the dean of the School of Architecture at Princeton, to advise them on their plans. Geddes has a distinguished practice in Princeton and Philadelphia but has never designed any big buildings in New York. He says he felt it was his "duty" to take the job. But his counterpart at Yale, Cesar Pelli, felt no such duty. Pelli is fa-

miliar with New York. At the moment he is working on the
tower that will rise above the Museum of Modern Art. "It
would be a disaster," says Pelli of the St. Bart's plan. "It's a
matter of conscience."

Geddes doesn't think so. He had been approached, he says,
by the rector and a committee from the vestry. The inspiration may have come from Marc Haas, who is a 1929 graduate
of Princeton and is said to be one of its major benefactors.
"Morally, I did not believe that I could say no to a vestry that
asked for help from the dean of an architectural school,"
Geddes said recently. He agreed to meet with the various architects working with the developers who had shown interest
in the sight. He drew up a report and expressed his feelings
about light and space. Because of time pressures, the competing architects were given only a few weeks to come up with
their plans.

Geddes was helpful. He suggested to some of the architects
that they use a "harmonious" facade on the skyscraper. He
did not mention glass. So it came as a surprise to many people
when Geddes picked as his first choice the design done by
Peter Capone of Edward Durrell Stone's firm. As it happened,
Capone's developer, Howard Ronson, had offered the most
attractive package too.

Capone's solution was a slim reflecting-glass structure on
the site of the Community House that would cantilever out
toward the domed church building. Geddes says that his own
concerns were "theological, architectural, and civic." "I realize there were strong feelings about it," he says. "But Mr.
Capone's work will have to stand on its own."

Father Bowers calls Capone's design "magnificent" and
"our gift to the city." He is fond of saying how Bertram
Goodhue was not appreciated in his day either. From the talk
it is possible to believe that the huge tower will be as delicate
in appearance as a footprint left by Peter Pan. That word—
footprint—is often used to describe how the building will fade

into the background of the church. The building's champions point with pride to the way Capone was able to tack on the facade of the present Community House at the base of the new building. However the model looks, it is necessary to imagine a building somewhat like the Grand Hyatt looming over St. Bart's, overpowering the domed church and delicate garden.

Will the building reflect its surroundings, as Capone suggests? Probably not. A first principle of architecture is that the angle of incidence equals the angle of reflection. Thus, on a crowded street like Park Avenue, the only way to see the church's reflection may be from a very high story of a nearby building. Capone denies this. "The underside of the cantilevers will be mirrored too," he says.

You have to feel sorry for Peter Capone. He is going against a dozen of his craft's most revered practitioners in a field that marries reality to art. It takes a certain mind-set to be able to cross mandarins like Philip Johnson or to ignore the bitching in architectural circles that he has become a "pariah," desperate for his own major commission in New York. The New York chapter of the American Institute of Architects is supporting Ralph Menapace.

"We are not in it for the bucks," Peter Capone says. "I am in it because of my responsibilities to the profession. The building means a lot to me." Capone had been Stone's protégé. He studied architecture at Pratt. He is only forty-one, but since Stone's death he has run things and owns, he says, a great deal of the firm. Stone's successor still respects his principles. "The old man always used to say, 'Keep an open mind.'" Capone says he wanted to turn the job down. "Then I thought about it. It would have been a lot easier for us to just walk away."

Some weeks ago, Philip Johnson was in his office in the Seagram building, a paragon of modern taste that he designed. Johnson had not yet seen the sketch of the proposed St. Bart's building. It was put in front of him as he sat at his conference table, the whole East Side of Manhattan thirty-seven stories below. Through his round glasses, he peered at the architectural "section" that seemed to show the Capone building projecting out toward part of the dome. An ominous quiet came over the room. When he finally spoke, his voice was grave. "It would be preferable to tear the church down. They have been very clever to do the proper kinds of renderings so it will not look overpowering, but clearly the building will hang over the dome. To overhang a church is to kill it." He paused. "Can you imagine erecting a glass tower over St. Peter's?"

If the project and its design are controversial, the developer, Howard Ronson, is more so. Originally, says John White, who made the deal, "there were nine developers who expressed interest. That group was then narrowed to three." The church was asking for a lot—about two thousand dollars a square foot. The lease was to be for a hundred years, at the end of which the church would get eleven million dollars early and more than five hundred million dollars in tax-free funds over the first forty years. In the final bidding the developers were the Cohen brothers; Donald Trump and his partner, Peter Kalikow; and Howard Ronson with his partner, Hal Rosen. John White had been approached by Marc Haas to represent the church. White says he had other reasons too. "I am personally committed to mission and outreach," he says. So too was he committed to finding the highest bidder for the rights to lease the land. That was Ronson, who was willing to make a fifty-million-dollar personal guarantee. It was terrific for Ronson when Robert Geddes decided he liked his design best as well.

Ronson has been buffeted about for his earlier activities in England. St. Bart's public-relations firm, Brennan and Brennan, recently issued a three-page statement about him: "To Set the Record Straight on Howard Ronson." This statement was an addendum to the four pages already circulated. The record is still not exactly straight. In England, the Ronson family is very secretive. But a decade ago, the English papers paid some attention to them. There are two Ronson families in England, ruled by brothers. One of these families controls the Heron Group, a vast complex of gas stations, car dealerships, and real estate. Howard Ronson's first cousin heads that group and his name, Gerald, is the same as Howard's father's. Often the families are confused. They are in no way connected in business. In fact, Howard's cousin Gerald told *The Guardian,* "We haven't had anything to do with the other side of the family in twenty years."

It was up to young Howard to prove himself in a family real-estate business that was far less grand than his cousin's. Howard can be very cavalier. Recently, when asked where he had attended university, he replied, "Carmel College," which is actually a private religious boarding school for Jewish boys thirteen to eighteen—a secondary school. From Carmel, Howard went right into the family business—"Like most twenty-year-olds I didn't have a lot of experience." Howard ran into problems, he says, when his father asked him to "liquidate two of the companies." Those companies had creditors, and when they didn't get paid, the creditors went to the Department of Trade, an outfit that Ronson calls a "nonlegal body." In fact, while not a judicial agency, the department functions very much like the Federal Trade Commission in the United States.

The investigation lasted seven years—a fact that is not especially meaningful, since in England, as slowly as life moves, so do the activities of the Department of Trade. But the result was intriguing: The sixteen hundred-page Department of Trade report "drew attention to evidence of fraud," according to *The Guardian,* which quoted the report as saying that Ronson's father was "misled by avarice and overoptimism." *The Guardian* said that the Ronsons were probably guilty of "a ruthless pursuit of profit without any adequate capital resources to justify it." And of Howard Ronson the report stated, "He mirrored and enlarged his father's arrogance." All of which led the Department of Trade to conclude there was "evidence from which a court might infer" the company intended to "defraud its creditors."

Howard Ronson has been fairly shy about seeing the New York press. Our meeting took place in his apartment, just off Fifth Avenue in the Seventies. It is a quiet building with just the right amount of marble. The decorators have been hard at work upstairs. It has smoked-glass walls, flannel-covered divans, sprays of Madison Avenue-arranged lilies. Next to the mantel is the predictable collection of silver-framed portraits—in this case, the architectural renderings of ten Howard Ronson projects in New York.

He is a large man who strains the confines of his Turnbull and Asser shirt. On a red-lacquered chinoiserie cocktail table in front of him was a collection of sterling trowels, souvenirs of European ground breakings. After the Department of Trade report, Ronson found it easier to work outside of England. Three years ago, he moved here. In New York, there has already been a lawsuit over two of the developments he shared with the William Kaufman organization. The people there found him "impossible." An architect who has worked with Ronson recently said, "It was a very bad experience. He was the kind of man who cut every corner, who would say, 'Why do you need eight elevators for this building when four would do?' "

In a one-hour meeting, Ronson was very smooth. He said he had paid off his creditors in England—five hundred thousand dollars was involved. Only once did he betray any emotion—on the subject of Donald Trump. His partner, Rosen, made an innocuous comment—"Donald Trump is acting like a jilted lover"—prompted by word that Trump has a theory that the St. Bart's tower deal will never get made. As I wrote this down, Ronson scowled furiously at his partner, looking a bit like an enraged Sydney Greenstreet. Then, once again, his face became as cool as glass. He said, "If the deal falls through, I'll be out two million dollars." He said this was not worrying him. In fact, he sounded philosophical. "It would be a tragedy if St. Bart's went bankrupt, because if it did, someone else will just tear it down and put up another tower there."

Father Bowers is philosophical too on the subject of Howard Ronson. "Every developer," he says, "has had these kinds of shady things in his past."

Even if the parish approves, it will be years before Ronson gets to put up his tower. The first step is the vote. Then Bishop Moore must make his ruling. The bishop says he is neutral. He refused to be interviewed for this article, even on the telephone. "I don't want to see anything I might say used against me in the courts," he said.

In private, the Right Reverend Paul Moore does not seem so neutral. The bishop is, in that fine vernacular of the 1960's, an "activist." He marched with Martin Luther King and against the Vietnam War. The rector and his bishop believe in the same kinds of things. But at the moment Paul Moore is also involved in building plans. He's trying to raise twenty million dollars to continue the work on the Cathedral of St. John the Divine's twin Gothic spires.

The diocese could use money now. Dozens of the city's Episcopal churches are struggling; their congregations have died off, moved away. Moore and Bowers reason that by aiding impoverished churches they will be aiding the poor of those neighborhoods as well.

In November 1980, Bishop Moore invited his old friend Sinc Armstrong up to the cathedral for tea. The bishop and Sinc Armstrong have known each other a very long time. They share similar backgrounds, schools and clubs. The bishop's family started Continental Can Company; for years his brother ran Bankers Trust. The bishop and Sinc Armstrong share a kind of shorthand and a history—the work at

St. Mark's in the Bowery and in Businessmen for Peace. "At tea, he asked me if my reason for the opposition to the St. Bart's plan was because I did not approve of the rector," remembers Armstrong. "He told me, 'I understand people don't like him because of his outreach programs, but I brought him here to shake up a parish that was essentially dead.' I said to him, 'Paul, have you got a financial interest in this project?' He said, 'Yes, I do.' The bishop said to me, 'Sinc, Trinity Church has a lot of land on Wall Street, and they support many churches in the diocese. I have five well-heeled churches, ten churches that are scraping along, and forty or so churches that cannot make ends meet. Bowers has promised to give me some of the money, and I expect to get twenty percent.' "

The deal has been sweetened considerably since Paul Moore asked Sinclair Armstrong up for tea. In the vestry report, the diocese is budgeted to receive thirty-three and a third percent of the proceeds from the lease. Before this white paper was published, Sinclair Armstrong sent the bishop a detailed memo about the rector and his tactics. "We had another three-hour meeting with the bishop," Armstrong says. "He said he deplored our criticism of Bowers and disagreed with our outlook. He said he thought Bowers had come up with a wonderful idea. We came away knowing that we did not have a chance with him."

"In that meeting in March the bishop said he would not rule on *any* of it until the church had all the government approvals. He even asked an adviser he had at the meeting, 'Don't you think I should wait for the approvals?' " Armstrong said. "It was pure sophistry and nothing else."

"What about the bishop's role in your tactics?" I asked the rector a few days later. Tom Bowers smiled. "Well," he said, "he sure hasn't told me to stop."

The other day, Father Bowers was not feeling in top form. Twenty-four hours earlier, Judge Greenfield had handed down his opinion. The evening before, there had been a rally against his plans at the Seventh Regiment Armory, up Park Avenue, and hundreds of people had shown up. That day had been busy. In the morning, the rector went ahead with the scheduled balloting even though the morning papers headlined the news that the courts had forbidden it. At the church, Father Bowers was very specific. "The only way I've heard about this thing is in the *Daily News*. You know how the newspapers are." In fact, says Leland Greene, the assistant to Judge Greenfield, he had spoken to the church's lawyer the day before. "I called him and told him about the judge's opinion and that there would be an injunction."

The next morning Bowers looked very, very down. "This fast track of New York is getting to be too much for me," he said. "I didn't think it would be this hard." For a moment, he seemed quite vulnerable sitting there in his paneled office, his boyish face grown puffy, his eyes tired, a little sad. The rector had walked me into his inner chamber by way of a small waiting room. In it hung a century's worth of oil studies of his predecessors. Dr. Finlay was there, and so was Father Norwood, who oversaw St. Bartholomew's at the height of its prestige, some fifty years ago. A proper iced aloofness radiated from these walls, as did traditional Episcopal rectitude. Father Bowers has yet to be hung in this shrine of his church's history. He sighed about it, and perhaps he was beginning to feel that, just like the real Saint Bartholomew, he was being flayed. Even so, he tried to make a joke. "The way I'm going around here," he said, "they're going to have to take a Polaroid of me and just put it in this corner . . . behind the door."

December 1981

* * *

By the spring of 1983, the vagaries of the real-estate market had done a great deal to soothe the situation on Park Avenue. Although the courts had lifted an

injunction against the church a year earlier, there was no sign
that the rector and wardens of St. Bart's would be able to go
ahead with their plans. New buildings had cropped up all over
midtown and office space abounded. Philip Johnson's new
AT&T building on Madison Avenue was offering extraordinary discount incentives to entice tenants, and the average
rental for the finest buildings on Park was about forty-five
dollars a square foot. "Nineteen million, five hundred forty
thousand square feet will be available in 1983," a memo from
Cross & Brown Realty noted.

In this atmosphere, the sixty dollars a square foot St. Bart's
would have had to earn from its tower seemed an impossibil-
ity, and Howard Ronson, the English developer who had been
filled with such bluster, walked away from his deal. This didn't
surprise many people. Nor did he come up with the one million dollars he had promised when the court lifted its injunction. "No other developer has come forth," reported Sinclair
Armstrong, head of the opposition group. As the real-estate
market has plunged, Armstrong's spirits have soared. "We've
gotten forty percent of the parish voting with us," he said.

So Armstrong, in festive spirits, went to call on Tom
Bowers and two of his wardens, Charles Scribner and Anthony Marshall. "It was the first time they had even recognized our existence," Armstrong said. "We went into the rector's office and said, 'Now that the deal is off, let's get on with
our church work.' "

Scribner, a tall, pompous man with a florid complexion, is
not known for his flexibility. "As far as we're concerned, you
people can leave the church," he told Armstrong. "We'll have
a reconciliation in the parish if you people agree to never oppose any building deal again."

"Is it your position that forty percent of your parish should
take off?" Armstrong asked Tom Bowers. The rector hesitated. At this meeting he did not mention that the million-
dollar endowment fund Marc Haas had given to St. Bart's in

the 1970's had been "substantially invaded," as the treasurer had reported at the annual meeting. Architects, lawyers, and public-relations campaigns can be expensive. "I don't want to lose any more of my flock," Bowers said. "Sometime in the next five years, we'll go ahead with our plans. For now, we're in a holding pattern."

The Deb of
the Year

Her most glorious night will come at her official party in June—the climax of a year of lesser parties—and although Cornelia Guest, the deb of the year, laughs at how seriously all the other debs are taking it all, she seems to be pretty serious about her coming out too. Cornelia's mother is Mrs. Winston Frederick Churchill Guest—her friends and readers know her as C.Z.—and she gives plenty of good advice in her syndicated gardening column. C.Z. Guest has good advice for her daugher as well. "Be polite, meet everybody, and have a wonderful time," she told Cornelia, who turned eighteen recently. Someday soon, C.Z. might regret the "meet everybody" part. Cornelia's godfather was the Duke of Windsor. He gave her advice also. When Cornelia was a little girl, he told her, "Manners are the most important thing in life."

Cornelia has paid a lot of attention to her mother and her godfather. So far, her manners have been pretty good—well, she did slip a bit at the New York Debutantes Ball and on New Year's Eve—but she's had a wonderful time and met a lot of people. Cornelia says that her "favorites" are Jerry Zipkin, Estée Lauder, Consuelo Crespi, and Francesco Scavullo

("He's a genius. An absolute genius."). These favorites were at her eighteenth-birthday party at Mortimer's, in November, as were Cheryl Tiegs and Peter Beard; Way Bandy, who did her makeup for the occasion; Kenneth Jay Lane; Lester Persky, the producer; Tawn and Howard Stein, the owner of Xenon; Doris Duke; Egon von Furstenberg; and John Bowes-Lyon, Queen Elizabeth's cousin. Cornelia says that being around this group is a lot more interesting than going to college. That she refuses to do.

"I don't want to learn anymore," she says. "I think men have to go to college, but women don't. It's really up to the person. You learn so much from the people you meet in New York every day. I learn so much from Scavullo, you wouldn't believe it." Presumably the deb of the year learns a lot from Tawn Stein too. Tawn and Cornelia are close friends. They work out together at The Vertical Club, near the Fifty-ninth Street bridge, the current gym of favor with the *haut* Xenon crowd. The two friends must make a striking tableau as they strain against the pressures of the de rigueur Nautilus equipment of their gym. Tawn Stein has the kind of looks that paralyze construction workers. She's a creature *nocturnis,* a dark vision of tangled Afro, wide-mouthed sensuality, and Spandex-perfect limbs. Cornelia is, shall we say, a study in contrasts: creamy-skinned and lanky, with that just-off-the-horse look, her blond hair streaked from the Palm Beach sun. In her day, as deb of the year, Brenda Frazier used to sit at the Stork Club with Fred and Adele Astaire. That was considered adventurous too.

Anyway, Cornelia has a lot on her mind. There's her big party in June. She's worried about that. She knows she wants it to be "very traditional, very white, *just white everywhere,*" and there's the problem, because it's all so subtle; she wants it to be traditional but she also wants to have a party with "spunk." Howard and Tawn and Francesco and Egon and Lester should provide that. Cornelia is thinking about doing something a little different, perhaps actually not wearing white. What about a perfect shade of pale green? *"Yech. Green? Never green. I look horrid in green. I hate green. Maybe hot pink . . . maybe."*

It's all still very early. Cornelia and her mother haven't planned "a thing" yet. Cornelia only knows that it will be at their "house in Old Westbury"—a girl whose father is second cousin to Winston Churchill understands (even without Briarcliff) that it is distinctly non-U to say "our estate." So, at "the house" in Old Westbury, on Long Island, Cornelia's mother will set up a tent, perhaps fashioned from ten thousand yards of ivory peau de soie, and in Cornelia's tent will go "pots and pots of orchids from Mummy's greenhouses" (there are three). The tent is where the worry comes in. Cornelia *hates* tents. "When it rains then you have to move everything inside and it's such a mess. I *hate* that. That's why I hate tents. You just never know what's going to happen." She might also worry how mummy and daddy are going to pay for it all—the Guests have been a bit overextended recently.

It would be nice to say that Cornelia Guest of the distinguished Guests—New York, Old Westbury, Palm Beach, and racetracks—was a classic deb, a throwback to Mimi Baker and Brenda Frazier, oh-so-madcap, taking the necessary year off to make her bow, unbothered by accusations of frivolity, spending her days flitting from fitting to fitting to lunch at Le Cirque, somehow still finding time to read both *The Wall Street Journal* and all of Proust. This isn't exactly the case. Cornelia is classic because she has a well-known last name and is very pretty and sweet and has a mouth just small enough to emit those clenched syllables of Old Westbury lockjaw. But she is also very much à la mode, a disco deb. For a while, she worked for Nicki Haskell's cable TV show. R. Coury Hay, the gossip writer of the *National Equirer,* has honored her with a party. Former Studio 54 owner, Steve Rubell was there. Nicki Haskell threw her a bash at The Underground.

Tawn and Howard gave one for her at Xenon. Cornelia's favorite escort is Francesco Scavullo. You have to wonder what the Duke of Windsor would have thought of all this.

Well, Cornelia has always been a little different. She dropped out of Foxcroft so that she could devote herself to riding. "The headmistress was really pretty rude about the whole thing," Cornelia said. "Everybody else got to go off to Paris for their break and when I wanted to ride she wouldn't let me. She said I was never going to achieve anything. Well, I got over to Paris and the whole thing was *such* a waste because all I saw was my mother's friends and I speak perfect French anyway and always have."

For a few years Cornelia, age fifteen, made the horse-show circuit—"One week you're in Ohio, the next week Lake Placid"—but the life didn't satisfy. She came back to Old Westbury and went to public high school and then finished up at the Professional Children's School, which gave her a chance to ride. Now she wants to act and be a model. ABC has given her a screen test. There's a chance that her friend Lester Persky will give her a role in *Hand-Carved Coffins,* based on the Truman Capote novella. She might take some acting lessons too.

"I'm really not into politics or anything like that," Cornelia says. "But I think the Reagans are fabulous. I keep up with them. Nancy—I mean Mrs. Reagan—is a really good friend of Mummy's. But some of these issues are so ridiculous. Like the ERA. That is *so* pompous. I just hate some of those women. I mean, the fact that they are trying to get through women in combat is absurd. I mean, it's been forever and ever that the men are supposed to go to battle and protect the women. That's the way it should be."

Her passions run to extremes. Besides Scavullo and Jerry Zipkin, Cornelia *loves* fox hunting, her thoroughbred, her mother's orchids, ball gowns in gold, silver, or black—especially if they're designed by her favorite designer, Fabrice—

and the ocean. Her hates are more interesting. Cornelia "really hates" swimming pools, all the "ruffles, ruffles, ruffles" other debs wear, "the way my mother's friends come up to me and pinch me on the cheek and tell me how much I've grown," people who keep birds that chirp for house pets, and her horse's name, Sweep-the-Market—"Well, I didn't name him," she says.

Cornelia's first big dance was over the holidays, the New York Debutantes Ball. She had refused to take part in the Junior League Ball, a month earlier. "That was around the time of my birthday, and if I had another party then I would have been just dead." The New York Debutantes Ball was quite enough, Cornelia says. "It was a fiasco! The woman who runs it was so terrible, screaming at all of us all the time during the rehearsals, and then we had to parade. Some of the girls had parasols, and they were supposed to do a little dance." A pause. "Well, that was kind of pretty, really it was, but the rest of us had to march around carrying these candles and then sit on the floor and sing Christmas carols. Well, some of these girls were acting like it was the biggest thing in the world, and it was so silly. I kept laughing, and my mother kept looking at me and laughing, and I was swinging my bouquet around till even my brother Alexander, who was my escort, told me to stop laughing. I know it's for a really good cause, that hospital downtown, but everybody was so serious. It was ridiculous."

A few days later she took off for Palm Beach "just to rest." "I opened the door to my room and there were just orchids everywhere, pots and pots, and it was beautiful, I couldn't believe how beautiful it was, and I said, 'Mummy, this is the most beautiful thing I have ever seen. I just want to stay here forever.' " Cornelia made sure to stay out of the sun. "I don't want to age my skin," she says. "Mummy makes me wear a big straw hat. There's nothing worse than all those horrible spots you can get from the sun."

She barely made it back in time for New Year's Eve. It was

touch and go for a while—on the plane, Cornelia had a bout of air sickness—but she rallied, and that night Scavullo took her to Regine's, where she sat with Lester Persky and partied with Karen Black, Elsa Martinelli, and Cher. The *Daily News* photographers wandered in and talked to Cornelia about her acting ambitions, and then Cornelia lifted her gown and let the *News* "People" page snap her limbs. Oh-so-madcap. Then it was "on to Studio and Xenon, and then they all wanted to go to this new club called the Red Parrot, but I was just dead, absolutely dead."

The next day, Cornelia was feeling a little tired. She was heading for Long Island and her "life-size doll's house"—a cottage, really, that her mother had built for her some years back. Cornelia's parents were still in Florida, but "Mamzelle" would be there. Mamzelle is Cornelia's governess. She now runs the house. "Everybody calls her Mamzelle," Cornelia says, "even Jerry Zipkin. It's the funniest thing. She's just Mamzelle."

The new year brings a lot to do. There's her new apartment in the East Seventies. Cornelia shares it with her best friend and the place is "an absolute mess. I've got to do something about picking fabrics," Cornelia says. And about the telephone. "It just rings and rings. Off the wall. It drives me crazy. People are calling me all the time. My poor roommate. When she has to tell people I'm out, they'll argue with her. They'll say, 'We know she's there and she just doesn't want to get on the telephone,' and sometimes when I'm taking naps they just don't believe it."

So far, the telephone has not brought a call from Mr. Right. Cornelia's brother Alexander is "another favorite escort because he's so handsome and nice." She also likes "my Phipps cousins whenever they come into town. . . . I wouldn't want to get married until I was twenty-six or twenty-seven," she says, "and then it has to be someone who is really good-looking with a good personality, someone who likes to have

fun, who is polite and a gentleman. Oh yes, he has to be successful. And he should be five or ten years older." Even the
right escort can be a problem. "I just hate those boys who sit
in the corner and don't know anyone, and when I just run
around, they hide somewhere."

Cornelia has given some thought to what it means to be a
deb. She says she is glad "that tradition has come back. I think
maybe it's come back because the right people now have kids
who are old enough to come out. I think good parties do a lot
to keep young people in line." Still, she realizes that the ethos
of the deb might have changed a bit with the times. "It used
to be that you introduced your daughter to the right families
and everyone got to meet you and then you lived happily ever
after. Well, I said, 'Daddy, I think you're stuck with me.'
Now I think it's just supposed to be fun." A pause. "I'm having a fabulous time."

January 1982

The Last
Chance Salon

*H*e's organizing again. This time, salons. That's what Jerry Rubin calls his weekly gatherings for ninety at his platform-and-pillow-filled apartment in the East Seventies. He doesn't have many souvenirs of the old Jerry Rubin around. The old Jerry used to organize teach-ins and wear Revolutionary War uniforms when he was testifying in front of HUAC. The new Jerry doesn't have any Yippie memorabilia on the walls. His only art is a blowup of Blondie. The minimal setting is perfect for the new Jerry. The new Jerry is quite a host. So far, he's had eleven gatherings. He's planning fifty a year. He says each salon will have a totally different cast. Jerry says his salons represent "networking." He believes the eighties will be a decade of accomplishment both for him and for his peers. That's why he thinks the salons are so important. He says he isn't social climbing. "I'm already so famous, where would I go?" he asks. He says he prefers to say he's redefining himself. Social redefinition this intense takes a lot of work, what with organizing the right caterer and the proper guest list, but Jerry seems to have every detail completely under control.

Moments before Jerry's tenth salon was to begin, everything was in place. His chrome-and-glass table was pushed against the wall to show off the mountain of cabbage, asparagus, raw mushrooms, and cauliflower Jerry's caterer had created. The waiter was in the kitchen with a stack of plastic glasses, ready to serve the powerful. Stanley Siegel, the former TV personality, was expected. So was the biggest venture-capital guy on Wall Street and the woman who runs the exercise studio, Lotte Berk. The host was putting on the second piece of the three-piece suit he says people now expect him to wear. The oatmeal plush carpet was freshly Hoover-ed. But there was a problem: A girl with a purple dress and a Henri Bendel pout wasn't quite ready to take her place, and her place was the most important place. She was on the door with the leather-bound guest book. Every guest must sign in. This is Jerry's rule. But at that moment, the sullen girl wandered around barefoot on Jerry's plush carpet and snapped at an early arrival, "You gotta sign. Name. Address. Home phone. Business phone." Soon, she would have her shoes on and be outside Jerry's door. The girl needed some work on her penside manner to be able to get reluctant salon-goers to enter the barest essentials of their curriculum vitae. Jerry says, "What am I supposed to do if I need to find someone again . . . rush after them to the elevator in the middle of the salon and yell, 'Hey, what's your name?' "

Jerry has always known how to organize things. He knows that if you're running what he calls "a success salon," a salon "for people who are into accomplishing and achieving," the follow-up is everything. He's a long way from marching on the Pentagon here. In those days, all he needed was a few vans and some bullhorns. Jerry is trying for the New York social big time now. He says he's after "the Donald Trumps of tomorrow." This takes work. He's had to run off thousands of fake Tiffany-script invitations that announce his purpose. "I am inviting the most interesting people to bring interesting people," the invitation reads. Inside, he clarifies. "Interesting:

compelling, fascinating, powerful, achieving, enthusiastic, intriguing, beautiful, dynamic, unforgettable, doers, leaders."
Before his invitations paper the city each week, he makes lists.
He aims for a "business and creative mix." He says that he has
so many people he wants to include that he is already planning
four salons ahead. He doesn't allow people to come to more
than two or three salons. "Otherwise I'd be just repeating a
weekly party."

Seven P.M. An hour into salon number ten, the room is
crowded. The atmosphere is early Maxwell's Plum. Jerry
rushes around introducing his guests. "This is the most important man in venture capital," he says of a slight figure with
glasses. Jerry beams. "Wow, it's an honor you're here. It
really is." Stanley Siegel sits on Jerry's platform, his agent
from William Morris close by. "I'm a very emotional person,"
Stanley says, crossing his legs. "I died on the transmitter on
October twenty-sixth. That was the end of me. Nobody appreciated me on the station. They moved me six different
times. Putting me near *Captain Kangaroo* was like opening a
cheese-and-pasta shop in the Bronx."

In other corners of the Rubin salon, the conversation is
equally elevated. "I delight in networking and matrixing," a
woman from Metromedia explains. "I'm not here to meet
men." From her perch, she is able to have a good look at the
crush coming through Jerry's door. She is suitably impressed.
"Look at this mix. Financial people! Media people! An actress. Bankers. A musical conductor. I'll leave tonight with at
least five more contacts." Jerry knows how important contacts
are to his guests. "Money is their pillow talk," he says. Boy
meets girl at Jerry Rubin's. "I do strategic planning," a man
in a suit tells a young woman. "Are you a friend of Albert's?"
she asks him. "Albert who?" "Well, if you don't know, then
you aren't," she snaps.

Jerry sails through his living room, helping his business
types and creative types to mix. His voice carries. "Why

aren't you meeting people? Don't just sit there!" "This is so-and-so. He's a top man at the Ford Foundation." A "top" computer expert on gold is introduced to a woman who has come up with "a revolutionary design for containers." A mushroom importer walks around with a bag of morels. Strangers exchange résumés, percentages, and engraved business cards. A real-estate lawyer in a Missoni T-shirt and a panama hat says, "I don't look like what I am." A copywriter squeals, "I've run into my whole life here. I've met a woman I'm sharing a summer house with. I've met George Lois!" The refugees of the Me Decade have found their niche in Jerry Rubin's Last Chance Salon. And Stanley Siegel still talks from his platform: "I guess my worst moment in life came on the Tom Snyder show when he started reading my man-that-fell-from-grace story that had been in *The New York Times.* Can you imagine? He just started reading it out loud. That was national humiliation. How could I come back from that?"

Maybe Jerry is onto something. He's not afraid to go right to the heart of where the new romance will spring from—the résumé. If he's shameless, so are lots of others at the Last Chance Salon. Jerry Rubin has never been accused of being subtle. Subtle personalities don't refer to themselves in the third person. "People want Jerry Rubin to be the old Jerry Rubin," he says. He's not. His days in Chicago with Abbie Hoffman are over. He's finished with his est training and yoga lessons. His marriage has broken up. Now he wants to be surrounded by those who think as he does—by those who equate ego with career. "I change lives every ten years," Jerry says.

In his new life, Jerry spends $350 a week to have the salons flow around him. He says his company isn't paying for them, although he is sure they are a "business expense." "A person who opens up a sizable account with John Muir will pay for one of these parties," Jerry says. "Already there's a myth that's grown around my salons. Like people think I'm running for office. Or they think I'm running a front for John Muir.

It's Jerry Rubin's party, but the salon now has a life of its own."

He's so busy that he can't even have any fun. "I have to be thinking all the time: Has anyone come in that I haven't greeted? Are the right people meeting the right people? People have said to me, 'You don't look like you're having a good time,' but they don't understand that this is intense. Would you go up to someone in the middle of a tennis match and ask him if he were having a good time?"

This night, Louise Lasser, the actress, comes in late and appears to be having a very good time. She is dressed in pale-blue Laura Ashley ruffles and looks beautiful. With her is a bearded man named Michael. Michael explains that he had been Louise's boyfriend when he was at Horace Mann and she was at Fieldston. Michael and Louise don't seem concerned with networking.

In the midst of Jerry's chaos, Louise and Michael are serene. About a year ago, Michael wrote Louise a letter. They hadn't seen each other since high school. In the letter he told her that all their old friends from high school were getting together—would she like to come? She didn't answer. His feelings were hurt. Then one day his phone rang. "Michael, what is this about getting together? I just found this letter stuck in a drawer." That happened a few months ago. After twenty years, they have come full circle.

Perhaps coming full circle will be Jerry's next incarnation. But not soon. Right now, he's having too much fun. "My ex-wife once said to me, 'Your life is nothing but one event after another,' " he says. This remark doesn't seem to bother him. Out of his attaché case comes his list for the next salon. "Look at these people. The Queens borough president. A socialite, Isabel Leeds. Frank Rich, the theater critic of *The Times*. I'm just expanding and expanding. I don't know who is going to come, and I don't know who they're going to bring. Anyone I hear about who's interesting, I add them to the list. If I didn't have a full-time job I could control it better. I just send invitations to anyone who I think might contribute."

On the day after salon number ten, Jerry glows from his success. "One hundred and thirty-seven people showed up," he says. "That was too many. But from the group that came last night you could network with anybody in the city. Marriages will come out of this. And business deals. Already a woman has gotten an invitation to the Kentucky Derby. Already a lawyer I know has gotten together with a really bright model."

Jerry points to the leather guest books lying on the restaurant table. "Look at these. *Filled.*" He flips through them. "Just look at some of these names. An art dealer. Suzy Chaffee . . . she had a great time! Big real-estate people. Ad agencies! The guy who gets the tables at Mortimer's. Do you know how important that is? Before, I'd go into Mortimer's and he'd look right through me. Now he'll know who I am." He searches the pages. "After each event is over I open the guest book and try to remember who each guest was. Then I call up all the people I found interesting or that I don't really remember and I talk to them for a while. Then, maybe we'll have some lunch or do some business."

Stacks of invitations come flying out of his briefcase. "And anyone who is really interesting I give invitations to, telling them to send them to forty friends. Like a few weeks ago, Trudy Mason, a woman who works with Richard Ravitch, head of the Metropolitan Transit Authority, came. I saw that she would have interesting friends. Now she's sending out invitations too."

Jerry is filled with plans. "You know the wine? I'm working right now to have it all for free. Like a wine importer could put his card on the table and he could get a lot of business just from the referrals. Or my caterer. I'll never understand the guy. I wish he were more entrepreneurial. Like if I were him I would say, 'Jerry, I'll do this for cost.' "

He smiles. It's late afternoon; downtown at Joanna, the moment's restaurant of favor, like other men of accomplishment and achievement, he's sipping Perrier, happy because already three people who have come into the bar smile and wave at him. "See that?" Jerry asks. "Everywhere I go now, people recognize me. It's all from the salons. Isn't that great?" He pauses. "You know, Abbie used to call me the catalyst when we were at the Chicago-Seven trial. I guess that's what I am."

June 1981

Like No Business
I Know

*A*nother opening, and this time a big one, *42nd
Street.* Two million dollars, tap dancing, sequins,
klieg lights. Only at this opening, something happened: The director, Gower Champion, died. The producer
announced the news as if it were the coda, after ten curtain
calls. But nobody onstage, except Jerry Orbach, knew his or
her role in this coda. All the performers could do was react
until Orbach brought the curtain down. The grief was real,
but the staging got out of hand. Perhaps what David Merrick,
the producer, the master of jest and mystery, needed to guide
him through his grief was a director. But this night, he had no
one to turn to.

As an unknowing Arthur Gelb and Frank Rich rushed up
the aisle to meet *The New York Times*'s deadline, Merrick, the
man of the theater, took center stage. The show was over, the
ovation wearing down, yet the cameras remained on—the TV
crews had been told Merrick would have an announcement of
some kind. They recorded him looking queasy, shattered,
green. They recorded him announcing death, embracing
Wanda Richert, the ingenue who had played the ingenue, the
dancer who had turned into a star and become the director's

girl friend. Before more than a thousand people at the Winter Garden Theatre, and the cameras, her surprise, her horror, and her anguish became a matter of public record.

Public grief in a public forum. In the front rows, the men in dinner clothes and the women in gowns could hear Merrick whisper, and the whisper traveled back over the audience from the high-status seats to the middle seats—critics, press, could-you-do-me-a-favor? tickets—then back to where the strangers were. And there were the questions in the rear as well—less reverent, bewildered, even cynical: "What did he say?" "Who's Gower Champion?" "They never would be tasteless enough to have the party, would they?"

But of course the party, like the show, would go on. Ruth Gordon arrived promptly in silver sequins and red trousers; Ethel Merman complained about Merrick's display, but she was there. Josh Logan wandered through two lobbies in the Waldorf-Astoria in search of the elevator to the Starlight Roof. People debated in taxis: "Should we get out at Fifty-first Street and see if other people are even going?" All those black ties wandered around Park Avenue in search of the right thing to do on an evening when there was no right thing to do.

In a sense, the night was historic. Because of the presentation, everyone in the Winter Garden Theatre was sucked into the tragedy. In an era of the Big Event, the size of this one, for the theatrical community anyway, went beyond Gower Champion's death. There was a great deal of money involved. The director had died at noon. Merrick felt he had to keep the fact secret—God knows how he kept it from Wanda Richert for nine hours, but he did. Few had even known Gower Champion was in the hospital. The word *virus* was tossed around, not Waldenström's macroglobulinemia, the rare and lethal blood disease that Champion died of. A simple tragedy was turned into high drama by David Merrick's behavior.

In front of the cameras, he did not choose to bring down

the curtain to shield the cast from our eyes. He did not stride out with his head held high, dignified and composed. His head was in his hands, even though he had known of the death for nine hours. Suddenly, everyone in the theater became a player in the theatrical family.

On to the party, then. Woody Herman and lamps with silk shades had been promised, and there was a long table with rows and rows of neatly penned dinner cards waiting to be picked up. Ed Asner. Mary Tyler Moore. Blake Champion. Valerie Harper. Henry Kissinger. Woody Herman's horns played "I Guess I'll Have to Change My Plan" and seemed uncommonly loud. Nobody wanted to dance. Pellets of information came like dispatches in the night. Gower Champion had lived with the young star. Carla Champion, Gower's ex-wife, had told the cast to come to the party. The Champion children were on their way. People wondered why, if Carla Champion was so close to Gower, Merrick had embraced Wanda Richert onstage? Why had he subjected Carla to that?

A subdued Merrick sat at his table with Neil Simon and Bob Fosse, Champion's closest friend. Merrick sat looking at his glass of wine, not focusing on anything or anyone, as Woody Herman, inches away, blasted him. Photographers surrounded everyone, blinding Merrick, catching him looking dazed or being consoled, congratulated, and comforted by the Broadway parade.

He wouldn't have been comforted to know how his own performance was being reviewed. His defenders said, "What was David to do? Cancel the show? Tell the cast before the show? Tell them at the party? Have them hear about it on the radio?" And his detractors were equally vehement. "Why were the TV people there? Why didn't he bring the curtain down?" "Merrick will do anything to sell tickets."

But it wasn't that at all. It was that Merrick, the man who always knows how to orchestrate everything, didn't know how to orchestrate this one. Nobody denied Merrick's grief was real, but Merrick is Merrick and it was as though all his stunts and crying wolf had gotten away from him and he had lost control. The two sides of his personality were at war. The reclusive, shy Merrick, who speaks in whispers and refuses interviews, was in a conflict with Merrick the bombastic. In a crisis, he had to do what he really knows how to do best, which is to have TV there, ready to catch his grief, his cast's grief, to grab the front pages everywhere, as much for the style of it all as for the event itself.

And after a time the show at the Starlight Roof wasn't his to orchestrate. Wanda Richert arrived looking sunny and composed in an off-the-shoulder purple dress. She took the stage, and smiling as brightly as the ingenue she plays in *42nd Street,* said, "Gower was a singular sensation," then announced that a group of dancers was going to dance *One* from *A Chorus Line*—not a Champion show—as a tribute to him. After that, with great relief, everyone took to the floor. At 2 A.M. they were still dancing, and then Merrick went on to Elaine's with a dozen friends, like Alan DeLynn, his movie partner; Dan Jenkins (Merrick had produced *Semi-Tough*); Ann Dowling, a political fund raiser; Wanda Richert; and some other members of the cast. Merrick told stories about Gower and the old days, the *Hello, Dolly!* and *Mack and Mabel* days.

Yet, always there was the worry of a producer overriding everything. With Gower Champion gone, who would oversee his last and finest numbers? Merrick was on the line with this show, his first in New York in five years, with two million dollars of his own money invested. Even at thirty dollars a ticket, *42nd Street* would have to sell out for a year to come close to breaking even.

So at five in the morning, the producer and his friends were still at Elaine's. In a few hours, millions of future New York City visitors and locals would read of this odd night on Broadway or see the producer himself on their TV screens. They would read about the director who died, and read the reviews, mostly raves, of the show. By noon at the Winter Garden Theatre, the line for tickets snaked three times through the lobby, out Fiftieth Street, around the block, even with the temperature at 94 degrees.

September 1980

A Night at
the Opera

They were all being very careful, what with the rain and the rawness of the night and the worry that had gone through the company because Placido Domingo had canceled the previous evening's *Don Carlos* premiere and the *Bohème* before it. James Levine was downstairs in his dressing room coughing away, and this night's Rodolfo, Dano Raffanti, in the house by 6:30 P.M., had missed one and a half *Bohème*s in the past nine days because he'd had the flu. Raffanti, a pleasant Italian tenor, was somewhat new to the Met and typical of a certain kind of singer the great hall attracts these days—a serviceable voice, better with Rossini than Puccini, no one to knock anybody out of a seat. Like most young artists, he had yet to learn to pace himself, and this *Bohème*, the fifty-ninth in the history of the Metropolitan Opera, would be the first he had sung all the way through with his Mimi, Linda Zoghby.

Not that that mattered. Just one of the ingenious aspects of the Franco Zeffirelli production of *La Bohème* was that it was so technically spectacular, meticulously directed, and filled with theatrical tricks that almost any journeyman singer would wander into the 1850's garret or the Café Momus and an audience would be pretty well satisfied. So by 6:45, as the artists were warming up with the Knabe pianos in each dressing room, the immense, efficient mechanism that is the Metropolitan Opera, the preeminent institution of its kind in the world, was running smoothly; no nerves showed.

The storm had forced Linda Zoghby to leave her Blackglama mink in the tiny walk-up apartment off Amsterdam Avenue she borrows from her brother. Her voice felt fine, however. This night would be only her fifth *Bohème* at the Met, although she had covered for Teresa Stratas almost since opening night. That had been on December 14, 1981, and Zoghby, well aware that the frail, neurasthenic Stratas had a tendency to skip performances, hung on till she got the call. It came a few months into last season's run, and the dark-haired soprano, who had left her baby and husband at home, in Mobile, Alabama, in anticipation of that moment, was in a taxi by 7:05. "Four hours later," she said, "I got a standing ovation." This season Zoghby was all too happy to understudy the part again, and was not disappointed. By February, Stratas had pulled out everything, pleading illness in her family. This didn't surprise anyone at the Met: The moody star has such "a profound interest in death," as she puts it, that, she once told *Opera News,* "when Lotte Lenya was dying, she remembered me as a redhead from my Jenny in *Mahagonny* at the Met. So I dyed my hair red again to make her feel more at home."

As divas go, Linda Zoghby seems less eccentric. "I thought Placido had canceled on me Saturday night to be in good voice for *Don Carlos,*" she told Victor Callegari, the head makeup man. Domingo's cancellation had been particularly annoying for Zoghby because that day a group of friends had come up from Mobile to hear her for the first time at the Met. She has had no trouble adapting to her surroundings. By seven, she was out of her pink blouse, tweed skirt, and beige slip and was in a black-satin robe with an enormous peacock embroidered on the back; she had listened to James Levine, the musical director, when he came in to give her a few suggestions, paying special attention when he told her to arch a certain bar in the *"Sono andati,"* in Act IV. Her shower was running to keep the air moist, and she'd requested hot water with lemon (a mild enough demand, considering that Martina Arroyo often cooks steaks in her dressing room). She kept up several conversations while she removed her makeup and pinned her hair back to be able to wear Mimi's wig.

A few doors down the hall, James Morris, who sings Colline, the philosopher, was putting on his tattered undershirt for the last time. Although Morris had been with this *Bohème* since opening night, it was time to move on; he would be heading in his van for Miami and *Falstaff* just after the performance. These comings and goings are nothing unusual; the days when Corelli, Tebaldi, and Tucker would camp out for season after season are long gone. But Morris's only sentiment had to do with the loss of his cherished undershirt. "You see where my sleeve is all charred and tattered? On opening night, Franco said, 'This isn't right. Too new.' And he took out his lighter and set the cuffs on fire. Then he tamped them out real fast and said, 'Better.' "

Although that incident was fairly characteristic of the kind of madness that accompanies any Zeffirelli production, another recent *Bohème* fire was not. This one had occurred ten days earlier onstage, when Dano Raffanti was lighting the garret's stove. Although the fire was simulated, the match was not; the head flew off and caught in some papers. "Jimmy didn't even stop conducting until Dennis the electrician came in with a fire extinguisher," Morris said. If Morris was flustered by the blaze, Levine was phlegmatic. "If I stay here long enough, I'll see everything," he had said earlier. From where Morris was standing in his dressing room, he could hear Mario Sereni warming up with the first notes of *"Sei sordo"* for Act I. Sereni, who is celebrating his twenty-fifth season at the Met, is known for his attention to musical detail: He routinely sings each note of his part before each act.

"I'm sorry, Mario," David Kneuss exclaimed as he raced

into the artists' dressing area. "I've just had potentially life-changing news. The Maggio Musicale called me from Florence! I'm going to be doing *Fidelio* in the '84 season."

Kneuss is one of seven staff directors at the Met. It was his responsibility, along with his assistant for this production, Lesley Koenig, a petite Harvard grad, to keep the Met's *Bohème* just as Zeffirelli intended. So although he was exuberant because of his own news, his mind was on Mario Sereni.

"Mario," David Kneuss said, "in Act One, be sure to get everything in the picnic basket before you hoist it up the rope." "Hmmph," Sereni said. "Why do not you tell the others to help me? I'm the one who's singing." This exchange underscored an ongoing opera debate: What is more important, singing or attention to stage business? Sereni comes from the old school; he is La Scala-trained, and the intense concern for acting in this production was sometimes tricky for him. Used to singing Marcello in decades of *Bohème*s, now he had been cast as Schaunard the musician, and often at rehearsals he would find himself slipping back. As if to italicize the point, at 7:09, James Levine went whizzing down the hall where Kneuss and Sereni were talking. Levine had finished giving all the artists last-minute instructions and was running to his dressing room, his ubiquitous, faded bath towel over his shoulder, to put on the first of three tuxedos he would wear that night. "Is everyone all right?" he asked without waiting for a reply.

From 7:10 to 7:43, Kneuss had stopped in Linda Zoghby's dressing room, where he reminded her to hold her place in the *"Grazie. Buona sera"* in Act I; checked the presence on the left stage of Rocco, the donkey, and Cinnamon, the horse; interrupted a modified towel fight in the boy's-chorus room; and gone back up to the artists' dressing rooms and advised Patricia Craig, who sings Musetta, to "be sure to throw your hat so it lands at Marcello's feet; last night it hit the pâté." He arrived, not the least bit out of breath, onstage in time to help

Koenig arrange flowerpots on the balcony of the garret for Act I, almost at the exact moment the vaporizers began spewing out billows of mist to damp down the dust for the singers. As the great clouds of fine spray filled the air above the Paris rooftops, seeping into the Bohemians' garret, David Kneuss said, "Stratas is such a perfectionist that this isn't enough spritz for her. She comes out with her own hand sprayer ten minutes before curtain to make sure there isn't one particle of dust left in the air."

Perhaps the story is apocryphal: About the time that the new Metropolitan Opera House opened at Lincoln Center in 1966, a guild member was touring backstage just as the 7:45 P.M. vapor began. "How lovely," she said. "Isn't that just like the Met to spray perfume for its singers." The vast grandeur of the Metropolitan is real enough, though. Ninety-nine years after the first night's *Faust,* each evening for a thirty-week season the lights dim, the chandeliers ascend, the conductor takes his place before the orchestra, and thousands of music lovers and tone-deaf socialites are still enraged or enthralled.

The Metropolitan Opera has survived a fire that gutted one house, a demolition, two near bankruptcies, labor disputes, a depression, world wars, furious musical debates, and a social reputation so daunting that in 1907 Henry James noted, "There was nothing, as in London or Paris, to go 'on' to; 'going on' is, for the New York aspiration, always the stumbling block. . . . Its presence is felt ummistakably, for instance, in the general extravagant insistence on the Opera, which plays its part as the great vessel of social salvation, the comprehensive substitute for all other conceivable vessels."

Henry James's "Opera" was the Met, though it has changed enormously since the days when any climber with the price could get within conversational range of an Astor, a Belmont, or the Duchess of Marlborough, who built a reputation because of the number of orchids with which she festooned the anteroom of her box. The Met's general manager, Anthony Bliss, takes great pride in being a descendant of this rarefied world, but his style of running things is more like that of I.B.M. About all that remains of the Diamond Horseshoe days is the Vanderbilts' scarlet-and-gold color scheme; the Met is now happy to sell anybody anything, and for its 1983 centennial, just about everything inside the house is on the block. A donation of $10 million will endow the stage or underwrite one new production a year; $25 million will endow the auditorium; $1 million the wig shop, prop shop, or makeup department; and $500,000 the greenroom or the gift shop. Out of the Met's $70-million budget, which finances 210 performances of 23 operas, a tour, the telecasts and Texaco radio broadcasts, young artists' programs, language lessons, et al., $24 million comes from gifts. There are more than 100,000 members of the Opera Guild alone.

So when James Levine decided that he would meet with Franco Zeffirelli about the idea of doing a new *Bohème*, he was optimistic. *La Bohème*, a staple of opera since its first performance, in 1896, was, as Levine says, "always a hot ticket." Although the critics of the time despised Puccini's fourth work, the opera about tragic student lovers in bohemian Paris, is, next to *Aïda*, the most popular of the Met's repertory. Its story is one of the most familiar of all the opera standards: In Act I, Rodolfo, a struggling writer, meets and falls in love with Mimi, a beautiful but frail neighbor, on Chrsitmas Eve. Act II takes place the same night, when Mimi and Rodolfo celebrate at the Café Momus and she meets his friends, Schaunard, Colline, and Marcello, who is in love with the temperamental Musetta. In the third act, Mimi and Rodolfo have quarreled, and she seeks help from Marcello, who is staying near the Paris Customs gate. At the end of the act, Mimi and Rodolfo decide to part. By the fourth act, Mimi is dying. She returns to Rodolfo to be near him at the end.

A new production would have been an extravagance—this

one cost $707,000—but Mrs. Donald Harrington agreed to donate a great deal of it. *"Grazie a Dio!"* Zeffirelli told his friend the archaeologist Iris Love. "At last, I've found my patron!"

Zeffirelli had at first been reluctant to restage *La Bohème*; his 1963 La Scala version was considered classic. "At first, Franco wasn't sure he could bring anything new to it," James Levine said. Zeffirelli is known for his spectacular staging of grand opera: In 1966, when he directed Samuel Barber's *Antony and Cleopatra* for the opening of the new house, he was delighted that the Met had a technical marvel, a revolving stage. "Let's add more supers, hundreds of them—camels, goats, another ballet company!" he cried. At the dress rehearsal, the enormous turntable revolved once, twice, three times, then broke completely, and didn't turn again for a year.

His vision of *Bohème* was almost as grandiose. Peter Hall, the Met's costume designer, flew to Positano to find his friend Zeffirelli immersed in the study of Gavarni's engravings of the period; the director's plan was to have 265 people on the stage in Act II, when the curtain opens to reveal all of Paris. That meant 280 costumes would be needed. *"Se avessi potuto!"* he told Love. "I would have four hundred, five hundred if I could!"

It was Zeffirelli's notion to reproduce, for Act II, the medieval city of Paris: the shops, Christmas crowds, pushcarts, dancing bears, gypsies, vendors, drunks, and tramps on three levels, with the Café Momus—normally the centerpiece—obscured by pushcarts until the last moment. "What Franco wanted," said Joseph Clark, the technical director, "would have entailed a forty-minute intermission." An alternative plan was developed that resulted, as Zeffirelli later said, in a *"coup de théâtre."* Acts I and II would be performed without intermission, since the dramatic action was continuous.

Although this could be arranged because of the Met's sophisticated equipment, the Zeffirelli *Bohème* had many other problems. The year before there had been a labor dispute; the season was shortened, and the time allotted for new productions was reduced. The final approval for Zeffirelli's elaborate plans did not come through until four days before construction of the sets had to begin. That took eleven weeks, when Zeffirelli was ill in Europe, and everything, says Clark, had "to be done almost by guesswork."

Zeffirelli arrived in New York in October to begin rehearsals, picking 150 supers for Act II, working twice as many hours as usual—on the lighting and the technical difficulties in the morning and with the singers in the afternoon. In spare moments, he would wander into the costume department and say, "That doesn't look right," ripping out a hem to make a shawl. Or, says Peter Hall, "He would tell me to dip a whole group of my dresses into bleach. He's blood, sweat, and tears to work with. But I guess he's worth it." The obsession with aesthetic detail extended to all areas; the Act III umbrellas were painted with snowflakes; Parpignol's toy cart was completely redecorated by Zeffirelli himself because, he told David Kneuss, "The blues are not lurid enough." When *La Bohème* was attacked by the critics for being too elaborate and too remote—his garret was high above the treetops, far from the audience—he had one response: "*Fa niente!* Was the set beautiful?"

8:01 P.M.: The supers' room is crowded with ballet dancers, corporate executives, and unemployed actresses in the process of becoming nineteenth-century bakers, middle-class ladies, vendors, fortune tellers, and drunks. I am there, too, being laced into a pea-green plaid taffeta ribbon-trimmed gown, resurrected from the ladies' chorus for Molly Rockefeller when she decided she would like to get onstage. Mrs. Rockefeller, whose husband, William, is chairman of the board of the Met, got, as Bill McCourt, the assistant stage manager who oversees the supers, says, "the special treatment." That meant she was allowed to use the principals' dressing area and make-up man.

I am not getting "the special treatment." Almost the moment my black wool dress hits the chair in the cramped room the supers share, the owner of the Alkit Camera Shop, on Third Avenue, orders, "Put your dress somewhere else." Our surroundings are not luxurious. Dozens of women fight for space in front of two large mirrors, but Judy Mortinson, who retired early from her job as head of PR for Du Pont so she could spend more time at the Met, hurries me into the ladies' room, where she advises me to put on the palest makeup possible. "Nineteenth-century bourgeois women did not wear Blush-On," she says.

"We don't allow people to super because it's fun or they think it's going to be camp. You have to be serious about it," Bill McCourt has warned me. McCourt, trained as a stage manager, has, as he says, "cleaned it up around here," which means he's gotten rid of the supers who would accost a principal during an intermission and say, "Your top sure wasn't on tonight," or who would wander into the Café Momus to better hear Musetta's waltz song. Constant vigilance is required. McCourt does not want to repeat certain nightmares, such as the time during a *Rigoletto* some years ago when "an ambitious super who was playing a servant was simply supposed to bring in a bowl of fruit." The problem, McCourt says, "was that my super wanted to be an actor, so I looked on the monitor just in time to see him lurching across the stage like a hunchback, doing a real *Phantom of the Opera* routine. When he got offstage, I screamed, 'What the hell was that all about?' He said, 'I didn't want Rigoletto to feel alone.' "

So there are strict rules for McCourt's supers, memos that say, "No standing in the wings without permission" or "No one allowed out front in costume." McCourt has a group of about twenty he uses regularly, and although the Met never advertises, he is flooded with résumés. The files bulge: There is the Barnard girl who had a ten-second bit in *Cavalleria Rusticana* who sent a still from the stage headlined "——at the Met." There are body builders, a porno star, as well as "two men I used years ago that someone sent me a Polaroid of decked out as drag queens.

"This *La Bohème* is easy for the supers," McCourt says. "All my crowd has to do is to find a pattern of movement onstage and then mill and lurk. *Don Carlos*—that's my horror! There are processions, everything is symmetrical, people are holding candles. It's marches, it's drills! The supers are paid according to how much business they have; the average fee for a performance and rehearsal is ten dollars cash."

I have no marches and no drills, but as I take my place at 8:31 on the huge rolling wagons that will lock into place and become Parisian stairsteps, my pattern seems as complicated as a *Don Carlos* parade. I am standing with Judy Mortinson and her husband, the town butcher, my flag hidden in my sleeve ready for the final moments. And then we hear the first notes of the chorus and the sound rushes around us—*"Aranci, datteri, caldi i marroni "* ("Oranges, dates, hot chestnuts")— and the great curtain is up, and the 4,000 people in the audience cheer Zeffirelli's spectacle. James Levine is singing "Falso questo Re!" along with Mario Sereni, smiling all the while, and all of us in bohemian Paris can see our conductor both in the pit and on the television monitors that line each side of the stage.

But I have a great deal to do: I must stop at the gypsy and have my palm read; circulate between the bakery, the butcher shop, and the silk merchant; stop in front of three different vendors to look for Christmas presents; and get down the great sweep of stairs in time for the entrance of the dancing bear and the man on stilts, a Golden Gloves boxer who will leave the performance and take on his second job, as bouncer at the Red Parrot. Timing is crucial: I must be back on the top level by the time Musetta sings her waltz, 'Quando me'n vo',' " when 245 people onstage freeze for two minutes.

8:50 P.M.: The waltz song is over, and from a distance we hear the first sounds of the marching band. At any moment, the twelve-piece band and the French sappers will fill the stage, moving from one end of Paris to the Café Momus, and all of the supers will be locked into place, prevented from traveling by the sweep of the parade. It has always been my plan to try to end up, at curtain, next to the principals. "Come with me," Judy Mortinson says. "Fast. Just follow me, I'll be running block." As the horns begin, the boy mascot in clear view, we cut in front, our flags waving maniacally, patriotic bourgeoisie to the end, to wind up almost on top of Richard Stilwell, who, as Marcello, is singing "Viva Musetta! . . . Gloria ed onor! onor e gloria del quartier latin!" I am not concerned with the glory of the Latin Quarter or Musetta, and I find myself just where I want to be, a breath away from Marcello and almost in the pit. Suddenly, the lights brighten for the audience to take in the entire majestic Zeffirelli tableau, the curtain begins to fall, Stilwell singing all the while, and I feel a sharp punch in my ribs. "Get your flag out of my face," Stilwell says. "Nobody can see me. Your damn flag is in my face."

9:11 P.M.: Snow covers the stage in readiness for Act III. The stagehands are moving the Customs gate into place. Linda Zoghby is getting ready to plead with Marcello to help her solve her problems, when a group of tourists, just before the Act III curtain, walk briskly through the confetti. "Right this way, Mrs. Cuomo," an Opera Guild member instructs the governor's wife. "Oh dear, how fascinating," Matilda Cuomo says. "I've never been backstage before." Mrs. Cuomo wanders through the set, treading on mounds of Styrofoam the stagehands use for snow fights.

"Oh my god," Linda Zoghby says moments before curtain. "I've left my gloves in the dressing room." This is not a minor problem, as Mimi's tattered gloves are crucial for the next scene. "David, please run to my dressing room to get them." Linda Zoghby is pleased to be through with the second act. "It's so noisy up on that stage I feel like I'm at Penn Station most of the time. I swear, the way Franco did it, you feel like you're singing in a zoo." As with all other Mimis, Act III is her favorite because her singing skills are shown off. "The one bad part about it," she says from the wings, "is that scrim. Look at it. Sure, it looks like winter to the audience, but it becomes impossible for me to see Jimmy or anyone else, so a lot of the time I feel like I'm singing in the shower."

Moments later, Linda Zoghby is onstage singing *"Speravo di trovarvi qui"* with Richard Stilwell, and offstage the stagehands shriek a few yards from the monitors. "Stop!" the stage manager shouts. "No!" one of the stagehands yells back. "I can't hear. They're making too much noise out onstage." Meanwhile, by 9:37, the same supers who were Christmas shopping in Act II are now working their way, in different clothes, through the Customs gate of Paris. "This is my fifth time circling around," Judy Mortinson says, carrying a basket. "I'm tired." Raffanti is struggling, too, reaching for the B flat on the *"mondo"* in *"Amo Mimi, sovra ogni cosa al mondo,"* and from the stagehands' cubicle, laughter is heard. "At least the old-timers are gone," David Kneuss says. "They used to yell out things like 'Bring back Tebaldi.' "

By 9:50, there is a blizzard onstage at the Customs gate, and Mimi and Rodolfo have decided to stay together until spring. Musetta and Marcello have just had a quarrel, the principals have taken their curtain calls, and Richard Stilwell and Linda Zoghby are on their way back to their dressing rooms. "Good fight tonight," Richard Stilwell says to Patricia Craig. "Mr. Stilwell," the stage manager says, "your check."

From the wings, the stage manager has appeared with four white envelopes, the nightly paychecks for the artists. This practice of paying the singers between the third and fourth acts of the opera began in the nineteenth century, when singers traveled from theater to theater and would not complete a performance until they were assured of payment. "In South America," says Linda Zoghby, "they still come in with baskets of cash and pay you counting it out before the last act." The Met cannot pay its principals what other, richer opera companies can—it is said the Houston Opera pays Placido Domingo $25,000, for example—so this night, Linda Zoghby will probably earn about $2,500.

By 10:05, Linda Zoghby is dying offstage as well as on, collapsing on the chaise in her dressing room, trying to orchestrate her movements so that she will be in no danger, forty minutes hence, of crushing Dano Raffanti when she leans back and cries out "To sleep." Victor, the makeup man, has been making her look even paler, and the dresser has helped her into the pale-blue silk gown covered with tiny rosebuds that the costume shop's two head cutters, who are married to each other, have created. This dress caused tremendous consternation upstairs. "When I saw that Franco's staging only allowed this dress to be seen for ninety seconds," Peter Hall says, "and that he wanted Mimi to come onstage, get under the sheets, and collapse—well, I could have just killed him."

"Bene, bene, bene . . . that's better, Dano," David Kneuss, practicing with Zoghby in the dressing room, says to Dano Raffanti. The worry has to do with Raffanti's position on the bed. *"Come si dice* 'behind'? I want Dano to be in back of Linda." Act IV is always difficult for Mimi because she must work off the monitors and still look realistic. "Linda," Kneuss says, "please, don't crumple over so much. You have to sort of collapse forward. As Franco would say, 'Now you are in coma.' " He turns to Victor Callegari. "She needs to be much paler." Out in the hall, Patricia Craig is rushing toward her dressing room carrying a hot plate, and Joan Dornemann, the

prompter, is racing back to her booth, her silk tunic billowing out behind her, her hair askew. "I'm exhausted tonight. They're all singing every which way, and I have to jump up and down to find them. I wish they would get together."

They've certainly tried. Two weeks before, Zoghby had her first staging rehearsal with Dano Raffanti. (These rehearsals go on daily at the Met; when *Die Walküre* is on the main stage, *Der Rosenkavalier* will be on the rear stage, and scenes from *La Bohème* will be getting blocked out in a small studio on the second floor. It is in these rehearsals that the principals get to know one another. "Why you not buy American Express warrants like I tell you to?" Mario Sereni asked Lesley Koenig in early February. "I double, I triple my money. I wish I know when to sell.") The morning after the one time Linda Zoghby had sung with Placido Domingo she came in early to work with Raffanti. The Zoghby-Domingo night had been extraordinary, but Zoghby was subdued when she appeared at rehearsal. "I'm told I looked like a truck driver during the Act One scene at the table," she said. The evening had been her first *Bohème* of the season, and she was worried that she hadn't studied Terese Stratas's performance well enough. "I'm trying to do everything exactly as Stratas did it," Zoghby said. "And Act Four is driving me crazy."

10:20 P.M.: Only death is left. In the soundproof directors' booth, at the rear of the orchestra, David Kneuss and Lesley Koenig have taken their seats to monitor the activities onstage. No singer is a hero to his director, and at times, says Kneuss, "We get so frustrated at what they're doing up there we start banging on the walls." Outside the directors' booth, far away from Mimi's final seizure, Lois Binetsky, the ticket taker who waits at the front door of the house, is ready to go home. Binetsky keeps very busy during the performances. She sculpts wax molds for the jewelry she designs in the basement of the Met. As Mimi and Rodolfo are reunited, she pulls out a silver stickpin. "I made this during *Il Trovatore*," she says.

Inside the booth, Lesley Koenig is complaining. "I've been in this house for fourteen hours and thirty-five minutes," she says. "All day long I've been studying the score of *Der Rosenkavalier*. I haven't had one call from the outside world. Mimi's death is not a moment too soon." But death does not come so fast. First, there is the dance. Marcello and Schaunard have choreography—a jig that has been rehearsed and re-rehearsed, and nineteenth-century horseplay that involves an overturned table, a run across the Paris rooftops, a fake duel, and a raw fish being thrown from friend to friend. "The raw fish is real," David Kneuss says. "We used to have a rubber one, but Franco didn't think it looked real enough, so he sent down a memo to the props department, 'Please send up a real trout.' So the props department gave him a real trout, a cooked trout, and during the dress rehearsal when Mario tossed it to Richard it exploded all over the stage."

Tonight there is no such incident to add to Metropolitan Opera lore, only a minor glitch noticed in the directors' booth. "Oh, for God's sake," says Koenig. "Linda still has confetti in her hair. Why didn't anyone catch that?" The snow is an irritation, and so is the nightly 10:20 P.M. worry about Mimi's pillow. If Marcello doesn't place it exactly right on the deathbed, the entire balance of the piece will be disturbed, and Mimi will not be able to sing properly. "Every single Mimi complains about that tattered pillow," Koenig says. This night the pillow is not a problem. As Koenig and Kneuss both cry out "Die Linda! Die, die, already," Linda Zoghby holds her hand in the air for what seems an eternity before it finally floats down, slowly, slowly, then drops like a hammer.

"Dormire," she gasps. The time is 10:49.

April 1983

Less Work for
Mother

*T*he phones, the phones, all day they ring, jangling her
nerves, aggravating her heart condition, hardly leaving her a moment to take her pills. Mrs. Frances Fox
doesn't need cover stories to tell her about the baby boom.
For forty-six years she's been matching baby nurses with
mothers-to-be, nannies with snobs and strivers, governesses
with the busy or the cavalier. And in all these years, she says,
there's never been demand like this. "If I could place ten percent of my requests, I could retire," Mrs. Fox says. But she
can't. All she can do is listen: "Mrs. Fox, find me a Scottish
one, a French one, an English one." "I'll settle for a nice Bra-
zilian with no accent and a college degree." Hundreds of times
a day, she listens. Sometimes she makes a note in her spiral,
sometimes not.

Mrs. Fox has her methods. No Touch-Tones at the Fox
Agency. For that matter, no agents either. Or computer or
switchboard or even an answering service. Just a tall, lanky,
blond seventy-four-year-old with perfect posture and sensible
shoes, an assistant, faded photos of the nannies' charges, and
two battered standard black telephones. When Mrs. Fox gets
fed up, which is often, she takes them off the hook. Sometimes

the clients don't understand why she sounds so churlish. "When they call up and say, 'Mrs. Fox, I spoke to you last Wednesday, and it's not the second one you sent me that I liked but the fourth one—what was her name?' well, how the hell am I supposed to remember?" So the spiral tells it all. If you need a baby nurse, you better be nice to Frances Fox. Fame, family credentials, a lavish D.& B. do not impress her. Politeness does. "If they're nasty to me on the telephone, they're not going to be nice to my nurses," says Mrs. Fox. One scream provokes an indelible black mark by the caller's name: "Hold"; "Sounds prejudiced"; "Impossible!" The screamer's quest is doomed.

Her racist-spotting radar is finely tuned. Mrs. Fox can divine an euphemism from East Sixtieth Street to Gracie Square. She knows all the tricks. "Racism is my number-one problem," she says. "It's worse now than when Martin Luther King was alive. It is sickening. It is so easy to spot the bigots, and, believe me, everyone in this town is prejudiced, not just the upper crust. I can always catch them. First they call me and say, 'Mrs. Fox, I only want *Europeans*'—that's the word they use. 'Oh? Only Europeans. That's a pity, becauses I have a lovely South American girl, a college grad with a degree in pediatrics.' Then they'll say, 'Well, that's fine too.' Then I say, 'But she's not a European. . . . Anyway, that girl is booked, but I do have a lovely Jamaican with a master's in child care. . . .' And then I get the silence. Or they'll say, 'It's not me, it's my husband. He doesn't want black help in the house.' Or they'll say my favorite line, which is, 'My maid is black and it will create problems.' I've never known what that means."

Mrs. Fox says she begs, she pleads, she wheedles, but only once in the last five years has anyone called up and requested black help. "That was a lovely person. She said, 'I imagine a sweet woman from the islands singing to the baby.' " More often, Mrs. Fox gets calls like the recent one from the Great

Neck matron who said, "I won't take any blacks!" Mrs. Fox knew how to deal with her. "I said, 'Then I can't help you, because I'm black!' And I slammed the phone down."

Mrs. Fox knows all the secrets. Horror stories from her favorite nurses float back to the one-room office on East Sixtieth Street. Mrs. Fox is protective of her nannies, takes each slight to them as her own. Each bit of pathos in the penthouse is reported; Frances Fox is aware of every rich child neglected in New York. The daughter of a famous entertainer, for example. That little girl, says Mrs. Fox, had to live with her nanny across the hall from her parents' vast apartment and wait for them to call. "Oh, phone, I will kiss you if you will let it be my mummy calling me to come see her," the child would say to the telephone. There was the son of a garment-center millionaire deserted by his mother soon after he was born. When the child abused his puppy, his father told Mrs. Fox's nurse, "I don't care if he kills the dog, as long as it keeps him quiet." And Mrs. Fox remembers all: sons of a famous financier who were cloistered in their nursery for days on end. Not only did they not get to see their parents, they were denied their parents' food—the nursery refrigerator was a wasteland of soggy hot dogs, TV dinners, sour milk.

"The worst treatment is when the mothers starve the nurses *and* the children," says Mrs. Fox. "I know a lot of cases where the nurses have to buy all the food for the child and then are not allowed to eat anything in the house. There was a woman on Central Park West who once bawled out one of my nannies because she drank a glass of Tropicana orange juice from a gallon container in her icebox. I know of cases where the family ate steak every night and made the nurse bring in pizza."

Things are very different now from when Frances Fox started out. That was in 1936. She had been struggling at an employment agency placing nurses while her husband struggled trying to distribute pharmaceuticals and then became a traveling saleman. Her mother put her foot down: "You will not live alone." She didn't. Instead, the Foxes started their own agency with a small assist from one of Frances Fox's clients. They struggled more. Walter Winchell was an early client ("You remember those two darling Koreans he adopted . . ."), and he recommended others: Lilli Palmer, H. B. Warner, and "that singer, what's-her-name, 'Over the Rainbow'—that's right, Judy Garland." Mrs. Fox says she never can remember names.

Numbers she does better with. In those days her nurses made seventy-five dollars a month. Now they make almost that in a day. Mrs. Fox still gets her ten percent. "I'll never forget the Irish girl who asked for sixty-five dollars a month just so she could have some work. I think that was during the war. I got her seventy-five dollars, the going rate. She came in to see me a few months later, and I said, 'How are you doing?' She said, 'Okay. I figure I'm making sixty-five dollars a month for wages and ten dollars a month for the abuse.' " Days off were different too: There weren't any. "The first system was that they would get Wednesday afternoon and evening off, then all day Wednesday—big deal!—but you had to be back that night," says Mrs. Fox. "Walter Cronkite was my client. Did you know he was the first to allow weekends off? It wasn't done for years after that by anybody else. Now, that's standard. Oh, it was terrible for my girls then."

Terrible now is takeout pizza and no orange juice and, for Mrs. Fox, getting her clients to adjust to changing social mores. The first-name issue is a current crisis. "The modern way is that my nurses do not want to be called by their first names unless they can call their employers by their first names. That causes a lot of problems. One of my clients started to cry when I tried to explain to her about my nanny Susan Pemberton. I said, 'Don't call her Susan. She likes to be called Miss Pemberton,' and the client just started to bawl. She said, 'I have manners, Mrs. Fox; I was raised in a nice home. . . . I don't think it's fair for you to think I wasn't brought up well.' "

Even Mrs. Fox can get confused. "I say, as a matter of routine, 'What is your name, and what is your husband's name?' because of all the working women. The other day a woman *screamed* at me on the telephone, 'I don't have a husband!'

"You know what else is crazy? Even men are calling me to look for work. That's part of the modern era too. First I have to say, 'Excuse me, are you a gentleman?' because sometimes a woman can have a gruff voice. If they say yes, I say, 'I haven't had a request for a male baby nurse for forty-six years,' and then I hang the phone up very fast before they can give me an argument. They usually call back and tell me how rude I've been, but I don't care. I'm not going to get into a fight with them."

Mrs. Fox is at her desk each morning at 7:30, and each morning she thinks, "Lord above, what will this day bring?" Strange requests arrive in the daily mail. "Yesterday I got a letter from a man who wanted 'college, a second language, tennis, baseball'—he had sons—'driving a car,' and at the end of this crazy letter he wrote, 'Oh yes, she must be able to help in the kitchen and be a good cook.' Well, I just threw that one in the trash can.

"Then a woman called up and said, 'Mrs. Fox, do you have anyone who likes cats? That's the most important thing. We have a great many cats, and we need somebody to be able to take care of them.' I said, 'Call the animal league.' "

The mothers hover, the mothers neglect, the mothers can demand their nurses iron shirts, scour tiles, sauté chicken breasts for dinner for sixteen. Frances Fox has heard it all. "I keep trying to tell the clients that the nurses are educated and educated persons are not maids. You don't ask the bookkeeper to help the salesperson, do you? A lot of these mothers think, 'What is this nurse doing while I am breast-feeding? Why can't she go scrub the tubs out?' But the nurses work twenty-four hours a day. These mothers can think the nurses want to sabotage them when they advise giving a supplementary bottle because the babies are screaming because they're starving. Or the mothers will chase my nurses out of the baby's room at eleven o'clock at night because their husbands have come home late from work."

Frances Fox is always searching. Her ads run all over the city: THE FOX AGENCY: ONLY BABY AND CHILD CARE. She mourns Immigration's crackdown on the foreign nanny—"a catastrophe," she calls it. It is so hard to meet her standards. A Fox nurse must be trained. "I always find out how much education someone has, but that too is delicate now. I have to say, 'How old were you when you stopped going to school?' In the past, if I would ask them, 'How much school do you have?' they would get furious. . . . Now I don't care if they're purple, as long as they're high quality."

She dreads retirement. "I don't knit, I don't crochet, I don't play bingo. People harass me to leave. I have angina, but what am I going to do, sit home and look out of my terrace? I'd jump through the window. There's a lot of pep in the old gal yet."

Bells are ringing. "Hello . . . Fox Agency . . . Yes? How did you make out? Did you see her? Oh . . . What did you think? All of our nurses are quality. . . . Yes, she has a little accent. Very slight. Does that bother you? What about the other one? She's a college grad. She taught school. Of course she can. And perfectly too. I think almost without an accent."

October 1982

Letter from the
Hamptons

Some of them were glad their summers were over. They couldn't wait to call the East Hampton mover, Home Sweet Home. They had summer houses and a beach club, extra cars, and that seasonal staple of the middle class, the mother's helper. The elite had their maids with them as well, city bodies propped up by the kiddie pool looking very much out of place. Only in New York does one need an entourage just to drive to the beach club. The mothers would sit by the baby pool at the Bridgehampton Racquet and Surf Club and complain. On the face of it, you wouldn't think these mothers had much to complain about. For three months every year, they could escape the city. Money was their ticket out. And the money marooned them in the potato fields and the dunes of Bridgehampton and Sagaponack, an easy bike ride from the strawberry-rhubarb pies of the farmer on Mecox Road or the wagon of homegrown tomatoes—the best of the season—on the Westervelts' front lawn on Main Street, Wainscott. The husbands would arrive on Friday morning, wondering what their wives had to gripe about. The husbands had worked hard to buy them their summers in the sun.

But for days during the final weeks there was no sun. Storm systems blew in and out. The clouds stalled. The air chilled. A strong wind whipped off the ocean, and the water temperature dropped. The mothers felt betrayed. In late August, when they thought they couldn't take their loneliness another moment, they couldn't deal with this Emily Brontë weather. The cold and gloom made them wonder why they were a hundred miles away from their husbands, their jobs, their organizations, and their back-to-school shopping. They would use words like "dislocated" and "abandoned" to describe how they were feeling after a summer at the beach. Tempers frayed. They railed at their children. "I don't want you running, and I don't want you eating, Jeremy." "You get ready this second, young man." Their calls were shrill, the unhappy ones, like pigeons trying to flee a roost. "We do it for the children," Darlene, a lawyer, said.

But it was more than that, of course. This kind of leisure is a traditional certification of upper-middle-class status. And maybe that was the problem. Most city wives aren't good with the notion of leisure. All their lives they have been drilled to be organized. Their mothers have taught them how to get things done. They are all so busy. In the city, they have to make lists to keep track of everything. In the country, during their long summers, there are no lists they can make that don't look ridiculous. "Drive Adam to swimming lessons. Pick up Joshua from day camp. Pick up *pasta primavera* at Loaves and Fishes. Try to relax." *Try.* A kind of terrible discontent can set in. A fear that they are turning, God forbid, suburban. "I'll do anything to avoid a car pool," one mother said. By the end of the summer, the books on the chaise longues seemed to reflect the malaise. *The White Hotel* was acceptable chaise reading this year. So was *The Cinderella Complex.* That fueled them. Surrounded by other women, they read about why they were dependent. Even Darlene grew inert. "You would think I would be able to walk the thirty steps to get to the beach," she said, waving in the general direction of the ramp to the ocean. "But somehow I never do."

The husbands would appear at the baby pool on Saturday.

They would cast mean eyes at foreign toddlers with the ability to dive. "How old is that child?" they would demand.

The Bridgehampton Racquet and Surf Club is unique for a Hamptons club. It has absolutely no social distinction. Nothing links the members except a desire to have an enormous pool and tennis courts and cabanas by the ocean and the wherewithal to be able to pay about fifteen hundred dollars to get them. So it was hard to figure out who people were. No one had gone to boarding school with anyone else. To social climb would have been laughable. Distances were kept. Inevitably, there was one troublemaker who minded everyone's business. Early in the season, she approached a rather artsy mother playing with her twin baby boys. "Oh, my God," the woman said. "Is that nail polish on your sons' fingers and toes?" "Yes," the mother said pleasantly. "Why have you put nail polish on them?" "Because they like it." "Don't you think that nail polish is going to affect their sexuality?" the woman persisted. "At eighteen months?" the mother asked. Later one of her baby boys threw a tantrum. Nothing the mother did would calm him down. Within moments, the woman was back again. "You must be a sick woman to torture your child the way you do."

In late July, there was an incident far more poisonous than any bickering over fingers and toes. The occasion was a swim meet at the Maidstone Club. Twice each season, the children of Bridgehampton Racquet and Surf compete with these children of East Hampton, and each time they do, it is with some dread. As egalitarian as one club is, so is the other not. The atmosphere between the two clubs is frosty in the extreme. This year, there was an explosion. "Look at the dirty Jew with the big star," a Maidstone employee reportedly said as the daughter of a Surf Club member walked through the bar. City children are well drilled in how to behave when these matters occur. Immediately, the parents were called in. An apology from the Maidstone management was demanded. None was forthcoming. Half the Surf Club members withdrew. The incident made the front page of the Bridgehampton *Sun.*

It was a public acknowledgment of a private truth that is very much a part of the social fabric out here. These Hamptons are no longer the preserve of Polish potato farmers, Irwin Shaw, and the Meadow Club and the Maidstone members. A lot of New Yorkers can afford the new rentals—even at twenty thousand dollars a season and up. Real-estate brokers like Tina Fredericks are having a wonderful time being quoted about their busiest season ever. You can't find a parking space in East Hampton. The movies sell out. Dean & DeLuca is mobbed. That irritates the Old Guard. Social pressure is intense. And the social lines are getting drawn a lot more clearly than they were ten years ago, when it was still fun to have new millionaires around. In private, those comments about "the Jews" are being heard again. The fat cats are no longer holding their tongues, another symptom of the times.

"The new chip is a billion dollars," a Southampton hostess said one night at dinner. "You can't even play at the table anymore unless you have a billion." Her dinner guests nodded at this and then the butler passed around more grilled swordfish. It was as if nothing startling had been said at her table. And maybe nothing had. This kind of remark passes from table to table. Lunches are discussed at dinners, Saturday nights on Sunday afternoons. The political conversations of another era have given way to an obsession with personalities; the scenes are like pages ripped from *The House of Mirth.* There's a lot of money talk mingled in with this, of course. How much Francois de Menil is pouring into his house—one uses that term lightly—on Further Lane. What's going on at Ahmet Ertegun's now that Swifty Lazar has camped out there for a month.

In all of this, there was a certain mood. The mood was that it was okay to throw money around again. That style has gotten the papal kiss from Washington, after all. But great extravagance is a complicated trait. Anyone who really tosses money around gets sneered at, but it's a sneer that is tinged with respect.

Take the party that Terry Kramer gave for her husband, Irwin, at the end of the season. This was a big deal, even by fat-cat standards. The Kramers can play at the table with the new billion-dollar chip. Mrs. Kramer is a producer, but more to the point, her father is Charles Allen, as in Allen & Company. Irwin Kramer's father was rich too—he owned hotels in New York. As Hollywood hands have always known, the son-in-law always rises, but in this case Irwin Kramer made a lot of money of his own on Wall Street. This summer the Kramers rented a house called the Ark. Fifty thousand dollars is the chip they threw down for their 1920's mansion on the sea. That figure whipped through the Southampton dinner circuit this month, as did the price Irwin and Terry were going to buy the house for: $2.5 million. The deal fell through. No matter. For Irwin's sixtieth birthday, no expense was spared. A few days before the party, Terry Kramer explained the excess to come. "I don't want to be the richest girl in the cemetery," she said.

She won't be. A pair of striped lemon-and-white tents went up in front of the Ark. Peter Duchin was found. Three hundred guests were to be seated and fed by Glorious Foods, which imported essence of roast beef and, for dessert, lacquer trays with their eleven artfully arranged blueberries all the way from New York. Magnums of Lafite-Rothschild 1967 were lined up on the sideboard. *Magnums.* That's $116 per. The tableclothes were splashed with free-form dahlias—hand painted. Warner Communications head Steve Ross waltzed with his new girl friend, Courtney Sale, looking as if he didn't have a care in the world. Chuck Scarborough and Anne Uzielli strolled through the tents, but you needed a Wall Street expert to tell you who the other guests were. They were, in effect, the richest of the richest, the true invisibles—

Salomon Brothers bosses, that kind of thing. On this level, you don't need to have your name in "Suzy." It was the kind of group that doesn't look especially glamorous until you see their Dun & Bradstreet ratings.

The hostess was nowhere to be seen. At the last second, her doctors made her stay in the city because of some minor surgery. Maybe if she had stayed in the country she could have controlled her butler a little better. But the Kramers are very secure. They don't mind importing a holiday butler who spends his summer making pungent remarks about their guests. This year's rent-a-butler, Alan, had become well known in Southampton for his aphorisms. Alan has a lot of training. "He used to work for Jock Whitney," says a Kramer friend. Maybe he's been to see *Arthur* too.

Just before dinner, a cluster of staff, including Alan, stood on the steps of the Ark as one woman in cream chiffon made her way to the loo. Their voices were loud and decidedly English. "Have you ever seen such unattractive people?" one of them said. "Oh, my God, no." "Well," sniffed the other servant, "I certainly hope dinner will be served early." Had the Kramers been around to hear this, they probably would have laughed. At a certain level, money buys a great deal— like hundred-thousand-dollar parties—but it also buys something infinitely more precious: the ability to be absolutely impervious to insult. That came in handy this year at the beach.

September 1981

*   *   *

Although it would be wonderful to be able to wrap up this collection neatly, making several tart observations about the nature of journalism or even creating a case, however flimsy, that these articles might have been related, that would be a trick, a wave of the scarf to put a flourish on what was happenstance—luck in some cases, killing effort in others. The method has never varied: You go, you ask questions, you look around, you ask more questions, and you come back. Then the real work, the slow death, begins. Finally, the piece is published; it appears, it disappears, and it's on to the next. Magazines and newspapers are hungry. One of my favorite newspaper expressions is "feeding the goat." The goat is who you work for, a creature endlessly ravenous for more and more copy; one decent meal will never do. "The goat" doesn't know the difference between *fois gras* and hay.

Once in a while, as in "Letter from the Hamptons," an idea evolved after the events themselves; that is, I was not "assigned" to go to Southampton to nose around. Which brings me to the point. That marvelously brittle observation of Joan Didion's, "Writers are always selling somebody out," has been and will be the epigram copied into journals, typed out and placed on bulletin boards by writers down through the decades. I've typed it out, too, but I've added my own parenthesis. "And then they must expect the consequences." This addendum is particularly true as a piece of reporting evolves from just hanging around, if one did not start out to do a story. And this is a murky area. What do you do if, in the day-to-day business of life, something happens that later will illustrate a theme? Here's what you do: You go with it. Up to a point. The question is, what is "the point"? Everybody's point, the terrain where the professional becomes the personal, is different. Columnists and essayists have carte blanche. My point is the truly intimate: marriage, family, close friends are off limits except for harmless fun. This is not everybody's point, nor should it be, but it is my point, and for me, real intimacy is a sacred trust with a statute of limitations that runs very long. But that's where my sanctimony ends—anything or anyone else is fair game.

"Letter from the Hamptons" brought me smack into this area. Reporters are often told, "You can write about this," or

"You are not allowed to write about that." These pronounce-ments are always ignored, since they involve a logic that usually goes, "If you say you are here to write—if you an-nounce your intentions—then you can write." I've always found these orders to be a perverse and (usually) opportunistic dictum that is determined by individual circumstances; you're granted "permission" if the subject feels he can control the environment or if he will be cast in a flattering light. In fact, you can write about anything. In fact, you do not have to an-nounce that you're working. I almost always announce my in-tentions, because there is usually no reason not to.

In Southampton, I was a guest at the party described, brought by friends of the hosts, whom I had never met. Some weeks later, I found that the party served as a perfect example of an idea. The host and hostess were not amused. So be it. On to the next piece.

This reminds me of a story. Several years ago, in London, I was listening to two reporters sitting around trying to impress each other. One of them was particularly arrogant, and within about ten minutes he had managed to mention about thirty-seven different heads of state, famous people, swells, wars, lo-cales, and big-deal events he had covered. "I filed nine pieces to the paper in the last week alone," he said.

"I see," his friend said. "Feeding the goat, again."

Somehow that put everything in perspective.